THE CHRISTIAN HERITAGE OF OUR NATION

HISTORY CURRICULUM - Ten National Memorials

Catherine Millard, D. Min.

Illustrator: Maxwell Edgar

Copyright ©1985, 1988, 1997 by Catherine Millard
ISBN: 0-9658616-1-9
Library of Congress Catalogue Card Number: 97-76099

Illustrator: Maxwell Edgar

Grateful acknowledgements:
To Mrs. Florian Thayn, Head of Art and Reference, Office of the Architect of the Capitol, for her invaluable assistance and encouragement during the many years of study and research in formulating this book from original sources.

Published by **Christian Heritage Ministries**
Distributed by **Christian Heritage Tours, Inc.**
6597 Forest Dew Court
Springfield, Virginia 22152
Telephone: 703-455-0333

Printed in the United States of America

Definitions of terms used frequently in the text:

Symbol–Something that stands for, or represents another thing; especially an object used to represent something abstract; an emblem; as, the dove is a symbol of peace, the cross is a symbol of Christianity.

Landmark–An event considered to be a high point or turning point of a period.

Monument–Something set up to keep alive the memory of a person or event, as a tablet, statue, pillar, building, etc.; a writing or the like serving as a memorial; a work, production, etc., of enduring value or significance; as, monuments of learning; vb . . . to erect a monument to the memory of; as to monument a noble deed.

Memorial–Anything meant to help people remember some person or event, as a statue, holiday, etc. (e.g. Exodus 3:15; 17:14; Joshua 4:7; Acts of the Apostles 10:4).

Aesthetics–The theory of the fine arts and of peoples' responses to them; the science or branch of philosophy which deals with the beautiful; the doctrines of taste.

(Webster's New 20th Century Dictionary–Unabridged–Second Edition)
Scripture parallels for the term "Memorial" added.

Cover Photograph: *The Iwo Jima Memorial.* Photo by John W. Wrigley

DEDICATION

To my students in Christian, public, private and Homeschools throughout America.

THE CHRISTIAN HERITAGE OF OUR NATION

HISTORY CURRICULUM - Ten National Memorials

TABLE OF CONTENTS

INTRODUCTION

While studying the inception and historical development of this great nation from original sources, it has been an amazing discovery to find that all current literature, including textbooks, history books, guidebooks and brochures pertaining to our blessed country have been robbed of their accuracy. Let me explain. In the earliest documentation we have on record at the Library of Congress of the United States, up through approximately 60 to 70 years ago, Christianity is woven into the warp and woof of this nation's history. The framers of the Constitution turned to Scripture and prayer for guidance in formulating a new system of government, while most of America's greatest leaders, statesmen and inventors gave all glory to Almighty God, as the source and strength of their power and ability.

The need for this curriculum is urgent, as we are now evidencing the removal of tangible items of our precious American Christian heritage from national landmarks, monuments, memorials and shrines where the hand of God in the affairs of this nation is so boldly proclaimed.

Hence, the removal of America's true history from the hearts and minds of today's youth — the leaders of tomorrow. More importantly, God's glory, and that of His Son Jesus Christ, in the foundations of America, is being removed. As founding father Thomas Jefferson wrote more than 200 years ago: "Can the liberties of a nation be secure when we have removed a conviction that these liberties are the gift of God? I tremble for my country when I reflect that God is just. That His justice cannot sleep forever."

The Purpose for this curriculum is to inculcate and perpetuate these great memorials of America's Christian heritage and history in the hearts and lives of present-day youth, in order that they, in turn, may emulate the lives and deeds of great American statesmen and heroes in adulthood.

The Inception and Development of our Capital City

Let us begin at the beginning:

In 1608 the area which now boasts the nation's capital, and one of the world's greatest power centers, was discovered by Captain John Smith. George Washington chose this site himself in 1790 for the new federal city. At that time it lay mid-way between the northernmost and southernmost states. A year later, Washington appointed a French engineer by the name of Pierre Charles l'Enfant, who had served under him in the Revolutionary War, to draw up a plan for the new city. This imaginative, avant garde designer mapped out the streets in a simple but practical manner. From the Capitol, he numbered the streets running north to south, lettering those which ran from east to west. Broad avenues, bearing the names of the states, run crosswise in a diagonal pattern. The original lands were a gift from the states of Virginia and Maryland. In 1846, however, Virginia took back her portion of land, making the present-day total area of the District of Columbia 69 square miles.

Letters and notes accompanying l'Enfant's plans show a definite purpose in every aspect of his design. He wrote:

> a street laid out on a dimension proportioned to the greatness which the capital
> of a powerful Empire ought to manifest . . . [1]

The magnificence of Versailles prompted l'Enfant's grandiose ideas for the young nation's capital.[2] His broadest avenue of 400 feet has now become the grassy expanse separating the northern and southern rows of buildings which comprise the Smithsonian Institution.[3] A unique privilege of excelling the height of the Capitol's dome was granted the Washington Monument. At 555 feet, 5 and one eighth inches the obelisk serves to salute the father and founder of this nation. An aluminum cap atop the monument shouts out its own song of praise and worship to our God and Father. An inscription upon it bears the Latin words *Laus Deo*, that is to say; "Praise be to God."

In 1800, the government moved from Philadelphia to Washington with its 126 workers, 32 Senators and 106 Representatives. Before the move, eight other capitals had been evidenced as follows: Albany, New York, Philadelphia, Baltimore, York, Princeton, Annapolis and Trenton.

Since *God's Signature over the Nation's Capital* was published ten years ago, we have evidenced, at a cataclysmic rate, the removal, blockage and/or inaccessibility of tangible items of our precious American Christian heritage from foremost national memorials and historic sites. The latter boldly proclaim the hand of God in the affairs of this nation. The purpose and function of this History Curriculum, is therefore to take you by the hand through ten fascinating lessons at the seat of government. We will study America's rich Christian foundations through the art, architecture, sculpture and inscriptions, in concert with the original historic documents of *this nation under God*.

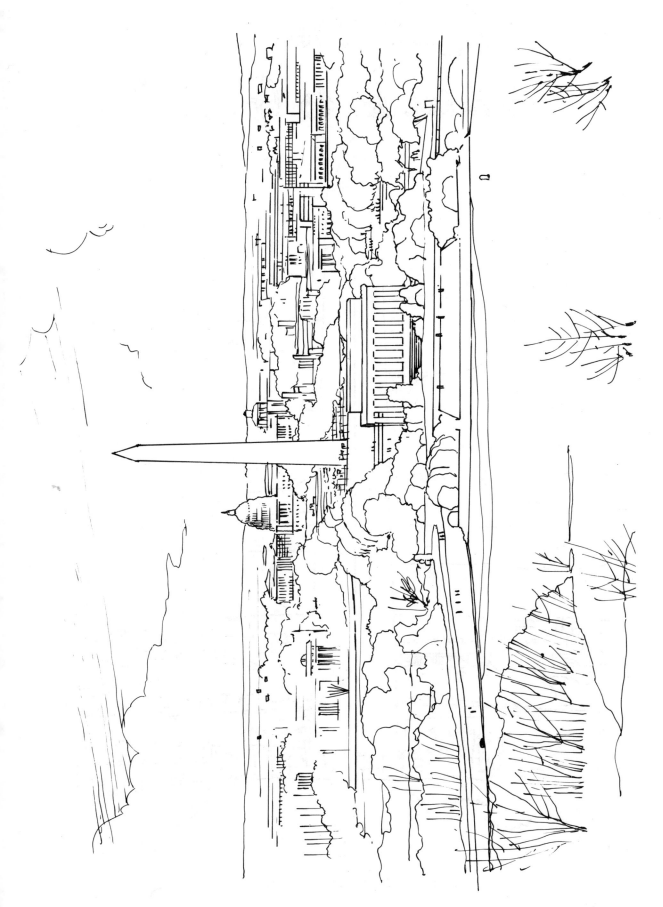

Our Nation's Capital from the Tidal Basin

Laus Deo
"Praise be to God!"

The Washington Monument

The Christian Heritage Of Our Nation - History Curriculum

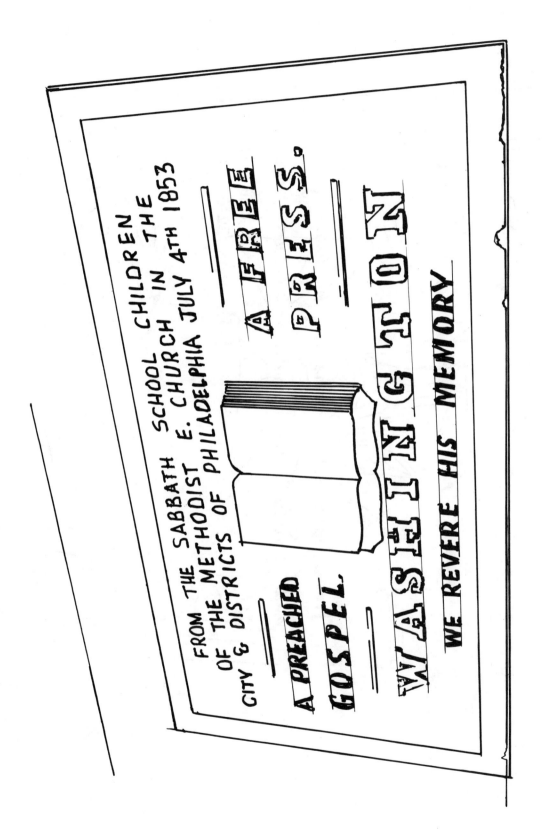

The Twenty-fourth Landing Memorial Stone

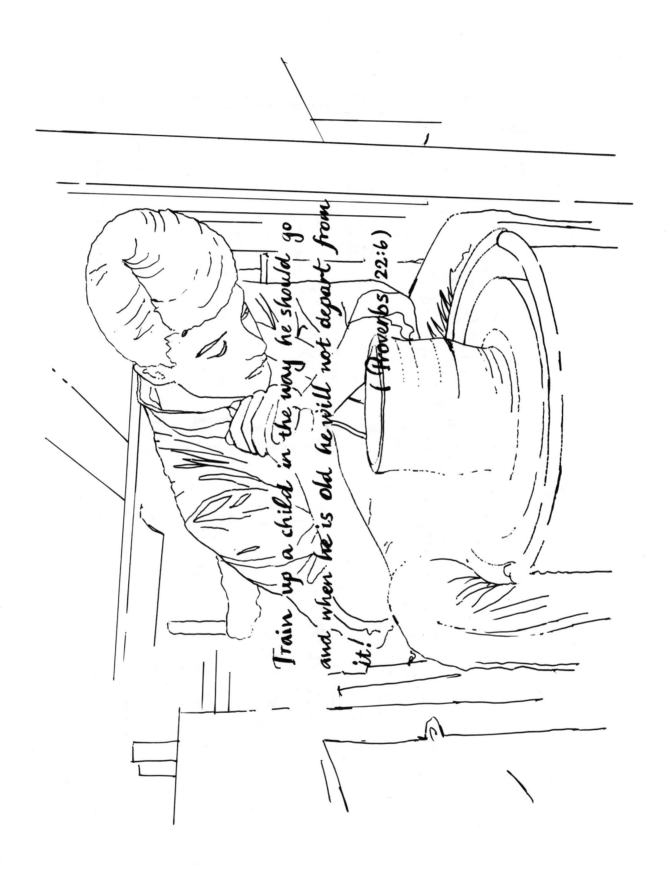

Train up a child in the way he should go and, when he is old he will not depart from it! (Proverbs 22:6)

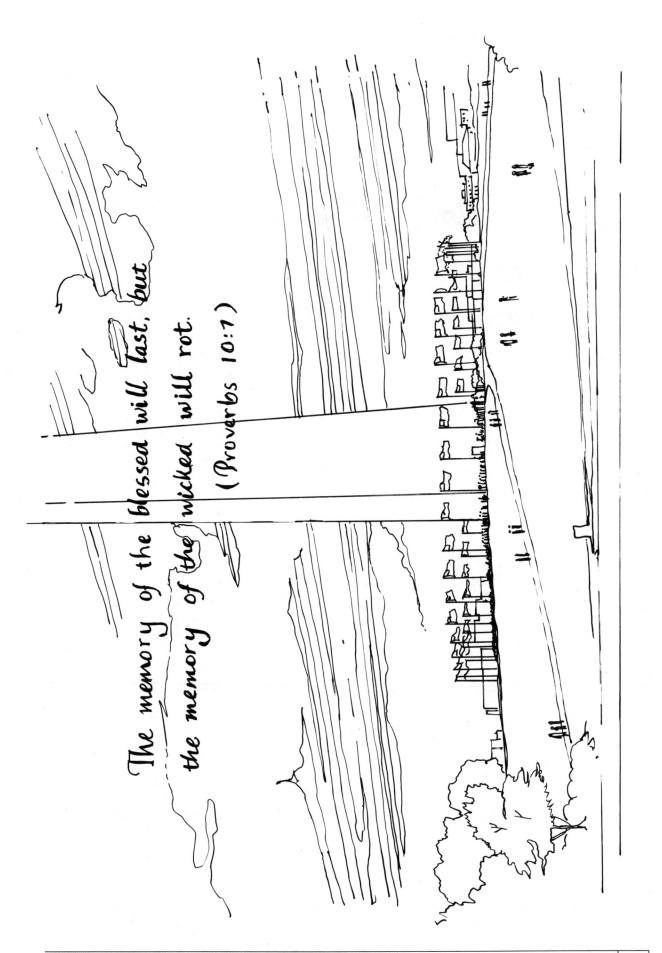

The memory of the blessed will last, but the memory of the wicked will rot. (Proverbs 10:7)

Suffer the little children to come unto me and forbid them not, for of such is the Kingdom of Heaven.

(Luke 18:16)

The Washington Monument from the Reflecting Pool

LESSON 1

THE WASHINGTON MONUMENT

...with its stately simplicity ... it is fitting that the aluminum tip that caps it should bear the phrase "Laus Deo."

William Howard Taft, President, United States of America[1]

On the aluminum cap atop the Washington Monument are inscribed the words *Laus Deo*, that is to say, "Praise be to God!"

At a height of 555-feet, 5 and one eighth-inches, the monument to the father of our nation overlooks the 69 square miles which comprise the District of Columbia, capital of the United States of America.

Resolution of the Continental Congress

The Continental Congress, on the 7th day of August, A.D. 1783, unanimously resolved (ten States being represented): "That an equestrian statue of George Washington be erected at the place where the residence of Congress shall be established in honor of George Washington, the illustrious Commander-in-Chief of the armies of the United States of America, during the war which vindicated and secured their liberty, sovereignty and independence."

On December 19, 1799, the day after the mortal remains of George Washington had been committed to the tomb, a committee of both Houses of Congress was appointed "to report measures suitable to the occasion and expression of the profound sorrow with which Congress is penetrated on the loss of a citizen first in war, first in peace, and first in the hearts of his countrymen."[2]

In pursuance of the foregoing resolution, both Houses of Congress passed the following resolution on December 24, 1799: "That a marble monument be erected by the United States in the Capitol, at the City of Washington, and that the family of General Washington be requested to permit his body to be deposited under it, and that the monument be so designed as to commemorate the great events of his military and political life."[3]

President John Adams was authorized to correspond with Mrs. Washington, asking her to consent to the removal and interment of her husband's remains beneath a monument, to be erected by the government in the Capitol.

Martha Washington's Letter

Mrs. Washington consented in the following beautiful words:

> Taught by the great example I have so long had before me, never to oppose my private wishes to the public will, I must consent to the request of Congress which you had the goodness to transmit to me; and in doing this I need not – I cannot – say what a sacrifice of individual feeling I make to a sense of public duty.[4]

Congress again made an application in 1832 to the proprietors of Mount Vernon for the removal and deposit of the remains of Washington in the Capitol, in conformity with the Resolution of 1799. The Legislature of Virginia protested against the movement, and John A. Washington declined the proposal.[5]

In the advertisements inviting designs for the Monument from American artists, it was recommended that they should "harmoniously blend durability, simplicity and grandeur."[6]

Design of the Washington Monument

The design originally selected for the Monument was that submitted by Robert Mills, comprising, in its main features, a vast stylobate, surmounted by a tetrastyle pantheon; circular in form, and with an obelisk 600 feet high rising from the center.[7]

Laying of the Cornerstone

When the cornerstone of the *Washington Monument* was laid on Independence Day, 1848, deposited within its recess were many items and documents of value. Among these are: a copy of the Holy Bible, presented by the American Bible Society, instituted in 1816; an American silk flag; the coat of arms of the Washington family; copies of the Constitution and Declaration of Independence; United States Presidents' messages to date of cornerstone laying; likenesses of all Presidents and their inaugural addresses to same date; a portrait of Washington taken from Gilbert Stuart's famous painting; and daguerreotype likenesses of Gen. and Mrs. Washington.

The inscription on the copper plate covering the deposit recess of the cornerstone reads:

> 4th July, 1776. Declaration of Independence of the United States of America.
> 4th July 1848. This cornerstone laid of a Monument by the people of the United States to the Memory of George Washington.[8]

Construction began on July 4, 1848, with President James Knox Polk presiding at the laying of the cornerstone, in accordance with the decision of the National Monument Society. The event took place in the presence of the members of the legislative and judicial branches of the government, foreign ministers and officers, and a vast concourse of citizens from all sections of the Union.[9]

An interval of almost 25 years ensued before the completion of the obelisk, which accounts for a slight change of color at a height of 150 feet. Stone continued to be quarried from the original site outside Baltimore, Maryland; but after a lapse of more than 20 years the level of stone had dropped, thus accounting for its change in hue. The monument is made up entirely of marble and granite with no steel shafts as interior support whatever. Its unique simplicity is enhanced by 50 United States flags proudly encircling the base, each one representing one of the 50 states in the Union.

Dedication of Washington Monument

On February 21, 1885, the Washington Monument was dedicated. Senator Sherman in the course of his oration, said:

> The Monument speaks for itself, — simple in form, admirable in proportions, composed of enduring marble and granite, resting upon foundations broad and deep, it rises into the skies higher than any work of human art. It is the most imposing, costly,[10] and appropriate monument ever to be erected in the honor of one man.

Prayer was offered by the Reverend Henderson Suter, Rector of *Christ Church*, Alexandria, Virginia, where Washington worshipped God. President Chester Arthur accepted the Monument, making a short dedicatory address, after which a procession formed and moved to the Capitol. Here orations were delivered by Robert C. Winthrop of Massachusetts, and John W. Daniel, Senator of Virginia. After the benediction had been pronounced, the President of the United States and members of the Supreme Court, and the invited guests retired from the hall at 5 o'clock.[11] A beautiful verse was composed for this auspicious occasion:

> Yonder shaft,
> Which States and peoples piled
>   the stones upon,
> That from its top the very winds
>   might waft
> To distant shores the name of
> Washington.

Inauguration of Washington Monument

October 9, 1888, marked the official inauguration and opening of this monument to the public. An original steam elevator took 15 minutes to reach the top, whereas the present electric one reaches the summit in a mere 70 seconds. A panoramic view of the city can be enjoyed at this elevation in height, with maps and sketches outlining each segment of the capital. Pierre Charles l'Enfant's original plan in operation is thus clearly seen. From this vantage point, a perfect cross can be traced over the Capital City, with the *White House* to the north; the *Jefferson Memorial* to the south; the *Capitol* to the east and the *Lincoln Memorial* to the west.

Memorial Stones of the Washington Monument

There are 898 steps and 50 landings within the Washington Monument. Of the 190 memorial stones inserted within its inner staircase walls, numerous glorify God in word and deed; many others extolling the Declaration of Independence and U.S. Constitution.[12]

On The First Landing (30 feet high), is inscribed:

Stone no. 5:   ***Delaware.*** First to adopt, will be the last to desert the Constitution.

The Second Landing (40 feet high) bears these words:

Stone no. 7:   Presented by the Columbia Typographical Society, Instituted January, 1815, "As a memento of the veneration of its members for the father of his country."

Stone no. 8:   Association of Journeymen Stone cutters of Philadelphia. July 9th, 1850. "United we Stand."

Stone no. 10:   ***Alabama***. A Union of Equality as adjusted by the Constitution.

Stone no. 11:   ***The State of Louisiana.*** Ever faithful to the Constitution and the Union.

The Third Landing (50 feet high):

Stone no. 17:   **State of Georgia.** The Union as it was. The Constitution as it is.

Stone no. 18:   **Indiana** knows no North, no South, nothing but the Union.

The Fifth Landing (70 feet high):

Stone no. 25:   Presented by the Grand Division, Sons of Temperance, **State of Virginia**. 1850. Hand in Hand Union.

Stone no. 26:   "God and our Native Land." United Sons of America. Instituted, 1845. **Pennsylvania**. "Usque ad Mortem." "Lente Caute Firme."

Stone no. 27:   Grand Division, Sons of Temperance, **North Carolina**. "Love, Purity, Fidelity."

The Sixth Landing (80 feet high):

Stone no. 34:   **Maryland.** The Memorial of Her Regard for the Father of His Country and of her Cordial, Habitual and Immovable attachment to the American Union. "Crescite et Multiplicamini."

Stone no. 35:   The City of Washington to its Founder.

Stone no. 36:   **Virginia** who gave Washington to America gives this Granite for his Monument.

The Seventh Landing (90 feet high):

Stone no. 40:   **The State of Mississippi** to the Father of his country. A.D. 1850.

Stone no. 41:   **The State of Ohio**. The Memory of Washington, and the Union of the States. "Sunte Perpetua."

Stone no. 42:   The Tribute of **Missouri.** To the Memory of Washington and a Pledge of her fidelity to the Union of the States.

The Eighth Landing (100 feet high):

Stone no. 46: "Hope" *Rhode Island.*

Stone no. 47: *North Carolina.* Declaration of Independence. Mecklenburg, May, 1775. "Constitution."

Stone no. 48: *Wisconsin.* Admitted May 29, 1848.

The Ninth Landing (110 feet high)

Stone no. 53: *Iowa.* Her Affections, like the Rivers of her Borders, Flow to an inseparable Union.

Stone no. 54: Nov. 12, 1852. From the Postmasters and Ast. Postmasters of the *State of Indiana.* Dedicated to the Washington Monument, Washington. May his Principles be Distributed, Broadcast over the Land and every American.

The Tenth Landing (120 feet high):

Stone no. 59: *California.* Youngest sister of the Union brings her Golden Tribute to the Memory of its Father.

The Eleventh Landing (130 feet high):

Stone no. 67: From the Alumni of Washington College, at Lexington, *Virginia.* The only College endowed by the father of his Country.

Stone no. 68: From the Grand Division, Sons of Temperance, *State of Connecticut.* A Tribute to the Memory of Washington. "Love, Purity, Fidelity."

The Twelfth Landing (140 feet high):

Stone no. 75: From Otter's Summit. Virginia's Loftiest Peak to Crown a Monument to Virginia's Noblest Son.

Stone no. 76:   From Fort Greene, Battle Ground of Long Island. A Tribute from the Fort Greene Guard of Brooklyn, 1854.

Stone no. 80:   Anno 1850. By the City of Baltimore. May Heaven to this Union continue its Beneficence; May Brotherly Affection with Union be Perpetual; May the Free Constitution which is the work of our Ancestors be sacredly maintained and its Administration be stamped with Wisdom and Virtue.

The Fourteenth Landing (160 feet high):

Stone no. 84:   *New York.* "Excelsior."

The Fifteenth Landing (170 feet high):

Stone no. 89:   *Vermont.* "Freedom and Unity."

Stone no. 92:   Charlestown. Bunker Hill Battle ground.

The Sixteenth Landing (180 feet high):

Stone no. 95:   "Liberty, Independence, Virtue." *Pennsylvania.* (Founded 1681). By Deeds of Peace.

Stone no. 96:   Declaration of Independence, Philadelphia, July 4th, 1776. Corporation of the City of Philadelphia.

Stone no. 98:   The Surest Safeguard of the Liberty of our Country - Total Abstinence from all that Intoxicates. Sons of Temperance of Pennsylvania.

The Seventeenth Landing (190 feet high):

Stone no. 100:   To the Memory of Washington. The Free Swiss Confederation MDCCCLII.

Stone no. 101:   Greece. (Greek inscription translated): "George Washington, the Hero, the Citizen of the New and Illustrious Liberty. The Land of Solon, Themistocles and Pericles–the

Mother of Ancient Liberty–Sends this Ancient Stone as a Testimony of Honor and Admiration from the Parthenon."

Stone no. 102:   Siam.

Stone no. 103:   Brazil, 1878.

Stone no. 104:   (Translation) "To Washington, the Great, Good and Just, by friendly BREMEN."

Stone no. 106:   Presented by the Governor and Commune of the Islands of Paros and Noxos, Grecian Archipelago. August 13th, 1855.

The Eighteenth Landing (200 feet high):

Stone no. 107:   From the Templars of Honor and Temperance. Organized Dec. 5th 1845. "Truth, Love, Purity and Fidelity." Our Pledge: "We will not make, buy, sell or use as a beverage, any spirituous or malt liquors, wine, cider, or any other alcoholic liquor, and we will discountenance their manufacture, traffic and use, and this pledge we will maintain unto the end of life." Supreme Council of the Templars of Honor and Temperance. 1846.

The Nineteenth Landing (210 feet high):

Stone no. 116:   Grand Division of Ohio, Sons of Temperance, "Love, Purity and Fidelity."

Stone no. 117:   Presented by the Grand Division on behalf of the Sons of Temperance of Illinois, January 1st, 1855. Grand Division, *State of Illinois*, Sons of Temperance. Inst. Jan. 8, 1847. "Love, Purity, and Fidelity."

Stone no. 121:   *Kansas*. Kansas Territory, organized May 20, 1851. State admitted January 29, 1861.

The Twentieth Landing (220 feet high):

Stone no. 122:   All for our Country. Nevada, 1881.

Stone no 123:   Nebraska's Tribute "Equality before the Law."

Stone no. 124:   (Chinese inscription translated): China. "Su-Ki-Yu, by imperial appointment, Lieut. Governor of the Province of Fuh Kun, in his universal geography says: It is evident that Washington was a remarkable man. In devising plans, he was more decided than Chin-Shing or Wu-Kwang, in winning a country, he was braver than Tsau-Tsau or Lin-Pi. Wielding his four-footed falchion, he extended the frontiers thousands of miles, and then refused to usurp the regal dignity, or transmit to his posterity, but first established rules for an elective administration. Where in the world can be found such a public spirit? Truly, the sentiments of the three dynasties have all at once unexpectedly appeared in our day. In ruling the state, he promoted and fostered good customs, and did not depend on military merit. In this he differed from all other nations. I have seen his portrait, his air and form are grand and imposing in a remarkable degree. Ah, who would not call him a hero? The United States of America regard it promotive of national virtue generally and extensively neither to establish titles of nobility and royalty nor to conform to the age, as respects customs and public influence, but instead deliver over their own public deliberations and inventions so that the like of such a nation one so remarkable does not exist in ancient or modern times. Among the people of the Great West can any man, in ancient or modern times, fail to pronounce Washington peerless?

This Stone is Presented by a Company of Christians and engraved at Ningpu . . . China, . . . the Reign of the Emperor Heen Fung.". . . (July 12th, 1853.)

Stone no. 126:   Tribute of **Wyoming Territory**. "To the Memory of him who by Universal consent was Chief among the Founders of the Republic."

Stone no. 127:   Holiness to the Lord.

Stone no. 131:   ***State of Oregon***. The Union.

The Twenty-first Landing (230 feet high):

Stone no. 133:   Under the Auspices of Heaven and the Precepts of Washington, **Kentucky** will be the last to give up the Union. "United we stand, divided we fall."

Stone no. 134:   *Georgia* Convention 1850. "Wisdom, Justice, Moderation."

Stone no. 137:   *Tennessee.* "The Federal Union, it must be Preserved."

The Twenty-second Landing (240 feet high):

Stone no. 139:   The General Assembly of the Presbyterian Church in the United States of America in session in Washington City, May, 1852.

The Twenty-third Landing (250 feet high):

Stone no. 151:   The Citizens of Stockton, San Joaquin Co., California. A Tribute of Respect to the Father of our Country, George Washington, 1859.

Stone no. 154:   A Tribute from the Teachers of the Buffalo Public Schools.

Stone no. 155:   The Young Men's Mercantile Library Association of Cincinnati. Organized A.D. 1805. A.D. 1853. 2,400 members. Proud to Honor Washington. Contributes its Humble Quota to the swelling tide of National Gratitude. *Ohio* - First born of the Ordinance of '87. Every pulsation of the heart beats high, beats strong, for Liberty and the Union.

The Twenty-fourth Landing (260 feet high):

Stone no. 156:   The Memory of the Just is Blessed. Prov.10:7. Presented by the Children of the Sunday Schools of the Methodist Episcopal Church, in the City of New York, Feb. 22, '55.

Stone no. 158:   From the Sabbath School Children of the Methodist E.

Church in the City and Districts of Philadelphia, 4th July, 1853. A Preached Gospel. A Free Press. Washington. We revere his Memory. "Search the Scriptures." Suffer little children to come unto Me and forbid them not, for of such is the Kingdom of God. Luke XVIII:16. Train up a child in the way he should go, and when he is old, he will not depart from it. Prov. XXII:6.

Stone no. 160: By the Pupils of the Public Schools of the City of Baltimore. A.D. MDCCCLI.

The Twenty-Sixth Landing (280 feet high):

Stone no. 169: To the Father of his Country. The Addison Literary Society of the Western Military Institute, Drennon, Kentucky. "Non nobis solum, sed patriae et amicis."

Stone no. 176: "All that Live must Die." A Tribute of Respect from the Ladies and Gentlemen of the Dramatic Profession of America. 1853.

One of the stones contributed to the Washington Monument was a block of marble from the Temple of Concord at Rome, and was a gift of the pope. It bore the inscription "Rome to America." In March 1854, the lapidarium, where the memorial blocks were kept, was forcibly entered, and this stone was taken and thrown into the Potomac.

George Washington's Formative Years

George Washington was the son of Augustine Washington and his second wife, Mary Ball. He was a direct descendant of King John of England and nine of the 25 Baron Sureties of the Magna Carta. His father died in 1743 when the boy was 11 years old. Therefore, until age 16, he lived with his half brother, Augustine, on the family estate in Westmoreland County, 40 miles from Fredericksburg, Virginia. Much of his education took place in the home.

At the age of 15, this exceptional young man copied in meticulous handwriting the *110 Rules of Civility and Decent Behaviour in Company and Conversation*. These maxims were so fully lived out in George Washington's life that historians have regarded them as important influences in forming his character. They are hereunder reprinted in their entirety:

GEORGE WASHINGTON'S
Rules of *Civility & Decent Behaviour*
In Company and *Conversation*

1st   Every Action done in Company, ought to be with Some Sign of Respect, to those that are Present.

2nd   When in Company, put not your Hands to any Part of the Body, not usually Discovered.

3rd   Shew Nothing to your Friend that may affright him.

4th   In the Presence of Others Sing not to yourself with a humming Noise, nor Drum with your Fingers or Feet.

5th   If You Cough, Sneeze, Sigh, or Yawn, do it not Loud but Privately; and Speak not in your Yawning, but put Your handkerchief or Hand before your face and turn aside.

6th   Sleep not when others Speak, Sit not when others stand, Speak not when you Should hold your Peace, walk not on when others Stop.

7th   Put not off your Cloths in the presence of Others, nor go out your Chamber half Drest.

8th   At Play and at Fire it's Good manners to Give Place to the last Commer, and affect not to Speak Louder than Ordinary.

9th   Spit not in the Fire, nor Stoop low before it, neither Put your Hands into the Flames to warm them, nor Set your Feet upon the Fire especially if there be meat before it.

10th   When you Sit down, Keep your Feet firm and Even, without putting one on the other or Crossing them.

11th   Shift not yourself in the Sight of others nor Gnaw your nails.

12th   Shake not the head, Feet, or Legs, rowl not the Eys, lift not one eyebrow higher than the other, wry not the mouth, and bedew no man's face with your Spittle, by approaching too near him when you Speak.

13th   Kill no Vermin as Fleas, lice, ticks &c in the Sight of others, if you See any filth or thick Spittle, put your foot Dexteriously upon it. If it be upon the Cloths of your Companions, Put it off privately, and if it be upon your own Cloths, return Thanks to him who puts it off.

14th   Turn not your Back to others especially in Speaking, Jog not the Table or Desk on which Another reads or writes, lean not upon any one.

15th   Keep your Nails clean and Short, also your Hands and Teeth Clean, yet without shewing any great Concern for them.

16th   Do not Puff up the Cheeks, Loll not out the tongue, rub the Hands, or beard, thrust out the lips, or bite them or keep the Lips too open or too Close.

17th   Be no Flatterer, neither Play with any that delights not to be Play'd Withal.

18th   Read no Letters, Books, or Papers in Company but when there is a Necessity for the doing of it you must ask leave: come not near the Books or Writings of Another so as to read them unless desired or give your opinion of them unask'd, also look not nigh when another is writing a Letter.

19th   Let your Countenance be pleasant but in Serious Matters Somewhat grave.

20th   The Gestures of the Body must be Suited to the discourse you are upon.

21st   Reproach none for the Infirmaties of Nature, nor Delight to Put them that have in mind thereof.

22nd   Shew not yourself glad at the Misfortune of another though he were your enemy.

23rd   When you see a Crime punished, you may be inwardly Pleased; but always shew Pity to the Suffering Offender.

24th   Do not laugh too loud or too much at any Publick Spectacle.

25th   Superfluous Complements and all Affectation of Ceremonie are to be avoided, yet where due they are not to be Neglected.

26th   In Pulling off your Hat to Persons of Distinction, as Noblemen, Justices, Churchmen &c make a Reverence, bowing more or less according to the Custom of the Better Bred, and Quality of the Person. Amongst your equals expect not always that they Should begin with you first, but to Pull off the Hat when there is no need is Affectation. In the Manner of Saluting and resaluting in words, keep to the most usual Custom.

27th   'Tis ill manners to bid one more eminent than yourself be covered as well as not to do it to whom it's due. Likewise he that makes too much haste to Put on his hat does not well, yet he ought to Put it on at the first, or at most the Second time of being ask'd; now what is herein Spoken, of Qualification in behaviour in Saluting, ought also to be observed in taking of Place, and Sitting down for ceremonies without Bounds is troublesome.

28th   If any one come to Speak to you while you are Sitting, Stand up 'tho he be your Inferiour, and when you Present Seats let it be to every one according to his Degree.

29th   When you meet with one of Greater Quality than yourself, Stop, and retire, especially if it be at a Door or any Straight place to give way for him to Pass.

30th   In walking, the highest Place in most Countrys Seems to be on the right hand, therefore Place yourself on the left of him whom you desire to Honour: but if three walk together, the middest Place is the most Honourable, the wall is usually given to the most worthy if two walk together.

31st   If any one far Surpassess others, either in age, Estate, or Merit, yet would give Place to a meaner than himself in his own lodging or elsewhere, the one ought not to accept it, So he on the other part should not use much earnestness nor offer it above once or twice.

32nd   To one that is your equal, or not much inferior, you are to give the chief Place in your Lodging and he to who 'tis offered ought at the first to refuse it, but at the Second to accept though not without acknowledging his own unworthiness.

33rd   They that are in Dignity or in office have in all places Precedency, but whilst they are Young they ought to respect those that are their equals in Birth or other Qualitys, though they have no Publick charge.

34th   It is good Manners to prefer them to whom we Speak before ourselves, especially if they be above us with whom in no Sort we ought to begin.

35th   Let your Discourse with Men of Business be Short and Comprehensive.

36th   Artificers & Persons of low Degree ought not to use many ceremonies to Lords, or Others of high Degree, but Respect and highly Honour them, and those of high Degree ought to treat them with affability & Courtesie, without Arrogancy.

37th   In Speaking to men of Quality do not lean nor Look them full in the Face, nor approach too near them, at lest Keep a full Pace from them.

38th   In visiting the Sick, do not Presently play the Physician if you be not Knowing therein.

39th   In writing or Speaking, give to every Person his due Title According to his Degree & the Custom of the Place.

40th   Strive not with your Superiors in argument, but always Submit your Judgment to others with Modesty.

41st   Undertake not to Teach your equal in the art himself Proffesses; it Savours of arrogancy.

42nd   Let thy ceremonies in Courtesie be proper to the Dignity of his place with whom thou conversest for it is absurd to act ye same with a Clown and a Prince.

43rd   Do not express Joy before one sick or in pain, for that contrary Passion will aggravate his Misery.

44th   When a man does all he can though it Succeeds not well, blame not him that did it.

45th   Being to advise or reprehend any one, consider whether it ought to be in publick or in Private; presently, or at Some other time in what terms to do it & in reproving Shew no Sign of Cholar but do it with all Sweetness and Mildness.

46th   Take all Admonitions thankfully in what Time or Place Soever given but afterwards not being culpable take a Time & Place convenient to let him know it that gave them.

47th   Mock not nor Jest at any thing of Importance, break no Jest that are Sharp, Biting; and if you Deliver any thing witty and Pleasent, abstain from Laughing thereat yourself.

48th   Wherein you reprove Another be unblameable yourself; for example is more prevalent than Precepts.

49th   Use no Reproachfull Language against any one, neither Curse nor Revile.

50th   Be not hasty to believe flying Reports to the Disparagement of any.

51st   Wear not your Cloths, foul, unript or Dusty, but See they be Brush'd once every day at least, and take heed that you approach not to any uncleaness.

52nd   In your Apparel be Modest and endeavour to accomodate Nature, rather than to procure Admiration, keep to the Fashion of your equals Such as are Civil and orderly with respect to Times and Places.

53rd   Run not in the Streets, neither go too slowly nor with Mouth open, go not Shaking yr Arms, kick not the earth with yr feet, go not upon the Toes, nor in a Dancing fashion.

54th   Play not the Peacock, looking every where about you, to See if you be well Deck't, if your Shoes fit well, if your Stokings Sit neatly, and Cloths handsomely.

55th   Eat not in the Streets, nor in ye House, out of Season.

56th   Associate yourself with Men of good Quality if you Esteem your own Reputation; for 'tis better to be alone than in bad Company.

57th   In walking up and Down in a House, only with One in Company, if he be Greater than yourself, at the first give him the Right hand and Stop not till he does, and be not the first that turns, and when you do turn let it be with your face towards him, if he be a man of Great Quality, walk not with him Cheek by Joul, but Somewhat behind him; but yet in Such a Manner that he may easily Speak to you.

58th   Let your Conversation be without Malice or Envy, for 'tis a Sign of a Tractable and Commendable Nature: And in all Causes of Passion admit Reason to Govern.

59th   Never express anything unbecoming, nor Act against ye Rules Moral before your inferiours.

60th   Be not immodest in urging your Friends to Discover a Secret.

61st   Utter not base and frivilous things amongst grave and Learn'd Men, nor very Difficult Questions or Subjects, among the Ignorant, or things hard to be believed. Stuff not your Discourse with Sentences amongst your Betters nor Equals.

62nd   Speak not of doleful Things in a Time of Mirth or at the Table; Speak not of Melancholy Things as Death and Wounds, and if others Mention them, Change if you can the Discourse. Tell not your Dreams, but to your intimate Friend.

63rd   A Man ought not to value himself of his Achievements, or rare Qualities of wit; much less of his riches, Virtue or Kindred.

64th   Break not a Jest where none take pleasure in mirth. Laugh not aloud, nor at all without Occasion, deride no man's Misfortune, tho' there seem to be Some Cause.

65th   Speak not injurious Words neither in Jest nor Earnest. Scoff at none although they give Occasion.

66th   Be not froward but friendly and Courteous; the first to Salute, hear and answer, & be not Pensive when it's a time to Converse.

67th   Detract not from others, neither be excessive in Commanding.

68th   Go not thither, where you know not, whether you Shall be Welcome or not. Give not Advice without being Ask'd, & when desired, do it briefly.

69th   If two contend together take not the part of either unconstrained; and be not obstinate in your own Opinion, in Things indifferent be of the Major Side.

70th   Reprehend not the imperfections of others, for that belongs to Parents, Masters and Superiours.

71st   Gaze not on the marks or blemishes of Others and ask not how they came. What you may Speak in Secret to your Friend deliver not before others.

72nd   Speak not in an unknown Tongue in Company but in your own Language, and that as those of Quality do, and not as ye Vulgar; Sublime matters treat Seriously.

73rd   Think before you Speak, pronounce not imperfectly nor bring out your Words too hastily but orderly & distinctly.

74th   When Another Speaks be attentive yourself, and disturb not the Audience. If any hesitate in his Words help him not nor Prompt him without desired, Interrupt him not, nor Answer him till his Speech be ended.

75th   In the midst of Discourse ask not of what one treateth, but if you Perceive any Stop, because of your coming you may well intreat him gently to Proceed: If a Person of Quality comes in while you're Conversing, it's handsome to Repeat what was said before.

76th   While you are talking, Point not with your Finger at him of Whom you discourse, nor Approach too near him to whom you talk, especially to his face.

77th   Treat with men at fit Times about Business & Whisper not in the Company of Others.

78th   Make no Comparisons, and if any of the Company be Commended for any brave act of Virtue, commend not another for the Same.

79th   Be not apt to relate News if you know not the truth thereof. In Discoursing of things you Have heard, Name not your Author always. A Secret Discover not.

80th   Be not Tedious in Discourse or in reading unless you find the Company pleased therewith.

81st   Be not Curious to Know the Affairs of Others, neither approach those that Speak in Private.

82nd   Undertake not what you cannot Perform, but be Carefull to keep your Promise.

83rd   When you deliver a matter, do it without Passion & with Discretion, however mean ye Person be you do it to.

84th   When your Superiours talk to any Body, hearken not, neither Speak nor Laugh.

85th   In Company of these of Higher quality than yourself, Speak not till you are ask'd a Question, then Stand upright, put off your Hat & answer in few words.

86th   In Disputes, be not So Desireous to Overcome as not to give Liberty to each one to deliver his Opinion and Submit to ye Judgment of ye Major

Part, especially if they are Judges of the Dispute.

87th   Let thy carriage be such as becomes a Man Grave, Settled and attentive to that which is spoken. Contradict not at every turn what others Say.

88th   Be not tedious in Discourse, make not many Digressions, nor repeat often the Same manner of Discourse.

89th   Speak not Evil of the absent for it is unjust.

90th   Being Set at meat, Scratch not, neither Spit, Cough or blow your Nose except there's a Necessity for it.

91st   Make no Shew of taking great Delight in your Victuals, Feed not with Greediness; cut your Bread with a knife, lean not on the Table neither find fault with what you Eat.

92nd   Take no Salt, or cut Bread with your Knife Greasy.

93rd   Entertaining any one at table, it is decent to present him with meat. Undertake not to help others undesired by ye Master.

94th   If you Soak bread in the Sauce let it be no more than what you put in your Mouth at a time, and blow not your broth at Table but Stay till Cools of itself.

95th   Put not your meat to your Mouth with your Knife in your hand, neither Spit forth the Stones of any fruit Pye upon a Dish, nor Cast anything under the table.

96th   It's unbecoming to Stoop much to one's Meat. Keep your Fingers clean & when foul, wipe them on a Corner of your Table Napkin.

97th   Put not another bit into your Mouth til the former be Swallowed. Let not your Morsels be too big for the Gowls.

98th   Drink not nor talk with your mouth full, neither Gaze about you while you are Drinking.

99th   Drink not too leisurely nor yet too hastily. Before and after Drinking wipe your Lips. Breathe not then or Ever with too Great a Noise, for it's uncivil.

100th   Cleanse not your teeth with the Table Cloth, Napkin, Fork or Knife but if Others do it, let it be done with a Pick Tooth.

101st   Rince not your Mouth in the Presence of Others.

102nd   It is out of use to call upon the Company often to Eat, nor need you Drink to others every Time you Drink.

103rd   In Company of your Betters be not longer in eating than they are, lay not your Arm but only your hand upon the table.

104th   It belongs to ye Chiefest in Company to unfold his Napkin and fall to Meat first, But he ought then to Begin in time & to Dispatch with Dexterity that ye Slowest may have time allowed him.

105th   Be not angry at Table whatever happens & if you have reason to be so, Shew it not but on a Cheerfull Countenance, especially if there be Strangers, for Good Humour makes one Dish of Meat a Feast.

106th   Set not yourself at ye upper of ye table but if it be your Due or that ye Master of ye house will have it So, Contend not, lest you Should Trouble ye Company.

107th   If others talk at Table be attentive, but talk not with Meat in your Mouth.

108th   When you Speak of God or His Attributes, let it be Seriously & with Reverence. Honour & Obey your Natural Parents altho they be Poor.

109th   Let your Recreations be Manfull not Sinfull.

110th   Labour to keep alive in your Breast that Little Spark of Celestial fire Called Conscience.

Finis [13]

Washington is Sworn into Office

The first President of the United States was sworn into office in New York on April 30, 1789. His left hand rested upon the Bible, which had been opened between the 49th and 50th chapters of Genesis. He then kissed the Bible and reverently said: "So - help - me - God."[14]

By this means, our first president set an unbroken Christian tradition for succeeding inaugurations of U.S. presidents, by which each president selects a Scripture of personal significance to him, and repeats, "So help me God" after swearing allegiance to the Constitution.

George Washington's First Inaugural Address

George Washington's first Presidential Inaugural Address, given to the U.S. Senate and House of Representatives on April 30, 1789, gives full allegiance and glory to Almighty God, as the author of our liberties in *this nation under God*. It is hereunder excerpted, for all Americans to understand that the foundational strength of our government comes from Almighty God, and His favor bestowed upon us:

. . . It would be peculiarly improper to omit in this first official act my fervent supplications to that Almighty Being who rules over the universe, who presides in the councils of nations, and whose providential aids can supply every human defect that His benediction may consecrate to the liberties and happiness of the people of the United States a government instituted by themselves for these essential purposes, and may enable every instrument employed in its administration to execute with success the functions allotted to his charge . . . No people can be bound to acknowledge and adore the Invisible Hand which conducts the affairs of men more than those of the United States. Every step by which they have advanced to the character of an independent nation seems to have been distinguished by some token of providential agency; and in the important revolution just accomplished in the system of their united government the tranquil deliberations and voluntary consent of so many distinct communities from which the event has resulted can not be compared with the means by which most governments have been established without some return of pious gratitude, along with an humble anticipation of the future blessings which the past seem to presage . . . I dwell on this prospect with every satisfaction which an ardent love for my country can inspire, since there is no truth more thoroughly established than that there exists in the economy and course of nature an indissoluble union between virtue and happiness; between duty and advantage; between the genuine maxims of an honest and magnanimous policy and the solid rewards of public prosperity and felicity; since we ought to be no less persuaded that the propitious smiles of Heaven can never be expected on a nation that disregards the eternal rules of order and right which Heaven itself hath ordained; and since the preservation of the sacred fire of liberty and the destiny of the republican model of government are justly considered, perhaps, as deeply, as finally, staked on the experiment entrusted to the hands of the American people . . .[15]

George Washington's Farewell Address

George Washington took his second oath of office in Congress Hall, in Philadelphia, and in 1796 delivered his famous *Farewell Address* praying for the nation as follows:

. . . May Heaven continue to you the choicest tokens of its beneficence: that your union and brotherly affection may be perpetual; . . . that the free Constitution, which is the work of your hands, may be sacredly maintained; that its administration in every department may be stamped with wisdom and virtue; that in fine, the happiness of the people of these states, under the auspices of liberty may be made complete by so careful a preservation and so prudent a use of this blessing as will acquire to them the glory of recommending it to the applause, the affection and adoption of every nation which is yet a stranger to it . . . It is of infinite moment that you should properly estimate the immense value of your national union to your collective and individual happiness. The name American, which belongs to you in your national capacity, must always exult the just pride of patriotism more than any appellation derived from local discriminations . . . [16]

Jefferson on Washington's Character

Thomas Jefferson's description of the character of George Washington, further shows his qualifications for the task to which he was called, as father of *this nation under God:*

> He was incapable of fear, meeting personal dangers with the calmest unconcern. Perhaps the strongest feature in his character was prudence, never acting until every circumstance, every consideration, was maturely weighed; refraining if he saw a doubt, but, when once decided, going through with his purpose, whatever obstacles opposed. His integrity was most pure, his justice the most flexible I have ever known, no motive of interest or consanguinity, or friendship or hatred, being able to bias his decision. He was, in every sense of the words, a wise, a good and a great man.[17]

Washington's General Orders

In an era when men are easily commended for good citizenship and right living, a backward glance at the origins and foundational strength of our country is exemplified in Washington's general orders, which reflect the caliber and moral rectitude which led to the formation of a unique republic, one which had the boldness to establish itself as the *one nation, under God.*

> All Officers, non-commissioned Officers and Soldiers are positively forbid playing at Cards, and other games of Chance. At this time of public distress, men may find enough to do in the service of their God, and their Country, without abandoning themselves to vice and immorality ... and it may not be amiss for the troops to know, that if any infamous Rascal in time of action, shall attempt to skulk, hide himself or retreat from the enemy without orders of his commanding Officer; he will instantly be shot down as an example of Cowardice: On the other hand, the General solemnly promises, that he will reward those who shall distinguish themselves, by brave and noble actions; and he desires every Officer to be attentive to this particular, that such men may be afterwards suitably noticed.

George Washington[18]

John Adams on Washington's Character

In addition to this, our second U.S. President extols the life and character of his friend and colleague, in an address delivered to the U.S. Senate shortly after his death:

December, 1799

. . . the life of our Washington cannot suffer by a comparison with those of other countries, who have been most celebrated and exalted by Fame. The attributes and decorations of Royalty, could only have served to eclipse the majesty of those virtues, which made him, from being a model citizen, a more resplendent luminary. Misfortune, had he lived, could hereafter have sullied his glory only with those superficial minds, who, believing that character and actions are marked by success alone, rarely deserve to enjoy it. Malice could never blast his honor, and envy made him a singular exception to her universal rule. For himself, he had lived enough, to lift and to glory. For his fellow citizens, if their prayers could have been answered he would have been immortal. For me, his departure is at a most unfortunate moment. Trusting, however, in the wise and righteous dominions of Providence over passions of men, and the result of their councils and actions, as well as over their lives, nothing remains for me but humble resignation. His example is now complete, and it will teach wisdom and virtue to magistrates, citizens and men, not only in the present age, but in future generations as long as our history shall be read . . . [19]

Such was the Christian example and moral direction given by the founder and first President of our unique republic. An oft-quoted question which arises at this juncture of America's history, is the following: Does Washington's concept, belief and intent for America reflect the United States of today? Was not his America the one country in the world established under the guidance, direction and banner of Almighty God, to whom was given all praise, honor and worship by the great men who formed and fashioned her pivotal foundations? The answer to this question is perhaps to be found in the inaugural Scripture chosen by the 40th President of the United States on January 20, 1981; and January 20, 1985, respectively: [20]

> . . . if My people who are called by My name, humble themselves and pray, and seek My face and turn from their wicked ways, then I will hear from heaven, and will forgive their sin, and will heal their land. II Chronicles 7:14

It is fitting here that we pause a moment to reiterate George Washington's prayer for America:

> Almighty God; We make our earnest prayer that Thou wilt keep the United States in Thy holy protection; that Thou wilt incline the hearts of the citizens to cultivate a spirit of subordination and obedience to government; and entertain a brotherly affection and love for one another and for their fellow citizens of the United States at large. And finally that Thou wilt most graciously be pleased to dispose us all to do justice, to love mercy, and to demean ourselves with that charity, humility and pacific temper of mind which were the characteristics of the Divine Author of our blessed religion, and without a humble imitation of whose example in these things we can never hope to be a happy nation. Grant our supplication, we beseech Thee, through Jesus Christ our Lord. Amen. [21]

LESSON ONE

PUPILS' GUIDE

The Washington Monument - "Laus Deo," Praise be to God!

I. Suggestions for Study

a) Read the lesson material carefully.

b) Look up Mount Vernon, Virginia; Delaware; Louisiana; Georgia; Indiana; Pennsylvania; North Carolina; Maryland; Virginia; Greece and China, on your maps of the United States and the world at home.

II. Lesson material

Text: Lesson 1 - The Washington Monument.

III. 1. The kind of man George Washington was:

i) How tall is the Washington Monument, and what phrase is inscribed upon the outer facade of its aluminum cap, facing our U.S. Capitol? (Circle one)

    a) 450 and a half feet - "Semper Fidelis"
    b) 555 feet 5 and one-eighth inches - "Praise be to God"
    c) 560 feet - "Equal Justice under Law"
    d) 580 feet - "A Tribute to Washington"

ii) What symbol can clearly be traced over the capital city of the United States from the top of the Washington Monument? (Circle one)

    a) A triangle
    b) The cross of Jesus Christ
    c) A pentagon
    d) A perfect square mile

iii) At the age of 15, George Washington penned his *110 Rules of Civility and Decent Behaviour in Company and Conversation*, which he meticulously practiced in adulthood. Some of these are as follows: (Consult your text and fill in the blanks)

    a) Rule 6: Sleep not when _____ _____ , sit not

when _____ _____ , speak not when you should
_____ _____ _____ , walk not on when
_____ _____ .

b) Rule 22: Shew not yourself _____ at the _____ of
_____ though he were your _____ .

c) Rule 108: When you speak of _____ or His _____ ,
let it be _____ and with _____ .
_____ and _____ your natural _____ , altho
they be _____ .

d) Rule 109: Let your_____ be _____ , not
_____ .

iv) What predominant characteristics does the above portray in the life and
conduct of George Washington? (Circle four)

a) self-centeredness
b) rudeness
c) godliness
d) consideration of others
e) mercilessness
f) righteousness
g) mercy

v) The Washington Monument's unique simplicity is enhanced by: (Fill in
the blanks)

a) _____ _____ _____ flags,
_____ encircling the _____ , each one
representing _____ of the _____ states in the
_____ .

vi) How many steps and landings, respectively, are there within the Washington
Monument? (Circle one)

a) 700; 30
b) 850; 45
c) 898; 50
d) 920; 60

vii) How many memorial stones are inserted within the inner staircase walls of
the Washington Monument? (Circle one)

a) 35
b) 120
c) 190
d) 205

viii) Numerous memorial stone inscriptions within the inner staircase walls of the Washington Monument glorify God and extol Christian virtues upon which this nation was founded. (Consult your text and fill in the blanks)

a) **Stone 26:** "_____ and our native _____." United _____ of America. Instituted 1845. _____ .

b) **Stone 27:** Grand Division, Sons of _____, North Carolina. "_____, _____, _____."

c) **Stone 95:** "_____, _____, _____." Pennsylvania. (Founded _____). By Deeds of _____ .

d) **Stone 98:** The _____ safeguard of the _____ of our Country - Total _____ from all that _____ . Sons of _____ of Pennsylvania.

e) **Stone 104:** "To Washington, the _____, _____ and _____, by _____ BREMEN."

f) **Stone 107:** From the _____ of Honor and _____. Organized Dec. 5th 1845. "_____, _____, Purity and _____." Our Pledge: "We will not _____ , buy, _____ or use as a beverage, any _____ or malt _____, _____, cider, or any other _____ liquor, and we will _____ their manufacture, _____ and use, and this pledge we will _____ unto the _____ of life." Supreme Council of the _____ of Honor and _____. 1846.

g) **Stone 124:** China. . . It is evident that Washington was a _____ man . . . Ah, who would not call him a _____ ? The _____ _____ of America regard it _____ of national _____ generally and _____ neither to establish _____ of _____ and royalty nor to conform to the _____, . . . but instead _____ over their own _____ _____ and inventions, so that the _____ of such a _____, one so _____, does not exist in ancient or modern _____. Among the _____ of the _____ _____ can any man, in ancient or modern _____, fail to _____ WASHINGTON _____ ? This stone is presented by a _____ of _____ and engraved at Ningpu . . . China. . . the reign of the _____ Heen Fung. . . (July 12th, 1853.)

h) **Stone 127:** _____ to the _____ .

i) **Stone 133:** Under the _____ of _____ and the _____ of Washington, Kentucky will be the _____ to give up the _____. "_____ we stand, _____ we fall."

j) **Stone 156:** The memory of the _____ is _____.
Prov. 10:7. Presented by the _____ of the _____
_____ of the _____ _____ Church,
in the City of New York, Feb. 22, '55.

k) **Stone 158:** From the _____ _____ children of
the _____ _____ Church in the City and Districts of
_____, 4th July 1853. A _____ Gospel. A free
_____. Washington. We _____ his memory. "Search
the _____." Suffer little _____ to come unto
_____ and forbid them _____, for of such is the
_____ of _____. Luke 18:16. Train up a _____
in the way he should _____, and when he is _____, he will
not _____ from _____. Prov. 22:6.

ix) Numerous memorial stone inscriptions within the inner staircase walls of the Washington Monument pay tribute to the sacredness, value and importance of the U.S. Constitution. They are as follows: (Consult your text and fill in the blanks)

a) **Stone 5:** Delaware. First to _____ , will be the
_____ to _____ the Constitution.

b) **Stone 10:** Alabama. A Union of _____ as
_____ by the Constitution.

c) **Stone 11:** The_____ of Louisiana. Ever _____
to the Constitution and the _____.

d) **Stone 17:** _____ of Georgia. The _____ as it
was. The Constitution _____ _____ _____.

e) **Stone 47:** North Carolina. Declaration of _____.
Mecklenburg, May, 1775. "_____."

f) **Stone 80:** Anno 1850. By the City of _____. May
_____ to this _____ continue its
_____; May _____ _____ with Union
be _____; May the Free _____, which is the
work of our _____ be _____ maintained and its
_____ be stamped with _____ and
_____ . (From George Washington's Farewell Address).

g) **Stone 96:** Declaration of _____, Philadelphia, July 4th,
1776. _____ of the City of _____.

x) What lies within the recess of the Washington Monument cornerstone? (Circle all correct answers)

a) A map of Washington, D.C.
b) The Holy Bible
c) Sports' equipment
d) Newspapers

e) An American silk flag
f) Indian arts and crafts
g) Copies of the U.S. Constitution and Declaration of Independence
h) U.S. Presidents' inaugural speeches up to 1848
i) A duplicate of Gilbert Stuart's renowned portrait of George Washington
j) A guide to restaurants
k) Daguerreotype likenesses of General and Mrs. Washington

xi) In George Washington's General Orders, our first U.S. President extols: (Circle all correct answers)

a) God
b) Self
c) Insubordination
d) Bravery
e) Disobedience
f) Patriotism
g) Laziness
h) Noble actions

xii) In George Washington's General Orders, our first U.S. President condemns: (Circle all correct answers)

a) All games of Chance
b) Faithfulness
c) Vice
d) Discipline
e) Immorality
f) Courage
g) Praiseworthiness
h) Skulking

xiii) George Washington prayed for the United States. In his prayer, he beseeches Almighty God to: (Fill in the blanks)

a) Almighty _____; We make our _____ prayer that
Thou wilt _____ the _____ _____ in
Thy _____ _____; that Thou wilt incline the
_____ of the _____ to cultivate a
_____ of _____ and _____ to
_____; and entertain a _____ affection and
_____ for one _____ and for their fellow
_____ of the _____ _____ at large.
And finally that Thou wilt _____ _____ be
pleased to _____ us all to do _____, to love

_____, and to _____ ourselves with that
_____, _____ and _____ temper of
_____ which were the characteristics of the _____
_____ of our blessed _____, and without a
_____ imitation of whose _____ in these things
we can never _____ to be a _____ nation.
Grant our _____, we beseech Thee, through
_____ _____ our Lord. Amen.

xiv) Founding father, Thomas Jefferson, describes the character of George Washington from first-hand knowledge, as follows: (Fill in the blanks)

a) He was _____ of fear, meeting personal _____
with the _____ unconcern. Perhaps the _____
feature in his character was _____, never acting until
every _____, every _____, was _____
weighed; refraining if he saw a _____, but, when once
_____, going through with his _____, whatever
_____ opposed. His _____ was most
_____, his _____ the most _____ I have
ever _____, no motive of _____ or
_____, or _____ or _____, being able to
_____ his decision. He was, in every sense of the
_____, a _____, a _____, and a
_____ man.

xv) In George Washington's _First Presidential Inaugural Address_, to whom does he give the glory as Ruler of the Universe? (Circle one)

a) Mohammed and his prophet
b) Garibaldi
c) Buddha
d) Almighty God of the Bible
e) Alexander the Great

xvi) George Washington delivered his famous _Farewell Address_ in 1796 from Congress Hall, Philadelphia, praying for the nation as follows: (Fill in the blanks)

a) . . . May _____ continue to you the choicest
_____ of its _____: that your _____ and
_____ _____ may be _____; . . . that
the free _____, which is the work of _____ hands,
may be _____ maintained; that its _____ in
every _____ may be _____ with
_____ and _____; that in fine, the happiness of

the _____ of these _____, under the
_____ of liberty may be made _____ by so
_____ a preservation and so _____ a use of this
_____ as will _____ to them the
_____ of _____ it to the _____, the
_____ and _____ of every _____ which is
yet a _____ to it . . .

xvii)   Our first U.S. President, in his *Farewell Address*, prays that Almighty God
        would sacredly maintain: (Circle one)

        a)   The pursuit of pleasure
        b)   Success and prosperity
        c)   The free Constitution
        d)   Liberty and happiness

xviii) Our first U.S. President, in his *Farewell Address*, prays for the following to
        be evidenced in the U.S. government's administration: (Circle all correct
        answers)

        a)   Wisdom
        b)   Corruption
        c)   Scandal
        d)   Virtue
        e)   Hypocrisy
        f)   Prudence
        g)   Greed
        h)   Liberty
        i)   Commendation
        j)   Deceit
        k)   Praiseworthiness
        l)   Esteem

xix)   Founding father, John Adams delivered a Eulogy to the U.S. Senate shortly
        after George Washington's death. In this Eulogy, what did Adams state the
        citizens of the United States had prayed for ? That: (Circle one)

        a)   George Washington resign his presidency
        b)   George Washington be impeached
        c)   George Washington be immortal
        d)   George Washington abandon his plantation home

xx)   In his Eulogy on George Washington, delivered to the U.S. Senate, founding
        father John Adams states that our first president's example will teach, to
        future generations, as long as America's history is read, the following: (Fill
        in the blanks)

a)   _____

b)   _____

2. Christian Character Traits

Select 10 Christian virtues, values and morals of this great American hero from the selected texts of original writings, documents and letters of George Washington and those who knew him. List them below:

a. _____   f. _____

b. _____   g. _____

c. _____   h. _____

d. _____   i. _____

e. _____   j. _____

IV. Illustrate your work with pictures, outline map, models and drawings.

V. Memory Verse: *(Inscribed upon Memorial Stone 158 of the Washington Monument):*

Train up a child in the way he should go, and when he is old, he will not depart from it.
                                      Proverbs 22:6.

The Lincoln Memorial

Original Marble Sculpture of Abraham Lincoln in the Lincoln Memorial by Daniel Chester French

Abraham Lincoln's Church - two blocks from the White House

The Christian Heritage Of Our Nation - History Curriculum

THE
BELIEVER'S
DAILY
TREASURE;

or,

Tecls of Scripture,
arranged for every day in the year.

The law of thy mouth is better unto me
than thousands of gold and silver.
Psalm cxix. 72.

FOURTH EDITION

LONDON:
THE RELIGIOUS TRACT SOCIETY;
Depository, 56, Paternoster Row, and
65, St. Paul's Churchyard;
AND SOLD BY THE BOOKSELLERS.

1852.

46   MARCH.

20.   INDWELLING OF THE SPIRIT.

Know ye not that ye are the temple
of God, and that the Spirit of God
dwelleth in you?   1 Cor. iii. 16.

Think what Spirit dwells within thee;
Think what Father's smiles are thine;
Think that Jesus died to win thee;
Child of heaven, canst thou repine?

21.   INTERCESSION OF THE SPIRIT.

The Spirit also helpeth our infirmities:
for we know not what we should pray
for as we ought : but the Spirit itself
maketh intercession for us with groan-
ings which cannot be uttered.   Rom.
viii. 26.

Let pure devotion's fervours rise,
Let every holy feeling glow;
Oh, let the rapture of the skies
Kindle in our cold hearts below.
Come, visit every humble mind;
Come, pour thy Spirit, come,
And make our hearts thy constant home.

BELIEVER'S PRIVILEGES.   47

22.   SANCTIFICATION BY THE SPIRIT.

Elect according to the foreknowledge
of God the Father, through sanctification
of the Spirit, unto obedience and sprin-
kling of the blood of Jesus.   1 Pet. i. 2.

Can aught beneath a power divine
The stubborn will subdue?
'Tis thine the eternal Spirit, thine,
To form our hearts anew.

'Tis thine the passions to recall,
And upwards bid them rise;
And make the scales of error fall
From reason's darkened eyes.

23.   THE FRUITS OF THE SPIRIT.

The fruit of the Spirit is love, joy,
peace, long-suffering, gentleness, goodness, faith, meekness, temperance:
against such there is no law.   Gal. v.
22, 23.

'Tis God himself the ground prepares,
His Spirit sows the land;
And every pleasant fruit it bears,
Is nurtur'd by his hand.

Lincoln's hand-autographed Devotional - "The Believer's Daily Treasure"

FOUR SCORE AND SEVEN YEARS AGO OUR FATHERS BROUGHT FORTH ON THIS CONTINENT A NEW NATION CONCEIVED IN LIBERTY AND DEDICATED TO THE PROPOSITION THAT ALL MEN ARE CREATED EQUAL.

NOW WE ARE ENGAGED IN A GREAT CIVIL WAR TESTING WHETHER THAT NATION OR ANY NATION SO CONCEIVED AND SO DEDICATED CAN LONG ENDURE · WE ARE MET ON A GREAT BATTLEFIELD OF THAT WAR · WE HAVE COME TO DEDICATE A PORTION OF THAT FIELD AS A FINAL RESTING PLACE FOR THOSE WHO HERE GAVE THEIR LIVES THAT THAT NATION MIGHT LIVE · IT IS ALTOGETHER FITTING AND PROPER THAT WE SHOULD DO THIS · BUT IN A LARGER SENSE WE CAN NOT DEDICATE — WE CAN NOT CONSECRATE — WE CAN NOT HALLOW THIS GROUND · THE BRAVE MEN LIVING AND DEAD WHO STRUGGLED HERE HAVE CONSECRATED IT FAR ABOVE OUR POOR POWER TO ADD OR DETRACT THE WORLD WILL LITTLE NOTE NOR LONG REMEMBER WHAT WE SAY HERE BUT IT CAN NEVER FORGET WHAT THEY DID HERE. IT IS FOR US THE LIVING RATHER TO BE DEDICATED HERE TO THE UNFINISHED WORK WHICH THEY WHO FOUGHT HERE HAVE THUS FAR SO NOBLY ADVANCED · IT IS RATHER FOR US TO BE HERE DEDICATED TO THE GREAT TASK REMAINING BEFORE US — THAT FROM THESE HONORED DEAD WE TAKE INCREASED DEVOTION TO THAT CAUSE FOR WHICH THEY GAVE THE LAST FULL MEASURE OF DEVOTION — THAT WE HERE HIGHLY RESOLVE THAT THESE DEAD SHALL NOT HAVE DIED IN VAIN — THAT THIS NATION UNDER GOD SHALL HAVE A NEW BIRTH OF FREEDOM — AND THAT GOVERNMENT OF THE PEOPLE BY THE PEOPLE FOR THE PEOPLE SHALL NOT PERISH FROM THE EARTH.

The Gettysburg Address

"Emancipation of a Race"
The Angel of Truth sets a slave free. Shackles fall off the arms and feet of the slave (to the right).

"Immortality" by Jules Guerin

"Justice and Law" by *Jules Guerin*

IF WE SHALL SUPPOSE THAT AMERICAN SLAVERY IS ONE OF THOSE OFFENSES WHICH IN THE PROVIDENCE OF GOD MUST NEEDS COME BUT WHICH HAVING CONTINUED THROUGH HIS APPOINTED TIME HE NOW WILLS TO REMOVE AND THAT HE GIVES TO BOTH NORTH AND SOUTH THIS TERRIBLE WAR AS THE WOE DUE TO THOSE BY WHOM THE OFFENSE CAME SHALL WE DISCERN THEREIN ANY DEPARTURE FROM THOSE DIVINE ATTRIBUTES WHICH THE BELIEVERS IN A LIVING GOD ALWAYS ASCRIBE TO HIM. FONDLY DO WE HOPE ~ FERVENTLY DO WE PRAY ~ THAT THIS MIGHTY SCOURGE OF WAR MAY SPEEDILY PASS AWAY · YET IF GOD WILLS THAT IT CONTINUE UNTIL ALL THE WEALTH PILED BY THE BONDSMAN'S TWO HUNDRED AND FIFTY YEARS OF UNREQUITED TOIL SHALL BE SUNK AND UNTIL EVERY DROP OF BLOOD DRAWN WITH THE LASH SHALL BE PAID BY ANOTHER DRAWN WITH THE SWORD AS WAS SAID THREE THOUSAND YEARS AGO SO STILL IT MUST BE SAID "THE JUDGMENTS OF THE LORD ARE TRUE AND RIGHTEOUS ALTOGETHER"

WITH MALICE TOWARD NONE WITH CHARITY FOR ALL WITH FIRMNESS IN THE RIGHT AS GOD GIVES US TO SEE THE RIGHT LET US STRIVE ON TO FINISH THE WORK WE ARE IN TO BIND UP THE NATION'S WOUNDS TO CARE FOR HIM WHO SHALL HAVE BORNE THE BATTLE AND FOR HIS WIDOW AND HIS ORPHAN ~ TO DO ALL WHICH MAY ACHIEVE AND CHERISH A JUST AND LASTING PEACE AMONG OURSELVES AND WITH ALL NATIONS ·

The third panel of Abraham Lincoln's second Inaugural Address

The Christian Heritage Of Our Nation - History Curriculum

"Reunion of the North and the South" by Jules Guerin

Reunion of the North and the South

"Charity" taking care of the orphans, the lame and the blind.

*"Fraternity" a woman enfolds a man, a woman & child in her arms, the nucleus family,
replenishing the abundance of the earth.*

The Christian Heritage Of Our Nation - History Curriculum

The "One Nation Under God" stained-glass window

One Nation Under God

The Reflecting Pool - Lincoln Memorial

I pledge allegiance to the flag of the United States of America and to the Republic for which it stands. One Nation Under God indivisible with liberty and justice for all.   1954

The Lincoln Memorial

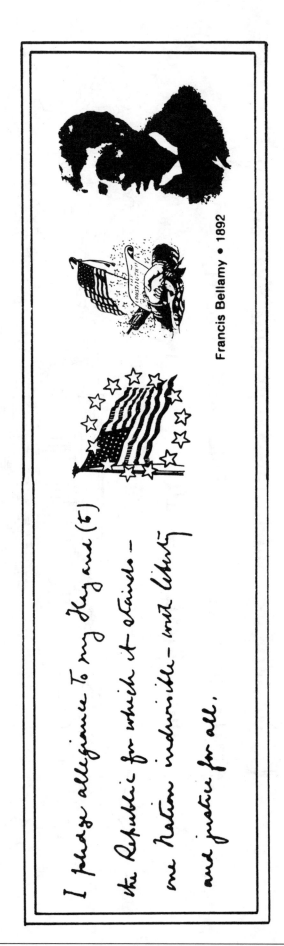

Francis Bellamy's originial "Pledge of Allegiance to our Flag" - 1892

The Christian Heritage Of Our Nation - History Curriculum

Rooted in the past
Building in the present
Reaching to the future
First Baptist Church - 1829
Little Falls, New York

LESSON 2

THE LINCOLN MEMORIAL

> . . . I do, therefore, invite my fellow-citizens in every part of the United States, and also those who are sojourning in foreign lands, to set apart and observe the last Thursday in November next as a day of thanksgiving and praise to our beneficent Father who dwelleth in the heavens.
>
> (signed) A. Lincoln.
October 3, 1863
>
> **Proclamation for Thanksgiving by the President of the United States.**[1]

On the 28th August, 1963, Dr. Martin Luther King Jr. delivered from the steps of the Lincoln Memorial, his now famous "I have a Dream" speech to over 200,000 people. The following is an excerpt:

> I have a dream that one day every valley shall be exalted, every hill and mountain shall be made low, the rough places will be made plains, and the crooked places will be made straight, and the glory of the Lord shall be revealed, and all flesh shall see it together. (from Isaiah 40:4-5)[2]

The cornerstone of the building was laid in 1915, and its dedication took place on Memorial Day, 1922. In completing this memorial, which honors the sixteenth President of the United States, Architect Henry Bacon made this observation: ". . . any emulation or aspiration engendered by the memorial to Lincoln and his great qualities is increased by the visual relation of the Washington Monument and the Capitol."[3] Both of these edifices are seen in a perfect straight line with the Reflecting Pool from the steps of the Lincoln Memorial, one of the loveliest views in Washington. Constructed to resemble the Parthenon in Athens, the thirty-six doric columns which form a colonnade around the edifice reflect the existing states in the Union at the time Lincoln was assassinated. Inscribed on the upper attic walls are names of the 48 states in existence at the time the memorial was inaugurated in 1922. The two remaining states to join the Union, Alaska and Hawaii, are honored upon a handsome bronze plaque, centrally located on the flagging directly in front of the Lincoln Memorial's main steps.

Within the building, a 19-foot-tall marble statue portrays the president seated in an armchair. His face is pensive and thoughtful. Sculptor Daniel Chester French spent four years carving this remarkable image of Abraham Lincoln from 28 blocks of white Georgia marble. Lincoln's expression is both powerfully introverted and drawn, indicating the intense struggle of the Civil War.

The building stands close to 80 feet tall, the central chamber measuring 74 feet in height and 60 feet in width. Bronze girders on the ceiling contain laurel and oak leaves, designed by Jules Guerin. The interior walls are constructed of Indiana limestone, while pink Tennessee marble comprises the inside floor and wall base. Each of the two handsome tripods flanking the entranceway to the doric colonnade is 11 feet tall.

The Gettysburg Address

The *Gettysburg Address* is featured on the inside South Wall. It reads as follows:

> Fourscore and seven years ago our fathers brought forth on this continent a new nation, conceived in liberty, and dedicated to the proposition that all men are created equal. Now we are engaged in a great civil war, testing whether that nation, or any nation so conceived and so dedicated can long endure. We are met on a great battlefield of that war. We have come to dedicate a portion of that field as a final resting-place for those who here gave their lives that that nation might live. It is altogether fitting and proper that we should do this. But in a larger sense, we cannot dedicate, we cannot consecrate, we cannot hallow this ground. The brave men, living and dead, who struggled here, have consecrated it far above our poor power to add or detract. The world will little note, nor long remember, what we say here, but it can never forget what they did here. It is for us, the living, rather to be dedicated here to the unfinished work which they who fought here have thus far so nobly advanced. It is rather for us to be here dedicated to the great task remaining before us, that from these honored dead we take increased devotion to that cause for which they gave the last full measure of devotion; that we here highly resolve that these dead shall not have died in vain; that this nation, *under God*, shall have a new birth of freedom, and that government of the people, by the people, for the people shall not perish from the earth.[4]

Lincoln was the first United States president to use the term: *This nation under God* in reference to our country. After his death, in 1865, on each succeeding February 12, a *Lincoln Day Observance Service* is held at the New York Avenue Presbyterian Church, his parish church, situated just two blocks from the White House. In 1954, Dwight D. Eisenhower was in attendance with his wife at this service. So moved was he by George Docherty's sermon entitled *Under God*, taken from Lincoln's words, that he initiated action in Congress to have it permanently made a part of the Pledge of Allegiance: "I pledge allegiance to the Flag of the United States of America and to the Republic for which it stands, *One Nation Under God*, indivisible, with liberty and justice for all."[5]

Francis Bellamy Pens Pledge of Allegiance to Our Flag

Francis Bellamy, the author of the Pledge of Allegiance to the Flag, was pastor of the *First Baptist Church of Little Falls*, in upstate New York from 1879-1885.[6] After graduating from the University of Rochester in 1876, Pastor Bellamy studied at *Rochester Theological Seminary.*[7] He was ordained to the Gospel ministry and installed as pastor of this church in 1879.[7] When Reverend Bellamy left Little Falls, he became pastor of the *Dearborn Street Baptist Church* of Boston. He subsequently became Advertising Editor of the weekly *Youth's Companion.*[8] In 1892, while serving as the chairman of the *National Public School Celebration of Columbus Day*, on the occasion of the 400th Anniversary of Columbus' discovery of America, he penned the final draft of the Pledge of Allegiance to the United States Flag. This beautiful Pledge was the result of many discussions between Reverend Bellamy and his superior, James B. Upham, and was designed to combat a growing movement aimed at destroying the national pride and patriotism of America's youth.[9]

Lincoln's Second Presidential Inaugural Address

On the North Wall of the Lincoln Memorial, his *Second Presidential Inaugural Address* takes its stance. It summarizes the state of the nation; the eradication of slavery being the reason and cause for the Civil War:

> At this second appearing to take the oath of the Presidential office there is less occasion for an extended address than there was at the first. Then a statement somewhat in detail of a course to be pursued seemed fitting and proper. Now, at the expiration of four years, during which public declarations have been constantly called forth on every point and phase of the great contest which still absorbs the attention and engrosses the energies of the nation, little that is new could be presented. The progress of our arms, upon which all else chiefly depends, is as well known to the public as to myself, and it is, I trust, reasonably satisfactory and encouraging to all. With high hope for the future, no prediction in regard to it is ventured.
>
> On the occasion corresponding to this four years ago all thoughts were anxiously directed to an impeding civil war. All dreaded it, all sought to avert it. While the inaugural address was being delivered from this place, devoted altogether to saving the Union without war, insurgent agents were in the city seeking to destroy it without war–seeking to dissolve the Union and divide effects by negotiation. Both parties deprecated war, but one of them would make war rather than let the nation survive, and the other would accept war rather than let it perish, and the war came.
>
> One-eighth of the whole population were colored slaves, not distributed generally over the Union, but localized in the southern part of it. These slaves constituted a peculiar and powerful interest. All knew that this interest was

somehow the cause of the war. To strengthen, perpetuate, and extend this interest was the object for which the insurgents would rend the Union, even by war; while the Government claimed no right to do more than to restrict the territorial enlargement of it. Neither party expected for the war the magnitude or the duration which it has already attained. Neither anticipated that the cause of the conflict might cease with, or even before, the conflict itself should cease. Each looked for an easier triumph, and a result less fundamental and astounding. Both read the same Bible and pray to the same God, and each invokes His aid against the other. It may seem strange that any men should dare to ask a just God's assistance in wringing their bread from the sweat of other men's faces, but let us judge not, that we be not judged.[10] The prayers of both could not be answered. That of neither has been answered fully. The Almighty has His own purposes. "Woe unto the world because of offenses; for it must needs be that offenses come, but woe to that man by whom the offense cometh."[11] If we shall suppose that American slavery is one of those offenses which, in the providence of God, must needs come, but which, having continued through His appointed time, He now wills to remove, and that He gives to both North and South this terrible war as the woe due to those by whom the offense came, shall we discern therein any departure from those divine attributes which the believers in a living God always ascribe to Him? Fondly do we hope, fervently do we pray, that this mighty scourge of war may speedily pass away. Yet, if God wills that it continue until all the wealth piled by the bondsman's two hundred and fifty years of unrequited toil shall be sunk, and until every drop of blood drawn with the lash shall be paid by another drawn with the sword, as was said three thousand years ago, so still it must be said "the judgments of the Lord are true and righteous altogether."[12]

With malice toward none, with charity for all, with firmness in the right as God gives us to see the right, let us strive on to finish the work we are in, to bind up the nation's wounds, to care for him who shall have borne the battle and for his widow and his orphan–to do all which may achieve and cherish a just and lasting peace among ourselves and with all nations.[13]

As was his custom, Lincoln quoted Scripture in his address, specifically Matthew 7:1; 18:7 and Revelation 16:7. Many references to God, the Bible and prayer were also incorporated.

Lincoln Memorial Mural Paintings

Above each address, a symbolic mural by Jules Guerin allegorizes Lincoln's ideals and principles of conduct.

Guerin's mural on the south wall is entitled *The Emancipation of a Race*. It is a tribute to Lincoln's *Emancipation Proclamation* signed on January 1, 1863. The central figure portrays the *Angel of Truth*, who sets a slave free. Shackles fall from the slave's arms and feet. The grouping to the left symbolizes *Justice and Law*. A sword of

Justice and the scroll of the Law are held by a central figure seated in the chair of the Law. Two upright guardians of the law hold torches of Intelligence.[14]

The grouping to the right depicts *Immortality*. *Faith*, *Hope*, and *Charity* stand by as a seated damsel receives the imperishable crown of immortality. The meaning here is that Eternal Life is acquired through faith in Christ, hope in Christ and Christ's love that is shed abroad in our hearts to others after the Holy Spirit indwells the believer at salvation.[15]

The north wall painting typifies *Reunion*. The central figure represents the *Angel of Truth*, who unites the North and the South by joining their hands together in a handclasp. To the left is a scene entitled: *Fraternity*. The central figure here is a woman who enfolds a man and a woman in her arms. This signifies the family nucleus replenishing the abundance of the earth. Vessels of wine and oil, symbols of Eternal Life, flank this grouping on either side.[16] The right grouping shows *Charity* in predominance. She is seen with her helpers, caring for orphans, the lame and the blind.[17] This is I Corinthians 13 in action. The artist used about 300 pounds of paint to execute his work, which was done on two pieces of canvas, each weighing 600 pounds. White lead and Venetian varnish were used to affix these canvases to the wall, making them entirely weatherproof. Forty-eight figures are represented in the two murals.[18]

Appropriately centered above the statue of Lincoln, in large capital letters, are engraved the words:

> In this Temple as in the hearts of the people for whom he saved the Union the memory of Abraham Lincoln is enshrined forever.

Abraham Lincoln's Formative Years

Abraham Lincoln, 16th president of the United States, was born in a lowly farm cabin near Hodgensville, Kentucky, on February 12, 1809. He was the first son and second child of Thomas Lincoln and Nancy Hanks, both of the Rockingham County, Virginia.[19]

Nancy Hanks' only book had been the Bible, from which Lincoln was taught and nurtured each day. She taught him to base his entire life upon the contents of that book. At his mother's untimely death when the boy was 10 years old, Lincoln knew much of the Word of God almost by heart. Many years later, as president of the United States, Lincoln is quoted as having said: "All that I am or hope to be, I owe to my angel mother. Blessings on her memory!"[20]

In 1819, Lincoln's father married Sarah Johnston of Kentucky. She brought cheer and kindness into the family, encouraging Abraham in his love for reading, which his father considered idleness. Lincoln had less than a year of formal school attendance, but learned to read and write and "cipher the rule of three," nonetheless.

He devoured books, beginning with the Bible. He worked at home, on neighboring farms, and became a clerk at Gentry's Store.[21]

At age 19 he accompanied the son of his employer to New Orleans on a flatboat trip.[22] It was there that he first saw an auction of slaves, and is reported to have said:

> By the grace of God I'll make the ground of this country too hot for the feet of slaves.[23]

In the book, *The Religion of Abraham Lincoln*, William W. Wolf wrote:

> No president has ever had the detailed knowledge of the Bible that Lincoln had. No president has ever woven its thoughts and its rhythms into the warp and woof of his state papers as he did.[24]

Abraham Lincoln's Family Bible

Abraham Lincoln's 1847 family Bible, one of the gems of America's Christian heritage, is in the custody of the Rare Book Collection of the Library of Congress. It displays the wording HOLY BIBLE upon its spine, and contains these beautiful illustrations: *Rebecca at the Well;* and *Samuel Praying*, showing the godly Old Testament hero kneeling in prayer at his bedside; and the baby Moses and his mother, captioned: "She took for Him an ark of Bulrushes and put the Child therein." (Exodus 11:3). The editor's preface to Lincoln's family Bible reads:

> . . . The sacred text is that of the Authorized Version, commonly called King James Bible, and is printed from the edition revised, corrected and improved, by Dr. Blayney, which from its accuracy, has been considered the Standard Edition, to which subsequent impressions should be made conformable. Forming an analysis and compendium of the Sacred Scriptures, of the Authenticity of the Scriptures: of the Inspiration of the Scriptures; of the Manuscripts and the Early Printed Editions of the Scriptures; of the Apostolic and Primitive Fathers; of the Jewish Sects; of the measures, weights and coins; of the modes of computing time in Scripture; Geography and History of the nations mentioned in Scripture . . .[25]

Four interior pages within this Bible contain Abraham Lincoln's *Family Record*, which includes this entry:

Abraham Lincoln and Mary Todd, married November 4, 1842.[26]

The Lincoln Marriage Certificate reads:

> The people of the state of Illinois – To any Minister of the Gospel, or other authorized person – Greetings. These are to license and permit you to join in the holy bands of Matrimony Abraham Lincoln and Mary Todd of the County

of Sangman and State of Illinois, and for so doing, this shall be your sufficient warrant.

Lincoln's Favorite Hymns

It was reported that Lincoln had favorite hymns that ministered to him. These old hymns glorified Jesus Christ, Son of God, Savior of the world. Among these are: *There is a Fountain Filled with Blood; When Shall I See Jesus and Reign with Him Above; Father, What E'er of Earthly Bliss Thy Sovereign Will Denies;* and *Rock of Ages.*[27]

Lincoln's Daily Devotional

Abraham Lincoln carried around with him in his vest pocket a small, hand-autographed leatherbound volume entitled, *The Believer's Daily Treasure.* This little devotional was read frequently by our 16th U.S. President. Reprinted below are some of the priceless gems of Scriptural Truth gleaned from its pages:

The Believer's Daily Treasure

January

**The
True Believer**

1

**The Believer the Object of
Divine Love**

In this was manifested the love of God toward us, because that God sent his only begotten Son into the world, that we might live through him. 1 John *iv. 9*.

> Pause, my soul, adore and wonder,
>   Ask, Oh, why such love to me?
> Grace hath put me in the number
>   Of the Saviour's family:
>   Hallelujah!
> Thanks, eternal thanks to thee.

2

Redeemed by the Blood of Christ

Forasmuch as ye know that ye were not redeemed with corruptible things, as silver and gold–but with the precious blood of Christ, as of a lamb without blemish and without spot. 1 Pet. *i. 18, 19.*

> Our sins and griefs on him were laid;
> He meekly bore the mighty load:
> Our ransom price he fully paid,
> By offering up himself to God.

3

Renewed by the Holy Ghost

Not by works of righteousness which we have done, but according to his mercy he saved us, by the washing of regeneration, and renewing of the Holy Ghost. Titus *iii. 5.*

> Vain is every outward rite,
> Unless thy grace be given:
> Nothing but thy life and light,
> Can form a soul for heaven.

4

Partaker of the Divine Nature

Whereby are given unto us exceeding great and precious promises: that by these ye might be partakers of the divine nature, having escaped the corruption that is in the world through lust.
2 Pet. *i. 4.*

> Blessed are the sons of God;
> They are bought with Christ's
> own blood;
> They produce the fruits of grace

In the works of righteousness:
Born of God, they hate all sin;
God's pure word remains within.

5

Justified Before God
Through Christ

By him all that believe are justified from all things, from which ye could not be justified by the law of Moses. Acts *xiii. 39.*

Jesus, thy blood and righteousness
My beauty are, and glorious dress;
'Midst flaming worlds, in these array'd,
With joy shall I lift up my head.

6

United to Christ

I am the vine, ye are the branches: he that abideth in me, and I in him, the same bringeth forth much fruit: for without me ye can do nothing. John *xv. 5.*

Lord of the vineyard, we adore
That power and grace divine,
Which plants our wild, our barren souls,
In Christ the living Vine.
For ever there may I abide,
And from that vital root,
Be influence spread through every branch,
To form and feed the fruit.

7

Joint-Heir with Christ

If children, then heirs; heirs of God, and joint-heirs with Christ. Rom. *viii. 17.*

Pronounce me, gracious God, thy son;
Own me an heir divine;
I'll pity princes on the throne,

When I can call thee mine:
Sceptres and crowns unenvied rise,
And lose their lustre in mine eyes.

8

Complete in Christ

For in him dwelleth all the fullness of the
Godhead bodily. And ye are complete in him.

Col. *ii. 9, 10.*

Thy saints on earth, and those above,
Here join in sweet accord:
One body all in mutual love,
And thou their common Lord.
Yes, thou that body wilt present
Before thy Father's face,
Nor shall a wrinkle or a spot
Its beauteous form disgrace.

9

Christ the Believer's Advocate

If any man sin, we have an advocate with the
Father, Jesus Christ the righteous.

1 John *ii. 1.*

Look up, my soul, with cheerful eye,
See where the great Redeemer stands
Thy glorious Advocate on high,
With precious incense in his hands.
He sweetens every humble groan,
He recommends each broken prayer;
Recline thy hope on him alone,
Whose power and love forbid despair.

10

Christ the Hope of the Believer

Paul, an apostle of Jesus Christ by the
commandment of God our Saviour, and Lord
Jesus Christ, which is our hope. 1 Tim. *i. 1.*

Jesus, my Lord, I look to thee;
Where else can helpless sinners go?

Thy boundless love shall set me free
From all my wretchedness and woe.

11

Christ the Life of the Believer

When Christ, who is our life, shall appear, then shall ye also appear with him in glory.
Col. *iii. 4.*

If my immortal Saviour lives,
Then my eternal life is sure;
His word a firm foundation gives,
Here let me build, and rest secure.
Here, O my soul, thy trust repose;
If Jesus is for ever mine,
Not death itself, that last of foes,
Shall break a union so divine.

12

Christ the Peace of the Believer

Now in Christ Jesus ye who sometime were far off are made nigh by the blood of Christ. For he is our peace. Eph. *ii. 13, 14.*

"He is our peace" – for by his blood
Sinners are reconcil'd to God;
Sweet harmony is now restor'd,
And man beloved, and God ador'd.

13

Christ the Righteousness of
the Believer

This is his name whereby he shall be called, The Lord our righteousness. Jer. *xxiii. 6.*

Saviour divine, we know thy name,
And in that name we trust;
Thou art the Lord our righteousness,
Thou art thine Israel's boast.

That spotless robe which thou hast wrought,
Shall clothe us all around,
Nor by the piercing eye of God
One blemish shall be found.

14

The Temple of the Spirit

Know ye not that your body is the temple of the Holy Ghost which is in you, which ye have of God. 1 Cor. *vi. 19.*

> Creator Spirit! by whose aid
>   The world's foundations first were laid,
> Come, visit every humble mind;
>   Come, pour thy joys on human kind:
> From sin and sorrow set us free,
>   And make us temples worthy thee.

15

Sanctified by the Spirit

God hath from the beginning chosen you to salvation through sanctification of the Spirit and belief of the truth. 2 Thess. *ii. 13.*

> Come, Holy Spirit, love divine,
>   Thy cleansing power impart;
> Each erring thought and wish refine
>   That wanders near my heart.

16

Upheld by the Spirit

That he would grant you, according to the riches of his glory, to be strengthened with might by his Spirit in the inner man.

Eph. *iii. 16.*

> Assisted by his grace,
>   We still pursue our way;
> And hope at last to reach the prize,
>   Secure in endless day.

17

The Spirit of Adoption Received

Ye have not received the spirit of bondage again

to fear; but ye have received the Spirit of adoption, whereby we cry, Abba, Father.

Rom. viii. 15.

> Assure my conscience of her part
>   In the Redeemer's blood,
> And bear thy witness in my heart
>   That I am born of God.

18

Comforted by the Spirit

When the Comforter is come, whom I will send unto you from the Father, even the Spirit of truth, which proceedeth from the Father, he shall testify of me. John *xv. 26.*

> In the hour of my distress,
>   When temptations me oppress,
> And when I my sins confess–
>   Sweet Spirit, comfort me.

19

Sealed by the Spirit

Grieve not the holy Spirit of God, whereby ye are sealed unto the day of redemption.

Eph. iv. 30.

> Forbid it, Lord, that we
>   Who from thy hands receive
> The Spirit's power to make us free,
>   Should e'er that Spirit grieve.
>
> O keep our faith alive,
>   Help us to watch and pray;
> Lest, by our carelessness, we drive
>   The sacred Guest away.

20

Taught by the Spirit

When he, the Spirit of truth, is come, he will guide you into all truth: for he shall not speak of himself; but whatsoever he shall hear, that shall he speak: and he will show you things to come. John *xvi. 13.*

Thine inward teachings make me know
The mysteries of redeeming love,
The emptiness of things below,
And excellence of things above.

21

Fellow-Citizen with the Saints

Now therefore ye are no more strangers and foreigners, but fellow-citizens with the saints, and of the household of God. Eph. *ii. 19.*

The kindred links of life are bright,
Yet not so bright as those
In which Christ's favoured friends unite,
And each on each repose:
Where all the hearts in union cling,
With Him, the centre and the spring.

22

Lives a Life of Faith in Christ

I am crucified with Christ: nevertheless I live; yet not I, but Christ liveth in me: and the life which I now live in the flesh I live by the faith of the Son of God. Gal. *ii. 20.*

Close to the ignominious tree,
Jesus, my humbled soul would cleave;
Despised and crucified with thee,
With Christ resolved to die and live:
There would I bow my suppliant knee,
And own no other Lord but thee.

23

Lives a Life of Consecration to God

I beseech you therefore, brethren, by the mercies of God, that ye present your bodies a living sacrifice, holy, acceptable unto God, which is your reasonable service. Rom. *xii. 1.*

Thine, wholly thine, I want to be;
The sacrifice receive:
Made, and preserved, and saved by thee,
To thee myself I give.

24

Lives a Life of Hope

Looking for the mercy of our Lord Jesus Christ
unto eternal life. Jude *21*.

> Rejoice in glorious hope;
>   Jesus, the Judge, shall come,
> And take his servants up
>   To their eternal home:
> Lift up your heart, lift up your voice;
>   Rejoice, he bids his saints rejoice.

25

Delivered from Condemnation

There is now no condemnation to them which
are in Christ Jesus, who walk not after the flesh,
but after the Spirit. Rom. *viii. 1*.

> O Love, thou bottomless abyss!
>   My sins are swallow'd up in thee;
> Cover'd is my unrighteousness,
>   From condemnation now I'm free;
> While Jesus' blood through earth and skies,
>   "Mercy, free boundless mercy!" cries.

26

Delivered from the Power of Satan

Forasmuch then as the children are partakers
of flesh and blood, he also himself likewise took
part of the same; that through death he might
destroy him that had the power of death, that
is, the devil. Heb. *ii. 14*.

> Dry up your tears, ye saints, and tell
>   How high your great Deliverer reigns;
> Sing, how he spoiled the host of hell,
>   And led the tyrant Death in chains.

27

Delivered from All Iniquity

Let Israel hope in the Lord: for with the Lord there is mercy, and with him is plenteous redemption. And he shall redeem Israel from all his iniquities. Psalm *cxxx. 7, 8.*

> Fix'd on this ground will I remain,
>   Though my heart fail, and flesh decay;
> This anchor shall my soul sustain,
>   When earth's foundations melt away:
> Mercy's full power I then shall prove,
>   Lov'd with an everlasting love.

28

Delivered from all Enemies

He delivereth me from mine enemies; yea, thou liftest me above those that rise up against me.
                    Psalm *xviii. 48.*

> Foes are round us, but we stand
>   On the borders of our land:
> Jesus, God's exalted Son,
>   Bids us undismay'd go on:
> Onward then we gladly press
>   Through this earthly wilderness.

29

Enjoys a Present Salvation

Which in time past were not a people, but are now the people of God: which had not obtained mercy, but now have obtained mercy.
                    1 Pet. *ii. 10.*

> Fill'd with holy emulation
>   Let us vie with those above:
> Sweet the theme—a free salvation,
>   Fruit of everlasting love.

30

Preserved unto Eternal Salvation

Who are kept by the power of God through faith unto salvation ready to be revealed in the last time.   1 Pet. *i. 5.*

> Saints by the power of God are kept
>   Till full salvation come;
> We walk by faith as strangers here
>   Till Christ shall call us home.

31

A Pilgrim to a Heavenly Country

Now they desire a better country, that is, an heavenly: wherefore God is not ashamed to be called their God: for he hath prepared for them a city. Heb. *xi. 16.*

> 'Tis true, we are but strangers
>   And sojourners below;
> And countless snares and dangers
>   Surround the path we go:
> Though painful and distressing,
>   Yet there's a rest above,
> And onward we are pressing
>   To reach that land of love. [28]

Abraham Lincoln's Death

Reverend Phineas Gurley, Abraham Lincoln's pastor at the New York Avenue Presbyterian Church in Washington, D.C., delivered the eulogy at his funeral, summarizing the life of a man who was loved by the people and who, in turn, loved his God and relied upon Him for everything in prayer:

"Have faith in God" — Mark 11:22
A Sermon delivered in the East Room of the Executive Mansion

Wednesday, April 19, 1865 at
The funeral of Abraham Lincoln,
President of the United States,
By: Rev. P.D. Gurley, D.D.
Pastor of the New York Avenue Presbyterian Church,
Washington, D.C.

As we stand here today, mourners around this coffin and around the lifeless remains of our beloved chief magistrate, we recognize and adore the sovereignty of God. His throne is in the heavens, and His kingdom ruleth over all. He hath done, and He hath permitted to be done, whatsoever He please.

. . . The people confided in the late lamented President with a full and loving confidence. Probably no man since the days of Washington was ever so deeply and firmly embedded and enshrined in the very hearts of the people as Abraham Lincoln. Nor was it a mistaken confidence and love. He deserved it—deserved it well—deserved it all. He merited it by his character, by his acts, and by the whole tenor, and tone, and spirit of his life. He was simple and sincere, plain and honest, truthful and just, benevolent and kind. His perceptions were quick and clear, his purposes were good and pure beyond question. Always and everywhere he aimed and endeavored to be right and to do right . . .

He saw his duty as the Chief Magistrate of a great and imperilled people, and he determined to do his duty, and his whole duty, seeking the guidance and leaning upon the arm of Him of whom it is written, "He giveth power to the faint, and to them that have no might He increaseth strength." Yes, he leaned upon His arm, he recognized and received the truth that the "kingdom is the Lord's, and He is the governor among the nations." He remembered that "God is in history," and felt that nowhere had His hand and His mercy been so marvelously conspicuous as in the history of this nation. He hoped and prayed that that same hand would continue to guide us, and that same mercy continue to abound to us in the time of our greatest need. I speak what I know, and testify what I have often heard him say, when I affirm that that guidance and mercy were the props upon which he humbly and habitually leaned; they were the best hope he had for himself and for his country. Hence, when he was leaving his home in Illinois, and coming to this city to take his seat in the executive chair of a disturbed and troubled nation, he said to the old and the tried friends who gathered tearfully around him and bade him farewell, "I leave you with this request: pray for me." They did pray for him; and millions of other people prayed for him; nor did they pray in vain. Their prayer was heard, and the answer appears in all his subsequent history; it shines forth with a heavenly radiance in the whole course and tenor of this administration, from its commencement to its close. God raised him up for a great and glorious mission, furnished him for his work, and aided him in its accomplishment. Nor was it merely by strength of mind, and honesty of heart, and purity and pertinacity of purpose, that He furnished him; in addition to these things, He gave him a calm and abiding confidence in the overruling Providence of God and in the ultimate triumph of truth and righteousness through the power and the blessing God . . .

Never shall I forget the emphasis and the deep emotion with which he said in this very room, to a company of clergymen and others, who called to pay him their respects in the darkest days of our civil conflict: "Gentlemen, my hope of success in this great and terrible struggle rests on that immutable foundation, the justice and goodness of God. And when events are threatening, and prospects very dark, I still hope that in some way which man cannot see all will be well in the end, because our cause is just, and God is on our side . . ."

He is dead; but the God in whom he trusted lives, and He can guide and strengthen his successor, as He guided and strengthened him . . . but the cause he so ardently loved survives his fall, and will survive it . . .[29]

LESSON TWO

The Lincoln Memorial – Abraham Lincoln, Emancipator of the Slaves.

I. Suggestions for Study

a)   Read the lesson material carefully.

b)   Look up Hodgensville, Kentucky; Springfield, Illinois; Washington, District of Columbia; Little Falls, New York and Boston, Massachusetts, on your United States map at home.

II. Lesson material

Text: Lesson 2 – The Lincoln Memorial - Abraham Lincoln, Emancipator of the Slaves.

III. 1. The kind of man Abraham Lincoln was:

i)   Inscribed upon the upper exterior attic walls of the Lincoln Memorial, at the time of its inauguration in 1922, are: (Circle one)

    a)   28 Olive branches
    b)   30 Grecian figures
    c)   48 States in the Union
    d)   45 Roman fasces*

ii)   What is honored, as inscribed upon the bronze plaque centrally located on the flagging in front of the Lincoln Memorial's main steps? (Circle one)

    a)   "The Civil War"
    b)   States' Sovereignty
    c)   North versus South
    d)   Alaska and Hawaii

iii)   The Lincoln Memorial pays tribute to a great American president and his heroic cause. These facts are engraved in marble above Abraham Lincoln's marble statue, as follows: (Fill in the blanks)

    a)   In this _____ as in the _____ of the
        _____ for whom he _____ the _____,
        the memory of _____ _____ is _____
        forever.

*The symbol for Roman Unified Government.

iv) Two national documents permanently effecting America's way of life were signed by President Abraham Lincoln. They are: (Circle two)

    a) Lincoln's First Inaugural Address, 1861
    b) The Emancipation Proclamation, 1863
    c) Lincoln's Autobiography, 1859
    d) Proclamation for Thanksgiving, 1863

v) Abraham Lincoln's famed proclamation, signed on October 3, 1863, concludes thus: (Fill in the blanks)

    a) I do, therefore, _____ my _____ in every part of the _____ _____, and also those who are _____ in foreign _____, to set apart and observe the _____ _____ in _____ next as a day of _____ and _____ to our _____ _____ who dwelleth in the _____.

vi) What famous American historic documents are inscribed in their entirety on the North and South walls of the Lincoln Memorial, respectively? (Circle two)

    a) Lincoln's *Independence Hall Address,* 1861
    b) Lincoln's *Second Inaugural Address,* 1865
    c) *The Gettysburg Address,* 1863
    d) Lincoln's *Springfield, Illinois letter,* 1861

vii) The three Scripture verses quoted by Abraham Lincoln in his *Second Inaugural Address* are: (Circle three)

    a) Deuteronomy 8:11
    b) Matthew 7:1
    c) Mark 7:6
    d) Matthew 18:7
    e) Luke 20:17
    f) Revelation 16:7
    g) James 1:27

viii) The three Scripture verses chosen by Abraham Lincoln for the American people in his *Second Inaugural Address,* read respectively: (Fill in the blanks)

    a) Let us _____ _____ that we be not _____.
    b) Woe unto the _____ because of _____; for it must needs be that _____ come, but woe to that _____ by whom _____ _____ cometh.

c) The _____ of the _____ are _____ and
_____ altogether.

ix) The Biblical offense against Almighty God, cited by Abraham Lincoln in his
Second Inaugural Address is: (Circle one)

   a)   Economic greed
   b)   Financial gain and avarice
   c)   War
   d)   American slavery

x) What attributes does Abraham Lincoln affirm that believers in a living God
have always ascribed to Him (in his *Second Inaugural Address*)? (Circle
three)

   a)   Judgment
   b)   Constancy
   c)   Truth
   d)   Omnipotence
   e)   Righteousness
   f)   Justice
   g)   Patience

xi) How many times does Abraham Lincoln extol Almighty God, directly or
indirectly, in his *Second Inaugural Address?* (Circle one)

   a)   3
   b)   5
   c)   7
   d)   16

xii) In his *Second Inaugural Address*, how many times, directly and indirectly,
does Abraham Lincoln cite the Bible and prayer? (Circle one)

   a)   6
   b)   3
   c)   5
   d)   9

xiii) In his famed *Gettysburg Address*, Abraham Lincoln states that: (Fill in the
blanks)

   a)   Fourscore and _____ _____ ago, our
        _____ brought forth on _____ _____ a
        _____ nation, conceived in _____, and _____
        to the proposition that _____ _____ are _____
        equal.

xiv) In the above Introduction of Lincoln's *Gettysburg Address*, our 16th United States President states that all men are: (Circle one)

a) Born equal (by birth certificate)
b) Treated as equal (by men)
c) Created equal (by Almighty God)
d) Considered equal (by society)

xv) In his *Gettysburg Address*, Abraham Lincoln states that those who died valiantly in the Civil War should not have died in vain; and that America would have a new birth of freedom because she is a nation under the authority of whom? (Circle one)

a) Mohammed
b) Confucius
c) Almighty God of the Bible
d) Zeus

xvi) Who wrote the *Pledge of Allegiance to our United States Flag*, and in what year? (Circle one)

a) James Knox Polk, United States President, 1848
b) Alexis de Toqueville, 19th Century author, 1835
c) Francis Bellamy, Minister of the Gospel, 1892
d) William Howard Taft, U.S. Supreme Court Chief Justice, 1823

xvii) Where did the phrase "Under God" originate, and who, by Act of Congress, had it inserted within the Pledge of Allegiance to our United States Flag? What year was this accomplished? (Circle one)

a) President Harry Truman's First Inaugural Address, 1940;
Harry Truman, 1940.
b) Abraham Lincoln's Gettysburg Address, 1863;
President Dwight D. Eisenhower, 1954.
c) President John F. Kennedy's State of the Union Address, 1962;
John F. Kennedy, 1962.
d) Secretary of the Treasury, Salmon P. Chase's letter to the Director of the Mint, 1863;
Salmon P. Chase, 1863.

xviii) Who conveyed the phrase "Under God" to the person chosen by Almighty God, to insert this phrase within the *Pledge of Allegiance to our U.S. Flag?* (Circle one)

a) A disciple of Buddha
b) A Hindu lecturer

c)   A minister of the Gospel, George Docherty

d)   A professor of Mohammedanism

xix)   In the Lincoln Memorial, the two mural paintings by Jules Guerin above Abraham Lincoln's *Gettysburg Address* and his *Second Inaugural Address*, respectively, are: (Fill in the blanks)

a)   _____

b)   _____

xx)   Who is centrally depicted in each of the mural paintings by Jules Guerin, above Lincoln's *Gettysburg Address* and his *Second Inaugural Address?* (Circle one)

a)   Liberty, enthroned

b)   The sage of the ages

c)   God's Angel of Truth

d)   A Greek statue

xxi)   In the Lincoln Memorial, the grouping to the right, in the mural painting by great master artist, Jules Guerin, "The Emancipation of a Race" is entitled, and described as: (Fill in the blanks)

a)   "_____." "_____," "_____" and "_____" stand by as a seated _____ receives the imperishable _____ of _____. The meaning here is that _____ _____ is acquired through faith in _____, hope in _____, and Christ's love that is shed abroad in our _____ to _____ after the _____ _____ indwells the believer at _____.

xxii)   Abraham Lincoln's 1847 family Bible is in the custody of whom? (Circle one)

a)   The White House

b)   The U.S. Supreme Court

c)   The Rare Book Collection, Library of Congress

d)   The federal government

xxiii)   List four of Abraham Lincoln's favorite hymns: (Consult your text and fill in the blanks)

a)   _____

b)   _____

c)   _____

d)   _____

xxiv)   Abraham Lincoln's pastor, Phineas Gurley, of the New York Avenue Presbyterian Church, delivered his eulogy in the East Room of the White House on April 19, 1865. In it, he affirmed of our 16th President's character: (Consult your text and fill in the blanks)

    a)   He saw his _____ as the _____ _____ of a great and imperilled _____, and he determined to do his _____, and his whole _____, seeking the _____ and leaning upon the _____ of Him of whom it is written: "He giveth _____ to the faint, and to them that have no _____ He increaseth _____." Yes, he _____ upon His _____, he recognized and received the _____ that the "_____ is the _____, and He is the _____ among the _____." He remembered that "God is in _____," and felt that nowhere had His _____ and His _____ been so marvelously _____ as in the _____ of this _____. . .

xxv)   On the 28th August, 1963, Dr. Martin Luther King, Jr. delivered from the steps of the Lincoln Memorial his world-renowned *I have a Dream* speech to over 200,000 people. This speech is based upon: (Circle one)

    a)   The writings of Confucius
    b)   The Koran
    c)   The Bible (Isaiah 40:4-5)
    d)   Shintoism

2. Christian Character Traits

Select 10 Christian virtues, values and morals of this great American hero from the selected texts of original writings and documents of Abraham Lincoln. List them below:

a. _____   f. _____

b. _____   g. _____

c. _____   h. _____

d. _____   i. _____

e. _____   j. _____

IV. Illustrate your work with pictures, outline map, models and drawings.

V. Memory Verse: Abraham Lincoln's Scripture verse upon which he based his denunciation of slavery, as an offense against God, bringing a woe upon our nation:

Woe unto the world because of offenses; for it must needs be that offenses come, but woe to that man by whom the offense cometh. Matthew 18:7

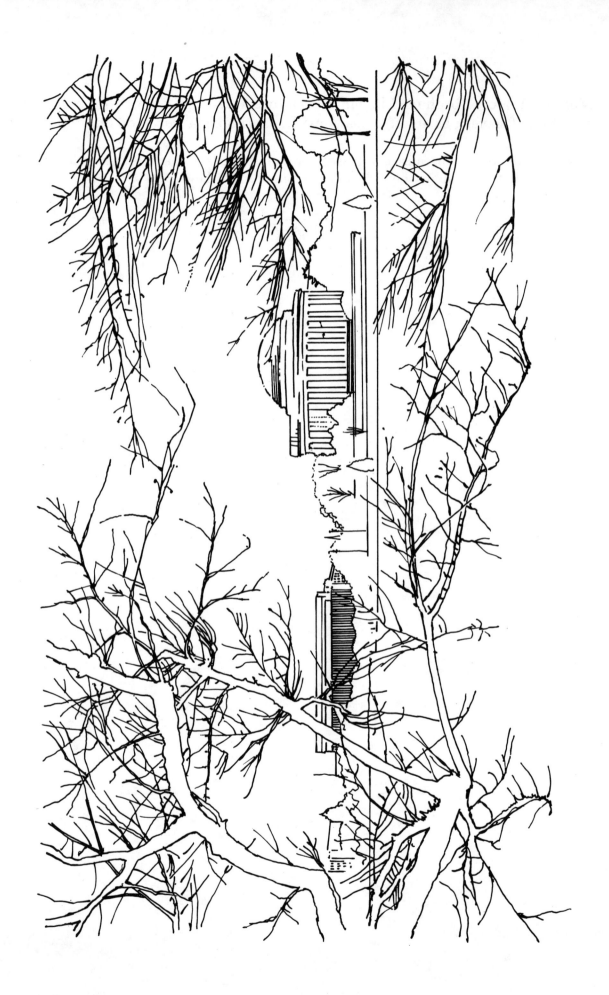

The Jefferson Memorial from the Tidal Basin

The Thomas Jefferson Memorial in our Nation's Capital

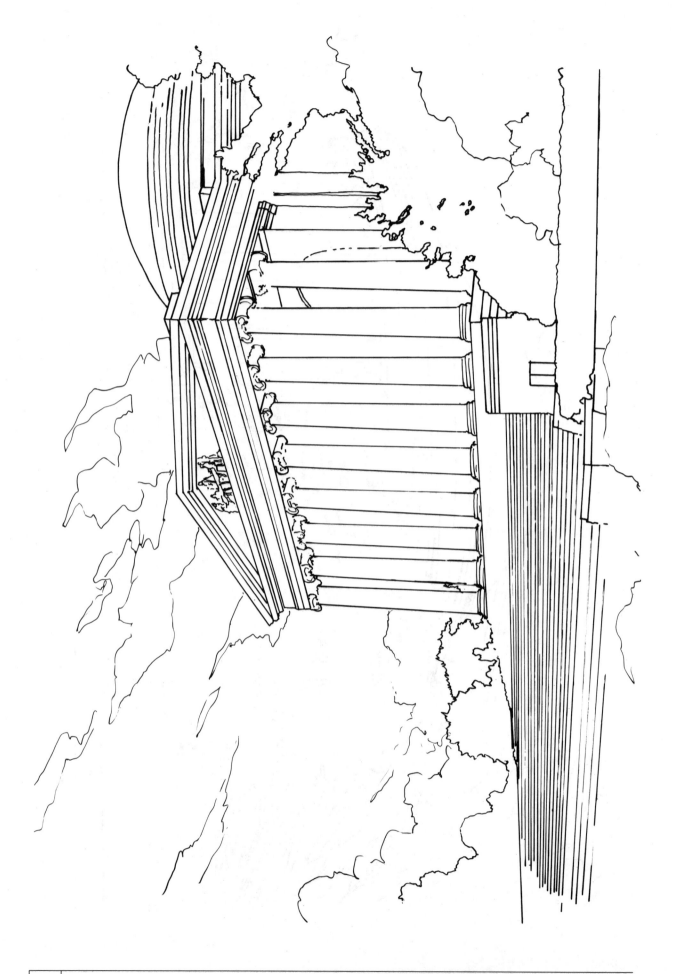

"Declaration of Independence"

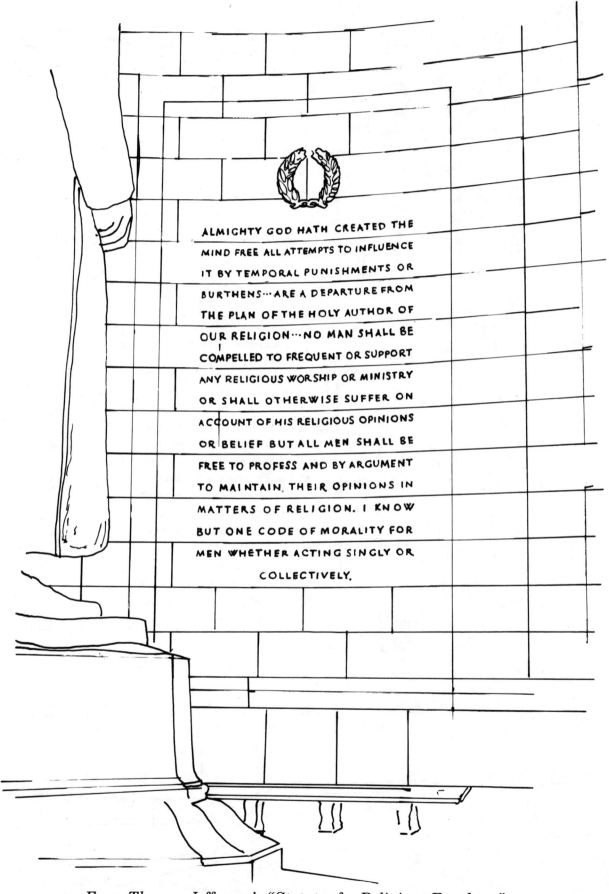

ALMIGHTY GOD HATH CREATED THE
MIND FREE ALL ATTEMPTS TO INFLUENCE
IT BY TEMPORAL PUNISHMENTS OR
BURTHENS...ARE A DEPARTURE FROM
THE PLAN OF THE HOLY AUTHOR OF
OUR RELIGION...NO MAN SHALL BE
COMPELLED TO FREQUENT OR SUPPORT
ANY RELIGIOUS WORSHIP OR MINISTRY
OR SHALL OTHERWISE SUFFER ON
ACCOUNT OF HIS RELIGIOUS OPINIONS
OR BELIEF BUT ALL MEN SHALL BE
FREE TO PROFESS AND BY ARGUMENT
TO MAINTAIN, THEIR OPINIONS IN
MATTERS OF RELIGION. I KNOW
BUT ONE CODE OF MORALITY FOR
MEN WHETHER ACTING SINGLY OR
COLLECTIVELY.

From Thomas Jefferson's "Statutes for Religious Freedom."

The Christian Heritage Of Our Nation - History Curriculum

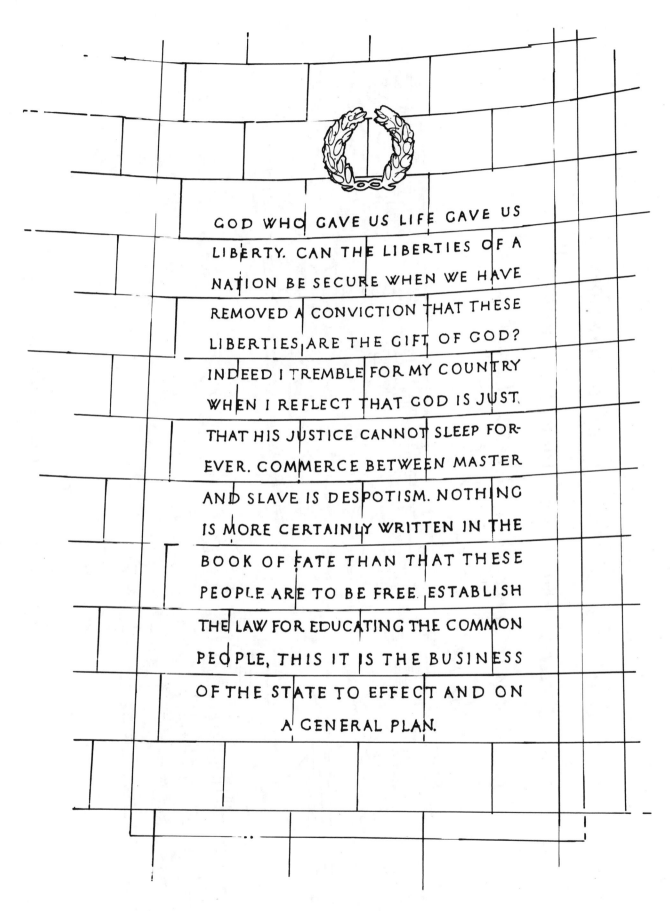

GOD WHO GAVE US LIFE GAVE US LIBERTY. CAN THE LIBERTIES OF A NATION BE SECURE WHEN WE HAVE REMOVED A CONVICTION THAT THESE LIBERTIES ARE THE GIFT OF GOD? INDEED I TREMBLE FOR MY COUNTRY WHEN I REFLECT THAT GOD IS JUST, THAT HIS JUSTICE CANNOT SLEEP FOREVER. COMMERCE BETWEEN MASTER AND SLAVE IS DESPOTISM. NOTHING IS MORE CERTAINLY WRITTEN IN THE BOOK OF FATE THAN THAT THESE PEOPLE ARE TO BE FREE. ESTABLISH THE LAW FOR EDUCATING THE COMMON PEOPLE, THIS IT IS THE BUSINESS OF THE STATE TO EFFECT AND ON A GENERAL PLAN.

From Thomas Jefferson's "Notes on Virginia" and his autobiography

Can the liberties of a Nation be secure when we have removed the conviction that these liberties are the Gift of God.?

The Jefferson Memorial overlooking our Nation's Capital

The Christian Heritage Of Our Nation - History Curriculum

LESSON 3

THE JEFFERSON MEMORIAL

I have sworn upon the altar of God eternal hostility against every form of tyranny over the mind of man.

Thomas Jefferson, President, United States of America

As first vice president and third president of the United States, Thomas Jefferson's genius extended itself into the realm of law, letters, invention and architecture. His penchant in architectural design is exemplified in the circular, dome-shaped colonnaded lines of the Jefferson Memorial. Its classic style reflects Jefferson's admiration for the Pantheon in Rome, as also evidenced in similar designs of the Virginia State Capitol, the Rotunda of the University of Virginia, and Monticello, his gracious home outside Charlottesville. John Russell Pope served as architect in its construction. In 1943, the 200th anniversary of Jefferson's birth was celebrated with the inauguration and grand opening of this building to the public.

A sculptured pediment above the entranceway steps to the memorial is the work of sculptor Adolf A. Weinman. Featured in the tableau is Jefferson reading his draft of the Declaration of Independence to the Committee appointed by the Continental Congress to evaluate the document: Benjamin Franklin, John Adams, Roger Sherman and Robert R. Livingston. Centered within the interior, domed structure, is a 19-foot-tall bronze statue of Jefferson standing upon a black granite pedestal. He directly faces the south facade of the White House, so it has been said that Jefferson is keenly aware of current proceedings in the President's House. He sports a fur-collared great coat, gift of his friend, General Thaddeus Kosciuszko.

The famous Declaration of Independence, forerunner to the U.S. Constitution is held in his left hand. Jefferson considered this document to be his greatest life work. Encircling the statue, one takes note of the two early symbols of colonial prosperity: corn and tobacco, which reflect Jefferson's love of agriculture. The 'capitals' above them indicate his interest in architecture. The sculptor is Rudulph Evans of New York. Viewed from the outside, the Vermont white marble exterior of the memorial reaches a height of 96 feet, the building being 152 feet in diameter. Its beauty is enhanced by 650 Japanese flowering cherry trees which adorn the Tidal Basin. They represent Yoshino (white) and Akebonos (pink) cherry trees, a gift from the city of Tokyo to the city of Washington. There were originally 3,000 of these given. The first two trees were planted on March 27, 1912, by Mrs. William Howard Taft and Viscountess Chinda, wife of the Japanese Ambassador to the United States.

Inscribed in a circular pattern within the inner dome, in bold letters, are Jefferson's famous words:

I have sworn upon the altar of God eternal hostility against every form of tyranny over the mind of man.

Four interior wall panels immortalize Jefferson's ideals and concepts. These quoted excerpts originate from the Declaration of Independence; the Statutes for Religious Freedom; Jefferson's anti-slavery views and his advocacy that institutions and organizations should advance with the progress of a civilization. Excerpts from the Declaration of Independence, his Statutes for Religious Freedom, and Jefferson's elaboration upon Slavery, viewed from God's eyes, read as follows:

The Declaration of Independence

We hold these truths to be self evident. That all men are created equal. That they are endowed by their Creator with certain inalienable rights. Among these are life, liberty, and the pursuit of happiness, that to secure these rights governments are instituted among men. We . . . solemnly publish and declare that these colonies are and of right ought to be free and independent states .
. . And for the support of this declaration, with a firm reliance on the protection of Divine Providence, we mutually pledge our lives, our fortunes and our sacred honour.

Statutes for Religious Freedom

. . . Well aware that Almighty God hath created the mind free; that all attempts to influence it by temporal punishments or burthens, or by civil incapacitations tend only to beget habits of hypocrisy and meanness, and are a departure from the plan of the Holy Author of our Religion, who, being Lord both of body and mind, yet chose not to propagate it by coercions on either, as was in his Almighty power to do; that the impious presumption of legislators and rulers civil, as well as ecclesiastical who being themselves but fallible and uninspired men, have assumed dominion over the faith of others, setting up their own opinions and modes of thinking as the only true and infallible, and as such endeavoring to impose them on others, hath established and maintained false religions over the greatest part of the world, and through all time: That to compel a man to furnish contributions of money for the propagation of opinions which he disbelieves, is sinful and tyrannical; that even the forcing him to support this or that teacher of his own religious persuasion, is depriving him of the comfortable liberty of giving his contributions to the particular pastor whose morals he would like to pattern, and whose powers he feels most persuasive to righteousness . . . be it therefore enacted by the General Assembly, That no man shall be compelled to frequent or support any religious worship, place or ministry whatsoever, nor shall be enforced, restrained, molested, or burthened, in body or goods, nor shall otherwise suffer on account of his religious opinions or belief; but that all men shall be free to profess and by argument maintain their opinions in matters of religion, and that the same shall in no wise diminish, enlarge, or affect their civil capacities . . .

The Christian Heritage Of Our Nation - History Curriculum

God, who gave us life gave us liberty. Can the liberties of a nation be secure when we have removed a conviction that these liberties are the gift of God? Indeed I tremble for my country when I reflect that God is just. That His justice cannot sleep forever. Commerce between master and slave is despotism. Nothing is more certainly written in the book of fate than that these people are to be free. Establish the law for educating the common people, this it is the business of the state to effect and on a general plan.

A fourth panel indicates the author's belief that laws and institutions within a society should advance hand in hand with the progress of the times.

The reader is struck by Jefferson's repeated mention and emphasis upon Almighty God and His attributes as man's Creator; The Holy Author of our Religion; the God of our life and liberty, our freedom coming as a gift from God; and the awesome justice of God. His was a profound respect and reverential awe of the Creator of heaven and earth, whom he acknowledged to be the founder and keeper of America's amazing republican way of life, her liberty and her freedom to pursue happiness; . . . that is, within the sphere of God's protective covering.

Thomas Jefferson, author of the famous Declaration of Independence, was a member of the Continental Congress. On January 11, 1776, he was appointed to the Committee of five assigned to draft the Declaration, which, in turn, unanimously selected him to actually write the document.[2] Before submitting it to the Committee, he sought out the criticism of two of the Committee members, Benjamin Franklin and John Adams, whose opinions he deeply respected. Jefferson wrote that they made only two or three verbal alterations. It was presented to the Committee and then to Congress on June 28, 1776.[3]

Attacks on the Declaration of Independence

In the debate which ensued in Congress over it, there were some who complained that it "contained no new ideas," that it was a "common-place compilation, its sentiments hackneyed in Congress for two years before," "its essence contained in Otis' pamphlet," and that "it was copied from Locke's treatise on government."[4]

Jefferson Defends His Declaration

In a letter written to James Madison years later in 1823, Jefferson defended his work as follows:

Otis' pamphlet I never saw, and whether I gathered my ideas from reading or reflection, I do not know. I know only that I turned to neither book nor pamphlet while writing it. I did not consider it as any part of my charge to invent new ideas altogether, and to offer no sentiments which had never been expressed before...[5]

John Adams Defends the Declaration

In spite of the hesitation of some to embrace the bold venture, there were those who stood firmly with Jefferson. He wrote regarding John Adams:

> . . . I will say for Mr. Adams, that he supported the Declaration with zeal and ability, fighting fearlessly for every word of it . . .[6]

John Witherspoon Defends the Declaration

And it was John Witherspoon, a minister of the Gospel and the president of Princeton College, who delivered the galvanizing speech that caused the members of the Continental Congress to rush forward to sign the Declaration of Independence, that historic July 4th in 1776.

Prior to the vote, a member had lamented, "We are not ripe for revolution," to which Witherspoon replied, "Not ripe, Sir, in my judgment, we are not only ripe, but unless some action is taken, we will be rotting." It was followed by a riveting speech.[7]

John Adams predicted that the event would "be celebrated by succeeding generations as the great anniversary festival commemorated as the day of deliverance by solemn acts of devotion to God Almighty from one end of the Continent to the other, from this time forward forevermore."[8]

Abraham Lincoln on the Declaration

In his famed 1861 Address from Independence Hall, which took place a short time before the Civil War, Abraham Lincoln referred to the significance of the Declaration stating that,

> It was not the mere matter of the separation of the Colonies from the motherland, but that sentiment in the Declaration of Independence which gave liberty, not alone to the people of this country, but hope to all the world, for all future time. It was that which gave promise that in due time the weights would be lifted from the shoulders of all men, and that all should have an equal chance. This is the sentiment embodied in the Declaration of Independence . . .[9]

Religious Freedom in America

Thomas Jefferson believed his greatest accomplishments were the writing of the *Declaration of Independence* and the passage of his *Act for Establishing Religious Freedom* in the state of Virginia in 1786. Jefferson fought against Virginia's state-supported clergy and church, as had been common practice in Europe. He believed that each individual should be free to contribute according to his conscience to a pastor and church of his own choice, and that one's religious beliefs should not in any way determine his suitability for civil government.

The following year, on September 17, 1787, the U.S. Constitution was written and signed. It included the important First Amendment Clause, that, "Congress shall make no law respecting an establishment of religion, or prohibiting the free exercise thereof." Jefferson's 1786 *Act for Establishing Religious Freedom* was a forerunner to the *First Amendment of the Constitution*.

Separation of Church and (from Interference by) the State—Jefferson's Letter to the Danbury Baptists

In recent years, those who would like to interpret the First Amendment in a manner our forefathers never intended, have made use of the term "Separation of Church and State" to mean that there could be no possible impact or influence of Christianity upon civil government — or even upon education.

The true meaning of the First Amendment or "Establishment" Clause can be stated in these terms — "Separation of Church from interference by the State." The only time the expression "Separation of Church and State" was used by a founding father, is in an off-the-record, non-political letter written by Thomas Jefferson to the Danbury Baptist Association. He wrote this letter on January 1, 1802 replying to their public address which applauded his stance for establishing religious freedom. Jefferson prefaces his statement with an assurance to the Danbury Baptists that he concurs with their belief of man being accountable to God alone for his mode of worship, without the government's coercion or interference:

> . . . Believing with you that religion is a matter which lies solely between man and his God, that he owes account to none other for his faith or his worship, that the legislative powers of government reach actions only, and not opinions, I contemplate with sovereign reverence that act of the whole American people which declared that their legislature should "make no law respecting an establishment of religion, or prohibiting the free exercise thereof," thus building a wall of separation between Church and State . . . [10]

The wall of separation between Church and State of which Jefferson speaks, is clearly in reference to protecting religious worship from the government's interference, and not the government being encroached upon by religious values. Furthermore, the

Declaration of Independence itself concludes with an emphasis upon this new nation's dependence upon God's protective care:

> . . . with a firm reliance upon the protection of Divine Providence, we mutually pledge our lives, our fortunes and our sacred honor.

It is seen, again and again in the founding fathers' writings, that they stressed the need of biblical principles and Christian values as the framework for good government, as attested to throughout this curriculum. While we do not have evidence of Thomas Jefferson having accepted Jesus Christ as his personal Lord and Savior, the only way to salvation, we can affirm that he governed his life by many Christian values and principles. Following are some examples from his writings to illustrate this:

Letters of Thomas Jefferson

A letter to Thomas Jefferson Smith, advising this young man on the course of life:

> *Adore God. Reverence and cherish your parents. Love your neighbor as yourself* and your country more than yourself. Be just. Be true. Murmur not at the ways of Providence. So shall the life, into which you have entered, be the portal to one of eternal and ineffable bliss . . . [11]

A letter to Peter Carr, dated August 10, 1787:

> . . . Above all things, lose no occasion of exercising your dispositions to be grateful; to be generous; to be charitable; to be humane; to be true, just, firm, orderly, courageous, etc. Consider every act of this kind as an exercise which will strengthen your moral faculties, and increase your worth. [12]

A letter to Samuel Adams, dated March 4, 1801:

> . . . When I have been told that you were avoided, insulted, frowned on, I could but ejaculate: *Father forgive them, for they know not what they do.* I confess I felt an indignation for you, which for myself I have been able, under every trial, to keep entirely passive. However, the storm is over, and we are in port . . . [13]

In a letter to Miles King, Jefferson stated that Christianity alone, regardless of denominational preferences, was the road to Heaven. However, the distinction not made by Jefferson was that one had to be "born again" into the family of God through faith in Christ Jesus as one's personal Savior, to inherit eternal life, regardless of church attendance. (In Christ's own words — John 3:3; 13-16.)

A letter to Miles King, September 26, 1814:

> . . . Nay, we have heard it said that there is not a Quaker or a Baptist, a Presbyterian or Episcopalian, a Catholic or a Protestant in Heaven; that on entering that gate, we leave those badges of schism behind, and find ourselves united in those principles only in which God has united us all. Let us not be uneasy then about the different roads we may pursue, as believing them the shortest to that our last abode; but, following the guidance of a good conscience, let us be happy in the hope that by those different paths we shall all meet in the end. And that you and I may there meet and embrace, is my earnest prayer. And with this assurance I salute you with brotherly esteem and respect.[14]

Jefferson's Catalogue of Biblical Paintings

Jefferson was the architect for his beautiful home, "Monticello," in Charlottesville, Virginia. As the home is the reflection of those who live in it, Jefferson's parlour or living room contained numerous evidences of the impact of Christianity upon his life and the culture of his day. This founding father drew up his own Catalogue of Paintings, Sculpture and Objets d'Art, replete with Scripture references and explanations on each of the biblical themes, quoting both chapter and verse from the Bible. Among the Scriptures given are: Matt. 21:12; Matt. 26:75; Luke 2:46; Mark 15:16-20; Genesis 22; Matt. 27:11-13; Matt. 14:11; Mark 6:28; Luke 3:21-22; Luke 23:44-45; Judges 11; Matt. 27:51-52.[15]

Among the paintings adorning these walls, were the *Ascension of Christ into Heaven; The Holy Family; The Transfiguration; The Prodigal Son; Jesus among the Doctors of the Law; Jesus driving the money-changers out of the Temple; Peter weeping in Repentance; John the Baptist heralding the Messianic Lamb of God; Christ before Pilate; The flagellation of Christ,* and *Christ's atoning death on the Cross of Calvary.* The Old Testament stories of *Abraham offering Isaac, with an angel of the Lord stopping his hand; Jephthah offering his Daughter* and *David and Goliath*, are also portrayed.

His Personal Library

Thomas Jefferson catalogued his own personal library of more than 6,000 volumes. Of the 190 entries under the title Religion (now in the Jefferson Collection of the Rare Book Division of the Library of Congress), 187 fit into the category of Christianity. A vast array of Old and New Testament Bibles, Concordances, Biblical sermons and writings, (such as John Witherspoon's sermons) were hand-initialled by Jefferson and made part of his collection. The three remaining books under Religion were: Boyse's and King's heathen gods, "to understand ancient poetry, coins and medals;" and a Sale's Koran — most probably to understand that philosophy.

In regard to the issue of slavery at the time of the founding of this nation, the question arises: If the founding fathers were against slavery as a great moral evil, why didn't they free the slaves?

Prior to the revolution, some of the colonial legislatures had attempted to prevent further importation through duties and prohibitions, but interference by the British government prevented them from doing so. Jefferson's sentiments and those of other colonists on the slavery issue are noted in his famous 1774 *A Summary View of the Rights of British America* (set forth in some Resolutions intended for the inspection of the present Delegates of the people of Virginia, now in Convention). It outlines the grievances of the colonies against England, as excerpted below:

> . . . The abolition of domestic slavery is the great object of desire in those colonies, where it was unhappily introduced in their infant state. But previous to the enfranchisement of the slaves we have, it is necessary to exclude all further importations from Africa; yet our repeated attempts to effect this by prohibitions, and by imposing duties which might amount to a prohibition, have been hitherto defeated by his majesty's negative: Thus preferring the immediate advantages of a few African corfairs (slaves) to the lasting interests of the American states, and to the rights of human nature deeply wounded by this infamous practice . . .[16]

After the Declaration of Independence, Jefferson was free to initiate a bill in Congress, which he did in 1779, proposing an initial attempt to deal with the slavery issue. In his autobiography, he wrote the following account of it:

> The bill on the subject of slaves was a mere digest of the existing laws respecting them, without any intimation of the plan for a future and general emancipation. It was thought better that this should be kept back, and attempted only by way of amendment, however the bill should be brought on. The principles of the amendment however were agreed on, that is to say, the freedom of all born after a certain day, and deportation at a proper age. But it was found that the public mind would not yet bear the proposition, nor will it bear it even at this day. Yet the day is not distant when it must bear and adopt it, or worse will follow . . .[17]

Jefferson could foresee the tremendous evil that would befall this country if the young nation did not eradicate this "infamous practice," which had deeply wounded human beings. He said that "commerce between master and slave is despotism," and gave this warning:

> It is still in our power to direct the process of emancipation and deportation peaceably and in such slow degree as that the evil will wear off insensibly and their place be pari passu filled with free white laborers. If on the contrary, it is left to force itself on, human nature must shudder at the prospect held up

... Commerce between master and slave is despotism.[18]

Unfortunately, Jefferson's admonitions as to what would befall this nation if the slavery issue was not fully resolved, became the reality of a tragic civil war within a century. Abraham Lincoln was God's instrument, raised up to totally eradicate this great moral evil from American soil. This he did with his *Emancipation Proclamation*, an immortal document, setting the slaves free on a permanent basis.

On the 28th of June, 1826, Jefferson lay at Monticello dying. Although his doctor had pronounced that he could not live through the night, Jefferson prayed that he might survive to celebrate the Jubilee of the *Declaration of Independence*. Miraculously, he lived on until the 4th of July, his last words to his family and friends being, "I have done for my country, and for all mankind all that I could do, and now I resign my soul, without fear, to my God, my daughter, to my country." And then he uttered distinctly two times like Simeon of old, "Lord, now lettest thou Thy servant depart in peace."[19]

LESSON THREE

PUPILS' GUIDE

The Thomas Jefferson Memorial – Author of the Declaration of Independence

I. Suggestions for Study

    a)   Read the lesson material carefully.

    b)   Look up Charlottesville, Virginia; Washington, District of Columbia, and France on your maps of the United States and the world at home.

II. Lesson material

    Text: Lesson 3 - The Thomas Jefferson Memorial.

III. 1. The kind of man Thomas Jefferson was:

    i)   What year was the Jefferson Memorial inaugurated, and what great landmark in America's history does it commemorate? (Consult your text and fill in the blanks).

        a)   In _____, the _____ anniversary of _____ birth was _____ with the _____ and grand _____ of this _____ to the public.

    ii)   The sculptured pediment on the front facade of the Jefferson Memorial, directly above the front steps, features what significant document undergirding the birth of our nation? (Consult your text and fill in the blanks).

        a)   Jefferson reading his draft of the _____ of _____ to the Committee appointed by the _____ _____ to evaluate the _____. They are: _____, _____, _____ and _____.

    iii)   How tall is the famous bronze statue of Thomas Jefferson within the interior of his memorial? Identify the great master sculptor who executed this work of art. (Circle one)

a) 15 feet; Lin-Sui, China
b) 17 feet; Sing Nagasaki, Japan
c) 19 feet; Rudulph Evans, New York
d) 20 feet; Santa Ana, Mexico

iv) According to founding father Thomas Jefferson, he considered his greatest work to be the document held in his left hand. It is: (Circle one)

a) *The Statutes for Religious Freedom*
b) His *Autobiography*
c) The Design of the University of Virginia
d) *The Declaration of Independence*

v) Inscribed within the inner dome of the Thomas Jefferson Memorial, in two-feet-tall lettering, are Jefferson's immortalized words: (Fill in the blanks).

a) I have _____ upon the _____ of _____ eternal _____ against every form of _____ over the _____ of _____.

vi) In the above statement, penned by Thomas Jefferson, whom does this founding father extol? (Circle One)

a) A Supreme Being
b) A Roman god
c) Almighty God of the Bible
d) A Greek deity

vii) Four interior wall panels within the Jefferson Memorial immortalize Jefferson's ideals and concepts. What are they? (Consult your text and fill in the blanks)

a) The _____ of _____; the _____ for _____ _____; Jefferson's _____ views; and his _____ that _____ and _____ should advance with the _____ of a _____.

viii) In Thomas Jefferson's *Declaration of Independence*, from where does this founding father state that our liberties as Americans originate? (Circle one)

a) Man's brilliant intellect
b) Individual self-achievement

c) The Continental Congress

d) Our Creator, Almighty God

ix) In his immortal document, the *Declaration of Independence*, Jefferson affirms that all men are: (Circle one)

a) Born equal (by birth certificate)

b) Regarded as equal (by society)

c) Created equal (by Almighty God)

d) Treated equal (by others)

x) Jefferson concludes his *Declaration of Independence* with a firm reliance upon the protection of whom? (Circle one)

a) Mohammed

b) Confucius

c) Zeus

d) Almighty God of the Bible

xi) Identify the three things which our founding fathers pledged for the support of the *Declaration of Independence*. They pledged their: (Circle three)

a) Gold watches

b) Houses

c) Lives

d) Horses

e) Plantations

f) Fortunes

g) Congressional votes

h) Sacred honor

xii) In Jefferson's *Statutes for Religious Freedom*, whom does this founding father state created the mind free? (Circle one)

a) Man

b) Teachers

c) Almighty God

d) The Board of Education

xiii) In Thomas Jefferson's *Statutes for Religious Freedom*, whom does this founding father state is Lord of both body and mind? (Circle one)

a) Secular Humanism

b) Atheism

c) Deism

d) The Holy Author of our Religion (Christianity)

xiv) In Jefferson's *Statutes for Religious Freedom*, whom does this founding father term fallible and uninspired men? (Circle two)

      a) Preachers of the Gospel
      b) Civil rulers
      c) Christian educators
      d) Ecclesiastical rulers

xv) In his *Statutes for Religious Freedom*, what does Thomas Jefferson state that these fallible and uninspired men compel a person to furnish, which is sinful and tyrannical? (Fill in the blanks)

      a) Contributions of _____ for the _____ of _____ which he _____.

xvi) In his *Statutes for Religious Freedom*, what does founding father Thomas Jefferson state these infallible and uninspired men deprive a person of the comfortable liberty of doing? (Consult your text and fill in the blanks).

      a) Giving his _____ to the particular _____ whose _____ he would like to _____, and whose _____ he feels most persuasive to _____.

xvii) What is the definition of the word "pastor" in *Webster's Dictionary*? (Circle one)

      a) A guru
      b) An eastern temple monk
      c) A minister of the Gospel of Jesus Christ
      d) A religious cult leader

xviii) What are synonyms for the word "morals" in Webster's Dictionary? (Circle one)

      a) Righteousness, virtue, good conduct
      b) Permissiveness
      c) Immorality
      d) Licentiousness

xix) Describe John Adams' prediction of the 4th July (Independence Day) celebrations, from 1776 onwards: (Fill in the blanks)

      a) The event would be _____ by succeeding _____ as the _____ _____ festival, _____ as

the day of _____ by solemn _____ of
_____ to God _____ from one end of the
_____ to the other, from this time forward
_____.

xx) In his famed 1861 *Independence Hall Address*, how did Abraham Lincoln evaluate the *Declaration of Independence?* (Consult your text and fill in the blanks)

    a) It was that which gave _____ that in due _____ the _____ would be _____ from the shoulders of _____ _____, and that all should have an _____ _____. This is the _____ embodied in the _____ of _____.

xxi) The *U.S. Constitution*, signed on September 17, 1787, included the important *First Amendment Clause*, which reads: (Consult your text and fill in the blanks)

    a) _____ shall make no _____ respecting an _____ of _____ or _____ the free _____ thereof.

xxii) The forerunner to the *First Amendment Clause* of the U.S. Constitution is: (Circle one)

    a) The *Magna Carta*
    b) Hugo Grotius' *Truth of the Christian Religion*
    c) Jefferson's 1786 *Statutes for Religious Freedom*
    d) Blackstone's *Commentaries*

xxiii) The true meaning of the *First Amendment* or *"Establishment" Clause* can be stated in these terms: (Circle one)

    a) Government control of the church
    b) Government control of the public schools
    c) "Separation of Church from interference by the State"
    d) An established, state-controlled church

xxiv) The only time the expression "Separation of Church and State" was used by a founding father, is: (Consult your text and fill in the blanks)

    a) In an _____, _____ letter, written by _____ to the Danbury _____ _____.

xxv) When and why did founding father, Thomas Jefferson write this letter to the Danbury Baptist Association? (Consult your text and fill in the blanks)

    a) Thomas Jefferson wrote this _____ on _____, replying to their _____ _____ which _____ his stance for _____ _____ _____.

xxvi) How does Thomas Jefferson preface his expression to the Danbury Baptists? Thomas Jefferson prefaces his expression with: (Consult your text and fill in the blanks)

    a) An assurance to the Danbury _____ that he _____ with their _____ of _____ being accountable to _____ alone for his _____ of _____ , without the _____ coercion or _____.

xxvii) Thomas Jefferson's *Catalogue of Paintings*, drawn up by himself, include the following Biblical events, replete with Scripture chapter and verse: (Circle all correct answers)

    a) The Parable of the Fig Tree
    b) The Holy Family
    c) The Parable of the Sower and the Seed
    d) Rebekah at the well
    e) The Transfiguration of Christ
    f) The Parable of the Prodigal Son
    g) Isaac and Rebekah
    h) Jesus driving the money-changers out of the Temple
    i) The Wedding of Cana in Galilee
    j) Peter weeping in Repentance
    k) John the Baptist heralding the Messianic Lamb of God
    l) The Parable of the Wheat and the Tares
    m) Christ before Pilate
    n) Christ's atoning death on the Cross of Calvary
    o) Abraham offering Isaac, an angel of the Lord stopping his hand

xxviii) In Thomas Jefferson's Personal Library, in the custody of the Rare Book Collection of the Library of Congress, the vast majority of Jefferson's entries under the title *Religion* fit into the category of Christianity. What are these entries? (Circle three)

    a) Universalism
    b) Deism
    c) Old and New Testament Bibles
    d) Atheism

e) Agnosticism
f) Concordances to the Bible
g) Secular Humanism
h) Biblical sermons and writings

xxix) The third panel in the inner wall of the Thomas Jefferson Memorial reiterates Jefferson's anti-slavery views. It reads as follows: (Consult your text and fill in the blanks)

a) _____ who gave us _____ gave us _____.
    Can the _____ of a _____ be secure when we have
    _____ a _____ that these _____ are
    the _____ of God? Indeed, I _____ for my
    _____ when I reflect that God is _____. That His
    _____ cannot _____ forever. Commerce
    between _____ and _____ is _____.

xxx) How many times does founding father Thomas Jefferson extol Almighty God, directly or indirectly, in his denunciation of slavery in America? (Circle one)

a) 2
b) 3
c) 4
d) 5

xxxi) In reading these four panels of Thomas Jefferson's famous writings, what personal attributes does he ascribe to Almighty God? (Circle all correct answers)

a) Man's Creator
b) Omniscient
c) The Holy Author of our Religion
d) Omnipresent
e) God of our life and liberty
f) Omnipotent
g) The Author of our freedoms
h) The Giver of gifts
i) Our Protector
j) Just
k) Longsuffering

xxxii) In his 1774 *A Summary View of the Rights of British America*, Thomas Jefferson wrote that the founding fathers were unable to free the slaves prior to Independence from England, because: (Consult your text and fill in the blanks)

a) ... The _____ of domestic _____ is the great object of _____ in those _____ where it was unhappily _____ in their _____ state. But previous to the _____ of the _____ we have, it is necessary to _____ all further _____ from _____; yet our repeated _____ to _____ this by _____, and by _____ duties which might _____ to a _____, have been hitherto _____ by his _____ negative: Thus _____ the immediate _____ of a few _____ _____ to the lasting _____ of the _____ states, and to the _____ of human nature _____ _____ by this _____ practise ..

xxxiii) In 1779, after the *Declaration of Independence,* Thomas Jefferson was free to initiate a Bill in Congress to emancipate the slaves. He writes about this important issue in his *Autobiography*, as follows:

a) It is still in _____ _____ to direct the _____ of _____ and _____ peaceably and in such slow _____ as that the _____ will _____ _____ insensibly and their place be _____ _____ filled with free _____ laborers. If, on the contrary, it is left to _____ _____ _____, human nature must _____ at the _____ held up ... Commerce between _____ and _____ is _____.

xxxiv) From the above original writings of Thomas Jefferson, the founding fathers considered American slavery to be: (Circle all correct answers)

a) Productive
b) Evil
c) Financially rewarding
d) Despotic
e) Deeply wounding to human beings
f) Advantageous to the American states
g) A disadvantage to the American states
h) Infamous
i) A great object of desire to abolish

xxxv)   What were founding father Thomas Jefferson's last words prior to his death, on the 4th July, 1826, exactly 50 years after the signing of the *Declaration of Independence?* (Consult your text and fill in the blanks)

a)   Lord, now _____ _____ Thy servant

_____ in _____.

xxxvi) From where do these words originate?

a)   The Koran
b)   Locke's Treaties
c)   Blackstone's Commentaries
d)   The Holy Bible (Luke 2:29)

2. *Christian Character Traits*

Select 10 Christian virtues, values, and morals inherent in the *Declaration of Independence, The Statutes for Religious Freedom,* and Thomas Jefferson's Autobiography. List them below:

a. _____   f. _____

b. _____   g. _____

c. _____   h. _____

d. _____   i. _____

e. _____   j. _____

IV. *Illustrate your work with pictures, outline map, models and drawings.*

V. *Memory Inscription:*   (Inscribed within the inner walls of the Thomas Jefferson Memorial)

God who gave us life, gave us liberty. Can the liberties of a nation be secure when we have removed a conviction that these liberties are the gift of God? Indeed I tremble for my country when I reflect that God is just. That His justice cannot sleep forever.

After the original bronze statue of Albert Einstein by Robert Berks

LESSON 4

THE ALBERT EINSTEIN MEMORIAL

The Albert Einstein Memorial on Constitution Avenue in our nation's capital is a bronze masterpiece of unique vintage. It portrays Einstein, one of the world's greatest master minds, seated, with his "Energy Formula" in his right hand.

The statue is the work of world-renowned sculptor Robert Berks. It was unveiled in 1979, being dedicated to the memory of this brilliant physicist and mathematician. It was the genius Einstein, a Jewish immigrant from Germany, who said that the more complex and intricate his calculations of the universe became, the more assured he was of the reality of a Supreme Creator.

Albert Einstein's Formative Years

Einstein was born in 1879 in the town of Ulm, Wurtemberg, Germany. His school days were spent in Munich, where he attended the *Gymnasium* until his 16th year. After leaving school at Munich, he accompanied his parents to Milan, whence he proceeded to Switzerland, six months later to continue his studies.[1]

From 1896 to 1900, Albert Einstein studied mathematics and physics at the Technical High School in Zurich, as he intended to become a secondary school (*Gymnasium*) teacher. For some time afterwards he was a private tutor, and having meanwhile become naturalized, he obtained a post as engineer in the Swiss Patent Office in 1902, which position he occupied till 1909[2]. The main ideas involved in Einstein's most important theories date back to this period. Amongst these may be mentioned: *The Special Theory of Relativity, Inertia of Energy, Theory of the Brownian Movement*, and the *Quantum Law of the Emission and Absorption of Light* (1905). These were followed some years later by the *Theory of the Specific Heat of Solid Bodies*, and the *Fundamental Idea of the General Theory of Relativity*.[3]

Einstein's Professional Years

During the interval 1909 to 1911 he occupied a post of Professor Extraordinarius at the University of Zurich, afterwards being appointed to the University of Prague, Bohemia, where he remained as Professor Ordinarius until 1912. In the latter year Professor Einstein accepted a similar chair at the *Polytechnikum*, Zurich, and continued his activities there until 1914, when he received a call to the *Prussian Academy of Science*, Berlin, as successor to Van't Hoff.[4] Professor Einstein was able to devote himself freely to his studies at the *Berlin Academy*, and it was there that he succeeded in completing his work on the *General Theory of Relativity (1915-17)*. Professor Einstein also lectured on various special branches of physics at the University of Berlin, and, in addition, he was Director of the Institute for Physical Research of the *Kaiser Wilhelm Gesellschaft*.[5]

A Kansas City Times Article

The Saturday, December 29, 1934 issue of the *Kansas City Times*, stated:

New Theory by Einstein

Mass and Energy Equivalent, Scientist Says
Simplified Equation is His First Important
Announcement Since Arrival in the United States.
By the Associated Press

Pittsburgh, Dec. 28. – Prof. Albert Einstein today announced a new and simplified proof that mass and energy are equivalent, and for many practical purposes identical.

His new equations are an encouragement for that branch of physical science which hopes in the next few years to lay the foundations for a world more secure and comfortable.

He got rid of the complicated electro-magnetic fields with which this equivalence of mass (or weight) and energy heretofore have been proven. He used instead the simple collision of two material particles to prove the same thing.

It was the first important speech in the United States, and his first important announcement in several years. It was made at the meeting of the American Association for the Advancement of Science, under auspices of the American Mathematical Society.

Tickets by Lot

While his audience of 400, the limit of the Little Theater of Carnegie Tech., most of them holders of tickets drawn by lot, filled the auditorium from back wall to stage, Einstein slipped in by the back door, and behind the stage curtain began covering two blackboards with figures and mathematical symbols.

As mathematical symbols they were unusually simple – ordinary letters and numerals.

The curtain rose with Einstein standing beside the two blackboards, his graying hair standing at all angles, a boyish grin on his face which set the audience of scientists to chuckling. They applauded heartily.

Einstein spoke English, for the first time at a lecture. But now and then he called on the audience to help him out with a word . . .

At a speed of 99 percent of the velocity of light, it has been calculated that your weight would be multiplied seven times. Human speeds are so slow that they would not add as much as a grain of sand to a man's weight.

Hot Substance is Heavier

A hot body weighs more than the same body when cool, because when hot the atoms are moving at faster speeds, or higher energy levels. Again, changes of this sort are too small to be measured in practical affairs.

But developments in the last three years in science have made this mass-energy equivalence of immediate importance investigating the nature of the nucleus of the atom.

It is from these nuclear investigations that material progress is expected. The atomic nuclei contain 99 percent of all matter, or all solid substances of earth, and its atmosphere. None of this nuclear material has been available for man's use.

Now nuclear chemistry, a new branch of science, is just beginning to learn how this hidden 99 per cent can be tapped.

In addition to the mass, 99 percent of the energy of all substances is locked in the nuclei, such as the power by which a single lump of coal could run a liner across the Atlantic . . .

A Test Case for Humanity - Einstein's Treaties

In October, 1939, Albert Einstein wrote the treaties *A Test Case for Humanity*. This work originally appeared in a 1944 issue of the *Princeton Herald*, New Jersey, in reply to an article by Dr. Philip K. Hitti, the Arab scholar. It is hereunder excerpted, as follows:

Both Jews and Arabs are said to stem from a common ancestor, from Abraham who immigrated into Canaan, i.e. Palestine, and so neither of them seem to have been earlier in the land than the others. Recent views assume that only part of the Israelites migrated to Egypt — as reflected in the Joseph story — and part of them remained in Palestine. So of the Canaanite population encountered by the Jews when they entered the promised land under Joshua were Israelites too. Therefore, the Arabs have no priority on the land.

To the Arabs Jerusalem is only the third holy city, to the Jews it is the first and only holy city, and Palestine is the place where their original history, their sacred history, took place. Besides, to the Arabs Jerusalem is a holy city only insofar as they trace their tradition back to Jewish origins, insofar as after the Arab conquest of Jerusalem in 637, the *Omar Mosque*, the *Dome of the Rock* was erected by the Omayyad Caliph Abd el Malek on the very place where the Jewish Ark of the Covenant and the Temple of Solomon had stood, on a rock *Even Shetiyah* (world foundation stone), which was considered by the Jews as reaching down to the bottom of the cosmic ocean, the navel of the world. And Jerusalem was a *qiblah*, a direction of prayer, under Mohammed only as long as he counted on the Jews as the main supporters of his new creed; he changed it, when his hopes failed, together with other institutions established out of pure consideration for his Jewish adherents, as, for instance, the fasting on the Jewish Day of Atonement—both are to-day abolished in their religious significance. It seems a little far fetched to use this abrogated rite as an evidence on which to base the Arab claim to Palestine.

If, finally, the Arab conquest of Palestine is considered holy it would be only fair to admit the corresponding holiness of the peaceful claim and the peaceful reclamation of the country by the Jews. To refer to the legitimacy of a "holy war" sounds rather queer for a people which denounces peaceful immigration as a violation of their rights.

No people, unfortunately, understands why it should contribute anything to the solution of the Jewish problem. The surface of the globe is everywhere occupied, and wherever the Jews could be given a piece of land to live under fair climate conditions, they would encroach on some property rights and sovereignties and would face friction with a population already firmly established on the spot. No country has been found where the Jews could possibly form an autonomous community, however small.

Palestine – Its Religious Foundation and Historic Tradition

There is still one difference between the other peoples and the Arabs. Every people has one country of its own which it developed with all the care of its generations and none of these countries has any connection with a specifically Jewish tradition or concern. The Arabs possess four major countries–Saudi Arabia, which harbours their holy places, Yemen, Iraq and Transjordania–if we leave aside Egypt, which is only partly Arab, Syria and all the North African colonies and provinces as yet not enfranchised from European rule. And the least and obviously most neglected of their settlements was the part they occupied in the tiny Palestinian country; only nine hundred thousand of fifty million Arabs live there. This tiny Palestinian country, on the other hand, is the only place in the world legitimately and most deeply connected with the Jewish people, its religious foundation and its historic tradition as an independent people.

In order to clarify the Palestinian problem let us compare the situation of the Jews with that of the Arabs. The Jews are and have always been numerically a small people. They have never exceeded fifteen and a half million. Deprived of their homeland through the ancient and medieval conquests of Palestine, they lived dispersed all over the world, and what they have suffered since by persecutions, expulsions and tortures of all kinds, are far beyond anything that other peoples had to endure. Of the fifteen and a half million computed in 1938, at least two millions have been slaughtered or starved to death by the Nazis, in the various European countries during the past few years. So the Zionist movement, or better the striving for a haven in the place of Jewish origin, is by no means an "exotic, artificially stimulated movement" (as Professor Hitti calls it), but a movement urged forward by utter need and distress. The promise held out to the Jews in the *Balfour Declaration* after the First World War has been whittled down bit by bit in the course of the British appeasement policy yielding to interests partly British, partly Arabian–a policy bitterly denounced by Mr. Churchill himself before he became Prime Minister. Palestine is a link in the lifeline of the British Empire between the Near East and India; and the Jewish people, by necessity a dependable ally of the British, have been sacrificed to the Arabs, who, by their numerical and political strength and the trump of the Islam portion of the Indian population, were in a position to sell dearly even their neutrality in the present conflict. The final result has been the complete prohibition of Jewish immigration into Palestine at the very moment when hundreds of thousands of Jews were threatened with annihilation.

Arab and Jewish Needs Compared

This is the Jewish situation; and there is no guarantee whatever against the persistence or recurrence of anti-Semitic outbreaks everywhere after this war. Even if we put aside the spiritual, religious and cultural ties making Palestine the only place in the world which persecuted Jews could consider their home, and develop with all the devotion a homeland inspires–there is not even any other country acceptable to human beings, which the numerous refugee conferences were able to offer to this hounded people. The Jews are prepared for extreme sacrifices and hardest work to convert this narrow strip which is Palestine into a prosperous country and model civilisation. What Jewish youth has already achieved in the few decades of Zionist settlement may be gathered from Mr. Lowdermilk's book.* They took over from the period of Arabian predominance, deserts and rocks and barren soil and turned them into flowing farms and plantations, into forests and modern cities. They created new forms of co-operative settlements and raised the living standard of the Arabian and the Jewish population alike. The Jews are willing and ready to give any guarantee of protection for the holy places and the civil rights, indeed the autonomy, of Arabs and Christians, a guarantee safeguarded by the overwhelming power of their neighbours, on whose co-operation they depend. They offer their assistance and their experience for the economic and scientific advancement of the Arab countries, for the lifting of the population to a modern standard of living.

But this, unfortunately, is just what the Arab leaders do not want. For the true source of Arab resistance and hostility toward a Jewish Palestine is neither

Palestine, Land of Promise by Walter Clay Lowdermilk. (Gollancz, 1944, 4/6.)

religious nor political, but social and economic. The Arabian population of Palestine is negligible in comparison with the vast number of Arab elements in the European provinces of North Africa and Asia. The Arabian chieftains did not arouse the Moslem world against Mussolini's regime in Libya: most of them were on splendid terms with him. The Mufti of Jerusalem and other Arab leaders were greatly honoured guests in Rome. The rich Arabian landowners did nothing to improve the nature, the civilisation, or the living standards of their countries. The large Arabian states are underpopulated, the masses of the people are held in a backward and inferior condition. "Life in the Damascus of the eighth century was not greatly different from what it is to-day," says Professor Hitti in his book about the Arabs. But the big Effendis fear the example and the impulse which the Jewish colonisation of Palestine presents to the peoples of the Near East, they resent the social and economic uplift of the Arab workers in Palestine. They act as all the fascist forces have acted: they screen their fear of social reform behind nationalistic slogans and demagogy. If it were not for these leaders and instigators, a perfect agreement and co-operation could be achieved between the Arab and the Jewish people.

Why a Jewish-controlled Palestine

The purpose of this statement is not a nationalistic one. We do not, and the vast majority of the Jews does not, advocate the establishment of a state for the sake of national greed and self-glorification, which would run counter to all the traditional values of Judaism and which we consider obsolete everywhere. In speaking up for a Jewish Palestine we want to promote the establishment of a place of refuge, where persecuted human beings may find security and peace and the undisputed right to live under a law and order of their making. The experience of many centuries has taught us that this can be provided only by home rule and not by a foreign administration. This is why we stand for a Jewish-controlled Palestine. We do not refer to historic rights, although if there exists something like an historic right on a country, the Jews, at least as well as the Arabs, could claim it on Palestine. We do not resort to threats of power, for the Jews have no power; they are, in fact, the most powerless group on earth. If they had had any power they should have been able to prevent the annihilation of millions of their people and the closing of the last door to the helpless victims of the Nazis. What we appeal to is an elementary sense of justice and humanity. We know how weak such a position is, but we also know that if the arguments of threats of power, of sacred egoisms and holy wars continue to prevail in the future world order, not only the Jews but the whole of humanity will be doomed . . .

Ancient Home of the People of the Bible

The Jews will never abandon the work of reconstruction which they have undertaken . . . I cannot believe that the greatest colonial Power in the world will fail when it is faced with the task of placing its unique colonising experience at the service of the reconstruction of the ancient home of the People of the Bible. The task may not be an easy one for the Mandatory Power, but for the success it will attain it is assured of the undying gratitude not only of the Jews but of all that is noblest in mankind.[6]

LESSON FOUR

PUPILS' GUIDE

The Albert Einstein Memorial - "The Energy Formula"

I. Suggestions for Study

a) Read the lesson material carefully.
b) Look up Germany; Switzerland; Bohemia; Israel (Palestine) and Pittsburgh, PA. on your map of the United States and the world at home.

II. Lesson material

Text: Lesson 4 - The Albert Einstein Memorial

III. 1. The kind of man Albert Einstein was:

i) The life-like bronze statue of Albert Einstein on Constitution Avenue in our nation's capital, portrays Einstein seated. What does he hold in his left hand?

   a) The Theory of Relativity
   b) The Atom Bomb
   c) The Energy Formula
   d) The Theory of the Specific Heat of Solid Bodies

ii) In his exploration of the intricacies and complexities of the Universe, it was the genius Einstein who said that: (Fill in the blanks)

   a) The more complex and _____ his calculations of the _____ became, the more assured he was of the _____ of a _____ _____.

iii) Identify the famous sculptor who executed the bronze masterpiece sculpture of Albert Einstein in our nation's capital: (Circle one)

   a) David D'Anger, French.
   b) Robert Berks, American.
   c) Jose Luis Sanchez, Spanish.
   d) Nehemiah Azaz, Israeli.

iv) What two professional posts did Einstein occupy between the years 1909-

1911 and 1911-1912, respectively? (Circle one)

    a)   Professor of Science at the *University of Berkley*, California.
    b)   Professor Extraordinarius at the *University of Zurich*, Switzerland.
    c)   Professor of Physics at *Yale University*, Connecticut.
    d)   Professor Ordinarius at the *University of Prague*, Bohemia.

v)   At what University did Albert Einstein succeed in completing his work on the *General Theory of Relativity*, and in what year? (Circle one)

    a)   *Harvard University*, Massachusetts, 1914.
    b)   *Columbia University*, New York, 1915.
    c)   *The Prussian Academy of Science*, Berlin, 1917.
    d)   *London University*, England, 1919.

vi)   In Einstein's *New Theory*, described by the Associated Press in the December 29, 1934 issue of *The Kansas City Times*; what was the new and simplified proof announced by Einstein? (Circle one)

    a)   That water and heat are equivalent.
    b)   That air and cold are synonymous.
    c)   That mass and energy are equivalent.
    d)   That weight and height are equivalent.

vii)   In Einstein's *New Theory*, what did this brilliant physicist get rid of? (Circle one)

    a)   Complicated water particles
    b)   Complicated mass substances
    c)   Complicated measurements
    d)   Complicated electro-magnetic fields

viii)   In Albert Einstein's *New Theory*, at a speed of 99 percent of the velocity of light, it has been calculated that your weight would be multiplied, how many times? (Circle one)

    a)   3 times
    b)   5 times
    c)   7 times
    d)   10 times

ix)   In Albert Einstein's *New Theory*, why is a hot substance heavier? (Consult your text and fill in the blanks)

a) A hot _____ weighs _____ _____ the same _____ when _____, because when _____ the atoms are moving at faster _____, or _____ _____ levels . . .

x) In Albert Einstein's *New Theory,* what could run a liner across the Atlantic? (Consult your text and fill in the blanks)

    a) In addition to the mass, 99 percent of the _____ of all _____ is _____ in the _____, such as the _____ by which a _____ _____ of _____ could run a liner across the Atlantic.

xi) Albert Einstein wrote a treaties, which was later published in the *Princeton Herald,* New Jersey, in response to an article by Arab scholar, Dr. Phillip K. Hitti. Identify the title of Einstein's treaties, the date it was written, and the date it first appeared in the *Princeton Herald:* (Circle one)

    a) *The One-World Order,* January, 1919; 1929.
    b) *The Emerging German Holocaust,* November, 1928; 1930.
    c) *A Test Case for Humanity,* October, 1939; 1944.
    d) *A Marxist Worldview,* April, 1927; 1935.

xii) In Einstein's *A Test Case for Humanity,* who are said to stem from a common ancestor? (Circle one)

    a) Both English and Americans
    b) Both French and Canadians
    c) Both Jews and Arabs
    d) Both Germans and Scandinavians

xiii) Who is this common ancestor, and to what land did he immigrate? (Circle one)

    a) William the Conquerer – England.
    b) Leif Erikson – Greenland.
    c) The Emperor Constantine – Turkey
    d) Abraham – Canaan (Palestine)

xiv) In Einstein's *A Test Case for Humanity,* to the Jews, Jerusalem and Palestine are, respectively: (Fill in the blanks)

a) The _____ and _____ holy _____, and _____ is the _____ where their _____ _____, their _____ _____, took place.

xv) In Einstein's *A Test Case for Humanity*, to the Arabs, Jerusalem is: (Fill in the blanks)

a) Jerusalem is _____ the _____ holy _____.

xvi) In Einstein's *A Test Case for Humanity*, Jerusalem is a holy city to the Arabs insofar as: (Fill in the blanks)

a) They trace their _____ back to _____ origins, insofar as after the _____ _____ of Jerusalem in 637, the "_____ _____" the "_____ of the _____" was erected by the _____ _____ _____ _____ _____ on the very place where the _____ _____ of the _____ and the _____ of _____ had stood . . .

xvii) In Einstein's *A Test Case for Humanity*, under Mohammed, Jerusalem was: (Fill in the blanks)

a) A _____, a direction of _____ only as long as he counted on the _____ as the main _____ of his new _____; . . .

xviii) In Einstein's *A Test Case for Humanity*, which is the least and obviously most neglected of the Arab settlements, and how many Arabs live there? (Circle one)

a) Saudi Arabia; 17 million.
b) Egypt; 60 million.
c) Syria; 16 million.
d) Palestine; 900,000.

xix) In Einstein's *A Test Case for Humanity*, what does this tiny Palestinian country represent to the Jewish people? (Fill in the blanks)

a) This tiny Palestinian country is the _____ place in the

_____ _____ and most _____
connected with the _____ _____, its
_____ foundation and its _____ tradition as an
_____ people.

xx) In Einstein's *A Test Case for Humanity*, why does the author stand for a Jewish-controlled Palestine? (Fill in the blanks)

a) In speaking up for a _____ _____, we want to promote the _____ of a place of _____ where _____ human beings may find _____ and _____ and the undisputed _____ to live under a _____ and _____ of their making. The experience of _____ _____ has taught us that this can be _____ only by _____ _____ and not by a _____ _____ . . .

xxi) In Einstein's *A Test Case for Humanity*, what does the author affirm that the Jews will never abandon? (Circle one)

a) Occupation of Arab countries
b) Mecca
c) Egypt
d) The work of reconstruction undertaken

xxii) In Einstein's *A Test Case for Humanity*, what does the author affirm the Jews bear the name of? (Circle one)

a) The people of ancient Egypt
b) The people of the Bible
c) The people of Roman mythology
d) The people of Arab occupation

IV. Illustrate your work with pictures, outline map, models and drawings.

V. Memory quotation:

"The more complex and intricate his calculations of the universe became, the more assured he was of the reality of a Supreme Creator."

The Martin Luther statue in our Nation's Capital

After the bronze statue of Martin Luther, his right, clenched fist rests resolutely upon a large leatherbound Bible

LESSON 5

THE MARTIN LUTHER MEMORIAL

On the triangular promonitory between Vermont and N Street, N.W., the statue of Martin Luther (1483-1546) stands out in originality and resolute muteness. His timeless message has been conveyed to passersby since the statue's inception, commemorating Luther's 400th birthday. Cast in Germany in 1884, it is a duplicate of the original by E. Reitschell, which stands in Worms, Germany. The eleven and a half-foot-tall bronze replica of one of the outstanding leaders of the 16th century Reformation holds a large leatherbound volume of the Scriptures in his left hand with his right, clenched fist resting upon its contents, as if to say "This is God's Word - Go by it alone! Let it be your guide in life!"

Luther wears a long, beltless cloak draped around him. His face is set as a flint with his eyes looking straight ahead. The sculptor portrayed this great man of God in the act of oratory — of which he was a master.

Inauguration of Luther's Statue

Interestingly enough, upon the inauguration of the bronze replica of Luther's famous statue in front of the *National Lutheran Church* in Washington, D.C., an article dated November 10, 1883 appeared in the *Washington Evening Star*. Its contents refocus upon the main points of contention between Scriptural truth and Roman Catholic dogma, as outlined in Martin Luther's 95 Theses.[1] The article is hereunder quoted:

The Protestant Reformation

The Protestant Reformation dates from the 31st October, 1517, the day on which Martin Luther nailed to the door of the church at Wittemberg his famous ninety-five theses. According to the historians of the Reformation, Pope Leo X in 1510 resorted to the plan of selling indulgences as a means of filling the empty treasury at Rome. This traffic was entrusted to a monk named John Tetzel and others. Luther's first knowledge of this traffic was brought to him by some of his own parishioners, who, living in Wittemberg, had gone to a neighboring town to purchase some of the new merchandise. They came to him and confessed great irregularities, and even crimes, which they had committed, and on being rebuked by Luther, they replied that they did not intend to abandon their sins. Luther was shocked and would not absolve them unless they promised to change their habits. They then showed him their letters of indulgence, believing in their efficacy. The poor dupes returned to Tetzel with complaints against their confessors, and he threatened to excommunicate and bring the most dreadful maledictions to bear against Luther and any others who dared question the efficacy of his indulgences.

Luther appealed to the bishops and to the pope. They would not interfere. Then he wrote out the ninety-five theses as subjects for discussion at the coming holyday of All Saints and nailed them to the door of the church. The principal points of these are as follows:

Martin Luther's Theses

1. Our Lord and Master, Jesus Christ, when He commands us to repent, intends that our whole lives shall be one of repentance.

2. This word cannot be understood of the sacrament of penance (i.e. confession and satisfaction) as administered by the priest.

3. Still the Lord does not mean to speak in this place solely of internal repentance, which is null if it produce not externally every kind of mortification of the flesh.

4. Repentance and sorrow that is true penitence lasts as long as a man is displeased with himself; that is, while he passes from this to eternal life.

5. The pope neither intends, nor can he remit any other punishment than that which he has imposed, according to his good pleasure, or in conformity with the canons - that is, to the papal ordinances.

6. The pope can forgive no debt, but can only declare and confirm the forgiveness which God Himself has given, except in cases that refer to himself. If he does otherwise, the debts remain unremoved and unforgiven.

7. God forgives the sins of no one whom he does not at the same time humble, and who is not willing to obey his confessor.

8. The laws of ecclesiastical penance ought to be imposed solely on the living, and have no regard to the dead.

21. Therefore, the preachers of indulgences are in error when they say that in consequence of the pope's indulgences, men are liberated from all sin and saved.

25. The same power that the pope has over purgatory throughout the church, each bishop possesses individually in his own diocese and each priest in his own parish.

27. They preach mere human folly who maintain that as soon as the money tinkles, avarice and love of gain arrive, increase and multiply. But the support and prayers of the church depend on God's will and good pleasure.

32. Those who fancy themselves sure of salvation by indulgences will go to perdition along with those who teach them so.

35. They are teachers of anti-Christian doctrines who pretend that to deliver a soul from purgatory or to buy an indulgence there is no need to either sorrow or repentance.

The Christian Heritage Of Our Nation - History Curriculum

36.   Every Christian who truly repents of his sins enjoys an entire remission both of the penalty and of the guilt, without any need of indulgences.

37.   Every true Christian, whether dead or alive, participates in all the blessings of Christ, or of the church, by God's gift, and without a letter of indulgence.

38.   Still we should not contemn the papal dispensation and pardon; for this pardon is a declaration of the pardon of God.

40.   True repentance and sorrow seek and love the punishment; but the mildness of indulgence absolves from the punishment and begets hatred against it.

42.   We should teach Christians that the pope has no thought or desire of compassing in any respect the act of buying indulgences with any mark of mercy.

43.   We should teach Christians that he who gives to the poor or lends to the needy does better than he who purchases an indulgence.

44.   For the work of charity increaseth charity, and renders a man more pious, whereas the indulgence does not make him better, but only renders him more self-confident and more secure from punishment.

45.   We should teach Christians, that whoever sees his neighbor in want and yet buys an indulgence does not buy the pope's indulgence, but incurs God's anger.

46.   We should teach Christians that if they have a superfluity they are bound to keep for their own household the means of procuring necessaries, and ought not to squander their money on indulgences.

47.   We should teach Christians that the purchase of an indulgence is a matter of free choice and not of commandments.

48.   We should teach Christians that the pope, having more need of prayers offered up in faith than of money, desires prayer more than money when he offers indulgences.

49.   We should teach Christians that the pope's indulgence is good if we put no confidence in it; but nothing is more hurtful if it diminishes our piety.

50.   We should teach Christians that if the pope knew of the extortions of the preachers of indulgences, he would rather the mother church of St. Peter were burnt and reduced to ashes than see it built up with the skin, flesh and bones of his flock.

51.   We should teach Christians that the pope (as it is his duty) should distribute his own money to the poor whom the indulgence sellers are now stripping of their last farthing, even were he compelled to sell the mother church of St. Peter.

52.   To hope to be saved by indulgence is a lying and an empty hope, although

even the commissary of indulgence – nay, farther, the pope – himself should pledge their souls to guarantee it.

53. Those who forbid the preaching of God's Word in other churches on account of the preaching of indulgences are enemies of Christ and of the pope.

54. Injustice is done to the word of God when as much or even more time is taken up in church in preaching indulgences than the Word of God.

55. The pope can have no other thought than this: If the indulgence, which is a lesser matter, be celebrated with ringing of a bell, with pomp and ceremony, much more should we honor and celebrate the Gospel, which is a greater thing, with a hundred bells and a hundred pomps and ceremonies.

56. The treasures of the church, out of which the pope distributes indulgences, are neither recognized nor pronounced satisfactory by the church of Christ.

59. St. Lawrence called the poor members of the Church, the Church's treasures, but he used the word as it was understood in his day.

62. The proper and true treasure of the Church is the holy Gospel of the glory and grace of God.

63. This treasure is for the benefit of the most hostile and the most hated, for it causes the first to be last.

64. But indulgences are for the benefit of the most worthy, for it causes the last to be the first.

65. Therefore the treasures of the Gospel are nets in which in former times the rich and respectable were caught.

66. But the treasures of indulgences are the nets by which in the present day the riches of the people are caught.

67. But the indulgence which the preachers hold up to the greatest grace must, of course, be esteemed a great favor, for it produces great gain and interest.

68. And yet this indulgence is certainly the very smallest token of grace when compared with the grace of God and the salvation of the cross.

69. It is the duty of bishops and pastors to receive with all respect the commissaries of the pope.

70. But it is still more their duty to ascertain with their eyes and ears that the said commissaries do not preach the dreams of their own imaginations, instead of the orders of the pope.

72. But blessed be he who speaks against the foolish and impudent language of the preachers of indulgences.

75. To esteem the pope's indulgence so high as to suppose that if a person were

(which is impossible) even to defile the holy mother of God, yet he should receive remission by those indulgences, is raving madness and folly.

76.   The indulgence of the pope cannot take away the smallest daily sin, as far as regards the guilt of the offense.

77.   To say that St. Peter, if he were now pope, could not give a more perfect indulgence, is blasphemy against St. Peter and the pope.

79.   It is blasphemy to say that the cross adorned with the arms of the pope is as effectual as the cross of Christ.

80.   The bishops, pastors and theologians who permit such things to be told the people will have to render an account of them.

81.   This shameless preaching, these impudent commendations of indulgences, make it difficult to defend the dignity and honor of the pope against calumnies of the preachers and the subtle and crafty questions of the common people.

86.   Why, say they, does not the pope, who is richer than the richest Croesus, build the mother church of St. Peter with his own money rather than that of poor Christians?

92.   Would that we were quit of all those preachers who say to the church, Peace! When there is no peace.

94.   We should exhort Christians to diligence in following Christ, their Head, through crosses, death and hell.

95.   For it is far better to enter into the kingdom of heaven through much tribulation than to acquire a carnal security by the consolations of a false peace.[2]

This inspiring article concludes with a description of Martin Luther's famed statue, together with an overview of the unveiling ceremonies:

It will be remembered that the statue represents Luther in a standing position in the clerical robes of that age. The right hand rests upon the Bible, and the facial expression is such as to impress the visitor with the Christian character of the man. The word "Martin Luther" will appear in bold relief on the pedestal. The unveiling will take place early in March, and the ceremony will be very impressive. People from all parts of the country are expected to participate and the President will be invited to officiate.[3]

Foxe's Book of Martyrs

For those who would seek to understand, in greater detail, the life, actions, works and words of Martin Luther, great Reformer of the Christian Church, the following account, penned by John Foxe in his world-renowned *Book of Martyrs*, is hereunder excerpted:[4]

Luther's Early Childhood

This illustrious German divine and reformer of the church, was the son of John Luther and Margaret Lindeman, and born at Isleben, a town of Saxony, in the county of Mansfield, November 10, 1483...

Luther was early initiated into letters, and at the age of thirteen was sent to school at Magdeburg, and thence to Eysenach, in Thuringia, where he remained four years, producing the early indications of his future eminence.

Luther Finds a Bible

In 1501 he was sent to the University of Erfurt, where he went through the usual courses of logic and philosophy. When twenty, he took a master's degree, and then lectured on Aristotle's physics, ethics and other parts of philosophy. Afterward, at the instigation of his parents, he turned himself to the civil law, with a view of advancing himself to the bar, but was diverted from this pursuit by the following accident. Walking out into the fields one day, he was struck with lightning so as to fall to the ground, while a companion was killed by his side; and this affected him so sensibly, that, without communicating his purpose to any of his friends, he withdrew himself from the world, and retired into the order of the hermits of St. Augustine.

Here he employed himself in reading St. Augustine and the schoolmen; but, in turning over the books of the library, he accidentally found a copy of the Latin Bible, which he had never seen before. This raised his curiosity to a high degree: he read it over very greedily, and was amazed to find what a small portion of the Scriptures was rehearsed to the people. He made his profession in the monastery of Erfurt, after he had been a novice one year; and he took priest's orders, and celebrated his first mass in 1507. The year after, he was removed from the convent of Erfurt to the University of Wittemberg; for this university being just founded, nothing was thought more likely to bring it into immediate repute and credit, than the authority and presence of a man so celebrated, for his great parts and learning, as Luther.

The Reformer Studies the Bible

In 1512, seven convents of his order having a quarrel with their vicar-general, Luther was chosen to go to Rome, to maintain their cause. At Rome he saw the pope and the court, and had an opportunity of observing also the manners of the clergy, whose hasty, superficial, and impious way of celebrating mass, he has severely noted. As soon as he had adjusted the dispute which was the business of his journey, he returned to Wittemberg, and was created Doctor of Divinity, at the expense of Frederic, elector of Saxony; who had often heard him preach, was perfectly acquainted with his merit, and reverenced him highly. He continued in the University of Wittemberg, where, as Professor of

Divinity, he employed himself in the business of his calling. Here then he began in the most earnest manner to read lectures upon the sacred books: he explained the epistle to the Romans, and the Psalms, which he cleared up and illustrated in a manner so entirely new, and so different from what had been pursued by former commentators, that, "there seemed, after a long and dark night, a new day to arise, in the judgment of all pious and prudent men." The better to qualify himself for the task he had undertaken, he applied himself attentively to the Greek and Hebrew languages; and in this manner was he employed, when the general indulgences were published in 1517.

Pope Leo X plans to build St. Peter's in Rome

Leo X who succeeded Julius II in March 1513, formed a design for building the magnificent church of St. Peter's at Rome, which was, indeed, begun by Julius, but still required very large sums to be finished. Leo, therefore, in 1517, published general indulgences throughout all Europe, in favour of those who would contribute any sum to the building of St. Peter's; and appointed persons in different countries to preach up these indulgences, and to receive money for them. These strange proceedings gave vast offence at Wittemberg, and particularly inflamed the pious zeal of Luther; who, being naturally warm and active, and in the present case unable to contain himself, was determined to declare against them at all adventures.

Luther's Theses Against Indulgences

Upon the eve of All-saints, therefore, in 1517, he publicly fixed up, at the church next to the castle of that town, a thesis upon indulgences; in the beginning of which, he challenged any one to oppose it either by writing or disputation. Luther's propositions about indulgences were no sooner published, than Tetzel, the Dominican friar and commissioner for selling them, maintained and published at Francfort a thesis, containing a set of propositions directly contrary to them. He did more; he stirred up the clergy of his order against Luther; anathematized him from the pulpit, as a most damnable heretic; and burnt his thesis publicly at Francfort . . .

In 1518, Luther, though dissuaded from it by his friends, yet, to show his obedience to authority, went to the monastery of St. Augustine at Heidelberg, while the chapter was held; and here maintained, April 26, a dispute concerning "justification by faith."

The Reformer Accused of Heresy

In the meantime, the zeal of his adversaries grew every day more and more active against him; and he was at length accused to Leo X as a heretic. As soon as he returned therefore from Heidelberg, he wrote a letter to that pope, in the most submissive terms; and sent him, at the same time, an explication of his propositions about indulgences. This letter is dated on Trinity-Sunday, 1518, and was accompanied with a protestation, wherein he declared, that "he did not pretend to advance or defend anything contrary to the Holy

Scriptures, or to the doctrine of the fathers, received and observed by the church of Rome, or to the canons and decretals of the popes: nevertheless, he thought he had the liberty either to approve or disapprove the opinions of St. Thomas, Bonaventure, and other schoolmen and canonists, which are not grounded upon any text."

The emperor Maximilian was equally solicitous with the pope about putting a stop to the propagation of Luther's opinions in Saxony; troublesome both to the church and empire. Maximilian, therefore, applied to Leo, in a letter, dated August 5, 1518, and begged him to forbid, by his authority, these useless, rash, and dangerous disputes; assuring him also, that he would strictly execute in the empire whatever his holiness should enjoin. In the meantime Luther, as soon as he understood what was transacting about him at Rome, used all imaginable means to prevent his being carried thither, and to obtain a hearing of his cause in Germany . . .

But Luther was soon convinced, that he had more to fear from the cardinal's power than from disputations of any kind; and, therefore, apprehensive of being seized, if he did not submit, withdrew from Augsburg upon the 20th. But, before his departure, he published a formal appeal to the pope, and finding himself protected by the elector, continued to teach the same doctrines at Wittemberg, and sent a challenge to all the inquisitors to come and dispute with him . . .

Luther Translates the New Testament into German

While the bull of Leo X executed by Charles V was thundering throughout the empire, Luther was shut up in the castle of Wittemberg; but weary at length of his retirement, he appeared publicly again at Wittemberg, March 6, 1522, after he had been absent about ten months. Luther now made open war with the pope and bishops; and, that he might make the people despise their authority as much as possible, he wrote one book against the pope's bull, and another against the order falsely called "the order of bishops." He published also, a translation of the "New Testament" in the German tongue, which was afterward corrected by himself and Melancthon. Affairs were now in great confusion in Germany; and they were not less so in Italy; for a quarrel arose between the pope and the emperor, during which Rome was twice taken, and the pope imprisoned. While the princes were thus employed in quarrelling with each other, Luther persisted in carrying on the work of the reformation, as well by opposing the papists, as by combating the Ana-baptists and other fanatical sects; which, having taken the advantage of his contest with the church of Rome, had sprung up and established themselves in several places . . .

Origin of the name "Protestant"

Fourteen cities joined against the decree of the diet protestation, which was put into writing, and published the 19th of April, 1529. This was the famous protestation, which gave the name of Protestants to the reformers in Germany.

After this, the protestant princes laboured to make a firm league among themselves, and with the free cities, that they might be able to defend each other against the emperor and the catholic princes . . .

Luther Bequeaths his "Detestation of Popery" in his Will

In 1533 Luther wrote a consolatory epistle to the citizens of Oschatz, who had suffered some hardships for adhering to the Augsburg confession of faith: and in 1534, the Bible translated by him into German was first printed, as the old privilege, dated at Bibliopolis, under the elector's own hand, shows; and it was published the year after. He also published this year a book "against masses and the consecration of priests." In February, 1537, an assembly was held at Smalkald about matters of religion, to which Luther and Melancthon were called. At this meeting Luther was seized with so grievous an illness, that there was no hope of his recovery. As he was carried along, he made his will, in which he bequeathed his detestation of popery to his friends and brethren. In this manner was he employed till his death, which happened in 1546.

Martin Luther – Founder of the Protestant Reformation

We will close this account of the great founder of the reformation, by subjoining a few opinions, which have been passed upon him, by both papists and protestants. "Luther," says Father Simon, "was the first protestant who ventured to translate the Bible into the vulgar tongue from the Hebrew text, although he understood Hebrew but very indifferently . . .

This is the language of those in the church of Rome who speak of Luther with any degree of moderation; for the generality allow him neither parts, nor learning, nor any attainment intellectual or moral. But let us leave these impotent railers, and attend a little to more equitable judges. "Luther," says Wharton, in his Appendix to Cave's *Historia Literaria*, "was a man of prodigious sagacity and acuteness, very warm, and formed for great undertakings; being a man, if ever there was one, whom nothing could daunt or intimidate. When the cause of religion was concerned, he never regarded whose love he was likely to gain, or whose displeasure to incur. He is also highly spoken of by Atterbury and others."

LESSON FIVE

PUPILS' GUIDE

The Martin Luther Memorial – "This is God's Word, Let it be your Guide in Life!"

I. Suggestions for Study

a) Read the lesson material carefully.
b) Look up Worms, Wittemberg, Augsburg, Magdeburg, Erfurt, and Francfort, Germany; and Rome, Italy, on your map of Europe at home.

II. Lesson material

Text: Lesson 5 - The Martin Luther Memorial

III. 1. The kind of man Martin Luther was:

i) Where is the famed bronze statue of Martin Luther to be found in America? Luther's statue is to be found in:

    a) Los Angeles, California
    b) Albuquerque, New Mexico
    c) Washington, D.C., our nation's capital
    d) Plymouth, Massachusetts

ii) What great event did the unveiling of this world-renowned statue commemorate?

    a) The birth of the Reformation
    b) The 1,883rd anniversary of the birth of Christ
    c) The 400th birthday of Martin Luther
    d) The 60th anniversary of the birth of Martin Luther King, Jr.

iii) At the time of the statue's dedication, a prominent article appeared in one of our nation's foremost newspapers. Identify the name of the newspaper, and date of the article: (Circle one)

    a) The *Los Angeles Times*, December 5, 1872
    b) The *Washington Evening Star*, November 10, 1883
    c) The *New York Herald Tribune*, September 17, 1887
    d) The *Mississippi Clarion Ledger*, January 20, 1891

iv) According to this prominent newspaper article, the Protestant Reformation dates from: (Circle one)

    a)   August 15, 1215 A.D.*
    b)   July 10, 1325 A.D.*
    c)   October 12, 1492, A.D.*
    d)   October 31, 1517, A.D.*

v) What cataclysmic, world-changing event characterized the launching of the Protestant Reformation? (Consult the text of the newspaper article and fill in the blanks)

    a)   The Protestant Reformation _____ _____ the _____ _____ _____, the day on which _____ _____ nailed to the _____ of the _____ at _____ his famous _____ _____.

vi) According to the historians of the Reformation, what was the plan Pope Leo X resorted to in 1510? (Consult your text and fill in the blanks)

    a)   Pope Leo X in 1510 resorted to the plan of _____ _____ as a means of _____ the _____ _____ at _____.

vii) Identify the name of the person to which this traffic was entrusted: (Circle one)

    a)   A friar named Melancthon
    b)   A priest named Benedict
    c)   A Cardinal named Petros
    d)   A monk named Tetzel

viii) Who first informed Martin Luther of this traffic? (Circle one)

    a)   Monastery monks at Wittemberg
    b)   The prelates of the diocese
    c)   Some of Luther's parishioners
    d)   The confessors of Rome

ix) Cite the actions which Tetzel threatened against Martin Luther due to his stance against the selling of indulgences: (Consult text and fill in the blanks)

    a)   Tetzel threatened to _____ and _____ the most _____ _____ to bear _____

(A.D. stands for Anno Domini in Latin, "The year of our Lord [Jesus Christ]".)

Luther and any _____ who _____ _____
the efficacy of his _____.

x) To whom did Martin Luther appeal and what response did he receive? Luther appealed to: (Circle one)

    a) The priests and prelates. They stopped this traffic
    b) The princes and dukes. They rebuked the trafficeers
    c) The Emperor. He banned this traffic
    d) The bishops and the pope. They refused to interfere

xi) What action did Martin Luther finally resort to in an attempt to stop the selling of indulgences? Martin Luther: (Consult your text and fill in the blanks)

    a) Martin Luther _____ _____ the _____
    _____ as _____ for discussion at the coming
    _____ of _____ _____ and
    _____ _____ to the _____ of the
    _____.

xii) Identify the following items of Luther's principal points in his 95 Theses: (Consult your text and fill in the blanks)

    1. Our Lord and Master, _____ _____, when He
    _____ us to _____, intends that our
    _____ lives shall be one of _____.
    2. This _____ cannot be _____ of the
    _____ of penance (i.e. _____ and
    _____) as administered by the _____.
    4. _____ and _____ that is _____
    _____ lasts as long as a _____ is _____
    with _____; that is, while he passes from _____ to
    _____ life.
    6. The _____ can _____ no _____ but can only
    _____ and _____ the forgiveness which
    _____ _____ has _____, except in cases that
    _____ to _____. If he does _____,
    the _____ remain _____ and _____.
    8. The _____ of _____ _____ ought to be
    imposed solely on the _____, and have no regard for the
    _____.
    21. Therefore, the _____ of _____ are in error
    when they say that in _____ of the _____
    _____, men are _____ from all _____
    and _____.

27. They _____ mere _____ _____ who maintain that as soon as the _____ _____, avarice and love of _____ arrive, _____ and _____. But the _____ and _____ of the _____ depend on _____ _____ and good pleasure.

32. Those who fancy _____ sure of _____ by _____ will go to _____ along with _____ who _____ them so.

36. Every _____ who truly _____ of his _____ enjoys an entire _____ both of the _____ and of the _____, without any _____ of _____.

37. Every true _____, whether _____ or _____, participates in all the _____ of _____, or of the _____, by _____ _____, and _____ a letter of _____.

45. We should teach _____ that whoever sees his _____ in want and yet _____ an _____, does not buy the _____ _____ but incurs _____ _____.

51. We should teach _____ that the _____ (as it is his _____) should distribute _____ _____ _____ to the _____ whom the indulgence _____ are now _____ of their last _____, even were he _____ to sell the _____ _____ of _____.

54. _____ is done to the _____ of _____ when as much or even more _____ is taken up in _____ in _____ _____ than the _____ of God.

56. The _____ of the _____, out of which the _____ _____ indulgences, are neither _____ nor _____ satisfactory by the _____ of _____.

xiii) In Martin Luther's 62nd Thesis, he states that the proper and true treasure of the church is: (Circle one)

    a) Indulgences
    b) St. Peter's in Rome
    c) The holy Gospel of the glory and grace of God
    d) The Archbishop's ring

xiv) In Martin Luther's 63rd Thesis, he states that the proper and true treasure of the church is for the benefit of whom and why? (Circle one)

    a)   The Aristocratic rulers. It causes the first to be first
    b)   The Hierarchy of Rome. It causes the hierarchy to be first
    c)   The beautiful people. It causes them to be celebrities
    d)   The most hostile and hated. It causes the first to be last

xv)   In Martin Luther's 64th Thesis, he states that indulgences are for the benefit of whom, and why? (Circle one)

    a)   The prelates of Rome. It increases their power
    b)   The unworthy rulers. It brings them fame
    c)   The most worthy. It causes the last to be first
    d)   The rich merchants. It causes their traffic to flourish

xvi)   In Martin Luther's 65th Thesis, what nets caught the rich and respectable in former times? (Circle one)

    a)   The nets of pride and prejudice
    b)   The nets of fishermen
    c)   The nets of the treasures of indulgences
    d)   The nets of the treasures of the Gospel

xvii)   In Martin Luther's 66th Thesis, the treasures of indulgences are used as nets, for what purpose?

    a)   To catch the poor and the sick
    b)   To catch the orphans and widows
    c)   To catch the riches of the people
    d)   To catch lost souls for Christ

xviii)   In Martin Luther's 68th Thesis, what does he state that an indulgence represents the very smallest token of, when compared with the grace of God, and the salvation of the cross?

    a)   money
    b)   riches
    c)   grace
    d)   profit

xix)   In Martin Luther's 79th Thesis, what does he say is blasphemy to state: (Consult your text and fill in the blanks)

    a)   It is blasphemy to say that _____ _____ adorned with the _____ of the _____ is as _____ as the _____ of _____.

xx) In his 94th Thesis, Martin Luther states that we should exhort Christians to diligence in following whom, and through what means? (Circle one)

a) The Emperor, through good citizenship
b) The Pope, through indulgences
c) Christ, their head, through crosses, death and hell
d) The Dukes and Barons, through the feudal system

xxi) In his 95th Thesis, how does Martin Luther advocate entrance into the Kingdom of Heaven? (Circle one)

a) The ringing of bells; pomp and ceremony
b) A horse-drawn carriage
c) The buying of many indulgences
d) Much tribulation

xxii) In his 95th Thesis, what does Martin Luther state are the consolations of a false peace? (Circle one)

a) To take care of the orphans and widows
b) To preach the Gospel of Jesus Christ
c) To acquire a carnal security
d) To help the sick and miserable

xxiii) Who was the first Protestant, according to Foxe's Book of Martyrs, who ventured to translate the Bible into the vulgar tongue (common language of the people) from the Hebrew text? (Circle one)

a) Pope Leo X
b) Martin Luther
c) The Emperor Maximillian
d) Tetzel

xxiv) Foxe's Books of Martyrs, quoting the Appendix to Cave's *Historia Literaria*, describes Martin Luther as: (Consult your text and fill in the blanks)

a) Luther was a man of _____ _____ and _____, very warm, and formed for _____ _____; being a _____, if ever there was one, whom _____ could _____ or _____. When the _____ of _____ was _____, he never _____ whose _____ he was _____ to _____, or whose _____ to _____ . . .

2. Christian Character Traits:

Select 10 Christian virtues, values and morals of this great Christian hero from the selected texts of the original writings of Martin Luther and those who documented his life. List them below:

a. _____   f. _____

b. _____   g. _____

c. _____   h. _____

d. _____   i. _____

e. _____   j. _____

IV. Illustrate your work with pictures, outline map, models and drawings.

V. Memory stanzas: (From Martin Luther's immortal hymn, "A Mighty Fortress is our God.")

A mighty fortress is our God
A bulwark never failing
A helper He amid the flood
Of mortal ills prevailing

For still our ancient foe
Doth seek to work us woe
His craft and power are great
And armed with cruel hate
On earth is not his equal

Did we in our own strength confide
Our striving would be losing
Were not the right Man on our side
The Man of God's own choosing . . .
Christ Jesus is His name.

FRANCIS ASBURY
1745 --- 1816
PIONEER
METHODIST BISHOP
IN AMERICA

THE FRANCIS ASBURY MEMORIAL, MERIDIAN HILL, NORTH/WEST

Francis Asbury - holds a Bible to his heart

FRANCIS ASBURY, PROPHET OF THE LONG ROAD
PORTRAIT by FRANK O. SALISBURY, C.V.O., R.P.S., LLD., D.F.A., IN THE WORLD
METHODIST BUILDING AT LAKE JUNALUSKA, NORTH CAROLINA, U.S.A.

LESSON SIX

THE FRANCIS ASBURY MEMORIAL

Henry Augustus Lukeman's bronze statue of Francis Asbury, pioneer of American Methodism (1745-1816), is a most unusual one. Broad-brimmed hat pulled over his brow, the rider's facial expression betrays noble features and a mouth set firmly in unswerving purpose. Asbury's left hand holds a loose rein, while his right clasps a Bible to his breast, fingers marking a particular reading. His horse fawns the ground, denoting incertitude, which is in direct contrast to the resoluteness of his master. Engraved on the marble pedestal upon which this work of art stands, are the words:

> If you seek for the results of his labor you will find them in our Christian civilization

> and

> His continuous journeying through cities, villages and settlements from 1771 to 1816 greatly promoted patriotism, education, morality and religion in the American Republic. (Act of Congress)

In keeping with the lines of suffering and deprivation traced upon his countenance, Asbury's mission in life is described upon the rear of the statue as: *The Prophet of the Long Road.*

Asbury's Journals

The Reverend Francis Asbury, Bishop of the Methodist Episcopal Church, wrote copiously of his travels. He was an itinerant preacher of the Gospel in America for 45 years, and 32 years a General Superintendent of the Methodist Episcopal Church. His Journal entries from 1771 to 1816, disclose the inner soul of this man of God, whose primary mission in life was to extend salvation to the lost. Some of these are reprinted below, for all to read:

Sunday, May 21st, 1792.

> I preached at Rehoboth on Isai. lv. 12. There was no great move: brothers H_____ and C_____ both spoke after me.

> Weary world, when will it end?

> My mind and body feel dull and heavy, but still my soul drinks deeper into God. We rode about one hundred and sixty miles from the Rich Valley to

Greenbrier conference; talking too much, and praying too little, caused me to feel barrenness of soul. We had a hope that not less than ten souls were converted during the conference: at preaching, I myself having a violent headach, retired; the Lord was with them at the sacrament; after which, the doors being opened, many came in and the meeting continued until nearly sunset.[1]

Tuesday, May 30, 1792.

We hasted to O_____ 's in the Cove, where we met with a most kind and affectionate reception. But O the flies for the horses, and the gnats for the men! And no food, nor even good water to be had. I slept well, although forced, ever and anon, to stir a little.

Wednesday 31.

We had a dreary path, over desperate hills, for fifty miles; no food for man or beast, which caused both to begin to fail very sensibly: my bowels continued to be disordered, and had I not procured a little wine, I suppose I should have failed altogether.

PENNSYLVANIA.

Thursday, June 1.

Both men and horses travelled sore and wearily to Union Town. O how good are clean houses, plentiful tables, and populous villages, when compared with the rough world we came through! Here I turned out our poor horses to pasture and to rest, after riding them nearly three hundred miles in eight days.

Friday 2.

Wrote letters to send over the mountains.

Saturday 3.

I began to feel lame, and had a severe touch of the rheumatism, accompanied with a high fever, which occasioned great pain to me while sitting in conference. I found it necessary to remove, by exchange, six of the preachers from this to the eastern district.

Sunday 11.

Having been too unwell to attend preaching through the week, I now ventured in public: a great crowd of people attended, and there was some melting and moving among them. I feel the death of this district; I see what is wanting here—discipline, and the preaching a present and full salvation, and the enforcement of the doctrine of sanctification. I have been variously tried, and was constrained to be cheerful.

We have founded a seminary of learning called Union School; brother C. Conway is manager, who also has charge of the district: this establishment is designed for instruction in grammar, languages, and the sciences.

I have had some awful thoughts lest my lameness should grow upon me, and render me useless. I sometimes have fears that I am too slack in speaking in public, at conferences; I also feel the want of time and places to pursue my practice of solitary prayer, being frequently obliged to ride all the day and late at night, that I may in time reach the appointed places to preach.

Tuesday 13.

We ascended Laurel-hill, and after forty miles riding reached M_____'s, quite weary. Came to I. C_____'s, and found the Lord was still in this house: I preached, and felt a melting heart, and there was some move in the congregation. I find myself recruited in body and mind; and I feel as if God would work once more amongst this people.[2]

MARYLAND.

I preached at Fort Cumberland, in our new house, to many people. Dined with Mr. D_____, at whose house I was entertained the first time I visited this town: O that each of the family may be everlastingly saved! It is now three years since I came down this road.—Swift-winged time, O how it flies! My body is in better health, and my soul in great peace; I feel no wrong temper. O that my whole heart might be running out in holiness after God!

Lord's day, 18.

We had a solemn meeting, whilst I enlarged on "Blessed are they that hear the word of God and keep it." It was a good season.

VIRGINIA

Monday 19.

Rode to Bath. Here I had the opportunity of writing to all the connected preachers in the district.

Friday 23.

In the evening I preached with some assistance on Luke xix.10.

NEW YORK.

Sunday, July 16.

Preached at our church on Staten Island. I was very close on the law and the Gospel—a few felt; but it was a dry time. Lord, help us.!

As very probably all of my life which I shall be able to write will be found in my journal, it will not be improper to relate something of my earlier years, and to give a brief account of my first labours in the ministry.

Asbury's Origins

I was born in Old England, near the foot of Hampstead Bridge, in the parish of Handsworth, about four miles from Birmingham, in Staffordshire, and, according to the best of my after-knowledge, on the 20th or 21st day of August, in the year of our Lord 1745.[3]

Asbury's Early Childhood

My father's name was Joseph, and my mother's, Elizabeth Asbury: they were people in common life; were remarkable for honesty and industry, and had all things needful to enjoy; had my father been as saving as laborious, he might have been wealthy. As it was, it was his province to be employed as a farmer and gardener by the two richest families in the parish. My parents had two children, a daughter called Sarah, and myself. My lovely sister died in infancy; she was a favourite, and my dear mother being very affectionate, sunk into deep distress at the loss of a darling child, from which she was not relieved for many years. It was under this dispensation that God was pleased to open the eyes of her mind, she living in a very dark, dark, dark day and place. She now began to read almost constantly when leisure presented the opportunity. When a child, I thought it strange my mother should stand by a large window poring over a book for hours together. From my childhood I may say, I have neither

"——dar'd an oath, nor hazarded a lie."

The love of truth is not natural; but the habit of telling it I acquired very early, and so well was I taught, that my conscience would never permit me to swear profanely. I learned from my parents a certain form of words for prayer, and I well remember my mother strongly urged my father to family reading and prayer; the singing of psalms was much practised by them both. My foible was the ordinary foible of children—fondness for play; but I abhorred mischief and wickedness, although my mates were amongst the vilest of the vile for lying, swearing, fighting, and whatever else boys of their age and evil habits were likely to be guilty of; from such society I very often returned home uneasy and melancholy; and although driven away by my better principles, still I would return, hoping to find happiness where I never found it. Sometimes I was much ridiculed, and called Methodist Parson, because my mother invited any people who had the appearance of religion to her house.

Asbury's Formative Years

I was sent to school early, and began to read the Bible between six and seven years of age, and greatly delighted in the historical part of it. My schoolmaster was a great churl, and used to beat me cruelly; this drove me to prayer, and it appeared to me, that God was very near to me. My father having but the one son, greatly desired to keep me at school, he cared not how long; but in this design he was disappointed; for my master, by his severity, had filled me with such horrible dread, that with me anything was preferable to going to school. I lived some time in one of the wealthiest and most ungodly families we had in the parish: here I became vain, but not openly wicked. Some months after this I returned home; and made my choice, when about thirteen years and a half old, to learn a branch of business, at which I wrought about six years and a half: during this time I enjoyed great liberty, and in the family was treated more like a son or an equal than an apprentice.

Asbury's Spiritual Birth in Christ

Soon after I entered on that business, God sent a pious man, not a Methodist, into our neighbourhood, and my mother invited him to our house; by his conversation and prayers, I was awakened before I was fourteen years of age. It was now easy and pleasing to leave my company, and I began to pray morning and evening, being drawn by the cords of love, as with the bands of a man. I soon left our blind priest, and went to West-Bromwick church: here I heard Ryland, Stillingfleet, Talbot, Bagnall, Mansfield, Hawes, and Venn, great names, and esteemed Gospel-ministers. I became very serious; reading a great deal—Whitefield and Cennick's Sermons, and every good book I could meet with. It was not long before I began to inquire of my mother who, where, what were the Methodists; she gave me a favourable account, and directed me to a person that could take me to Wednesbury to hear them. I soon found this was not the church—but it was better. The people were so devout—men and women kneeling down—saying Amen.—Now, behold! They were singing hymns—sweet sound! Why, strange to tell! The preacher had no prayer book, and yet he prayed wonderfully! What was yet more extraordinary, the man took his text, and had no sermon-book: thought I, this is wonderful indeed! It is certainly a strange way, but the best way. He talked about confidence, assurance, &c.—of which all my fights and hopes fell short. I had no deep convictions, nor had I committed any deep known sins. At one sermon, some time after, my companion was powerfully wrought on: I was exceedingly grieved that I could not weep like him; yet I knew myself to be in a state of unbelief. On a certain time when we were praying in my father's barn, I believe the Lord pardoned my sins, and justified my soul; but my companions reasoned me out of this belief, saying, "Mr. Mather said a believer was as happy as if he was in heaven." I thought I was not as happy as I would be there, and gave up my confidence, and that for months; yet I was happy; free from guilt and fear, and had power over sin, and felt great inward joy. After this, we met for reading and prayer, and had large and good meetings, and were much persecuted . . .

Francis Asbury, Preacher

I then held meetings frequently at my father's house, exhorting the people there, as also at Sutton-Cofields, and several souls professed to find peace through my labours. I met class awhile at Bromwick-Heath, and met in band at Wednesbury. I had preached some months before I publicly appeared in the Methodist meeting-houses; when my labours became more public and extensive, some were amazed, not knowing how I had exercised elsewhere. Behold me now a local preacher; the humble and willing servant of any and of every preacher that called on me by night or by day, being ready, with hasty steps, to go far and wide to do good, visiting Derbyshire, Staffordshire, Warwickshire, Worcestershire, and indeed almost every place within my reach for the sake of precious souls; preaching, generally, three, four, and five times a week, and at the same time pursuing my calling.—I think, when I was between twenty-one and twenty-two years of age I gave myself up to God and his work, after acting as a local preacher near the space of five years: it is now

The Christian Heritage Of Our Nation - History Curriculum

the 19th of July 1792.—I have been labouring for God and souls about thirty years, or upwards.

Sometime after I had obtained a clear witness of my acceptance with God, the Lord showed me in the heat of youth and youthful blood, the evil of my heart: for a short time I enjoyed, as I thought, the pure and perfect love of God; but this happy frame did not long continue, although, at seasons, I was greatly blest. Whilst I was a travelling preacher in England, I was much tempted, finding myself exceedingly ignorant of almost every thing a minister of the Gospel ought to know. How I came to America, and the events which have happened since, my journal will show.

NEW YORK.

Yesterday I preached in New-York, on "Who is on the Lord's side?"—I had some life in speaking, but there was little move in the congregation. O Lord, hasten a revival of thy work! This city has been agitated about the choice of Governor: it would be better for them all to be on the Lord's side.—The standard is set up — who declares for the Lord?—The wicked; the carnal professors; carnal ministers, and apostates, are the Lord's enemies.

Sunday 23.

Was a melting time with many hearts in the old church: my subject, I John 1. 6,7. In the afternoon, although very unwell, I laboured hard in the new church, but the people were exceedingly insensible. There was a little shaking under brother Hull in the old church in the evening . . . [4]

Monday, November 18, 1799.

We rode twenty-six miles into the state of Georgia, crossed Rocky River, properly so called, likewise the Savannah at the Cherokee Ford: it was wide, deep, and there were large rocks in it, and I had no guide.

Saturday and Sabbath day, December 7, 8.

We held our quarterly meeting at Mark's meeting house: I had dreaded this appointment. I had some pain and some pleasure. The state of religion is low here. Hope Hull preached on Saturday upon Jer. x, 8: we had some signs to show that life had not entirely departed, in the love feast and sacrament. Benjamin Blanton preached Sabbath day, from Isa. xxviii, 8, and I gave a gloss upon Joshua xiv, 8: "Nevertheless, my brethren that went up with me made the heart of the people melt; but I wholly followed the Lord my God." In the introduction peculiar attention was paid to the dealings of God with Israel from the beginning to the end; the influence pious characters had in the case before us, two prevailing against ten; that the well-being of future generations required that a decided tone to the morals, manners, and religious opinions should be given by the first settlers of the country. The weight of the discourse was opened in two divisions: First, what God had done for many Christians;

Secondly, their unfaithfulness and complaints (like the Israelites), and their bad influence upon the camp of Israel, as at the present day . . .[5]

SOUTH CAROLINA

Wednesday, January 1, 1800.

We began our conference in Charleston, twenty-three members present. I had select meetings with the preachers each evening, who gave an account of the dealings of God with their own souls, and of the circuits they supplied the past year.

Saturday, 4.

After determining by a large majority that our next meeting together (by Divine permission) should be in Camden, the conference rose.

Asbury's Description of George Washington

Slow moved the Northern post on the eve of New Year's day, and brought the heart-distressing information of the death of Washington, who departed this life December 14, 1799.

Washington, the calm, intrepid chief, the disinterested friend, first father and temporal saviour of his country under Divine protection and direction. A universal cloud sat upon the faces of the citizens of Charleston; the pulpits clothed in black—the bells muffled—the paraded soldiery—a public oration decreed to be delivered on Friday, 14th of this month—a marble statue to be placed in some proper situation. These were the expressions of sorrow, and these the marks of respect paid by his feeling fellow-citizens to the memory of this great man. I am disposed to lose sight of all but Washington: matchless man! At all times he acknowledged the providence of God, and never was he ashamed of his Redeemer: we believe he died, not fearing death. In his will he ordered the manumission of his slaves—a true son of liberty in all points.[6]

Minutes of Asbury's Conversations

Of further interest to history-loving Americans, are the *Minutes of Several Conversations between the Reverend Thomas Coke, L.L.D., The Reverend Francis Asbury and others*, at a Conference begun in Baltimore, in the State of Maryland, on Monday the 27th of December, in the year 1784. It composed a *Form of Discipline* for the Ministers, Preachers and other members of the Methodist Episcopal Church in America. This priceless document majors upon the issue of *Slavery*, as also, *Personal Holiness*, among other matters:

Q.   42.   What methods can we take to extirpate slavery?

A.   We are deeply conscious of the impropriety of making new terms of communion for a Religious Society already established, excepting on the most pressing occasion: and such we esteem the practice of holding our Fellow-Creatures in Slavery. We view it as contrary to the Golden Law of God on which hang all the Law and the Prophets, and the unalienable Rights of mankind, as well as every principle of the Revolution, to hold in the deepest Debasement, in a more abject Slavery than is perhaps to be found in any part of the world except America, so many souls that are all capable of the image of God. We therefore think it our most bounden duty, to take immediately some effectual method to extirpate this abomination from among us: And for that purpose we add the following to the rules of our Society, viz:

1. Every member of our Society who has slaves in his possession shall within twelve months after notice given to him by the assistant (which notice the assistants are required immediately and without any delay to give in their respective circuits) legally execute and record an instrument, whereby he emancipates and sets free every slave in his possession who is between the ages of forty and forty-five immediately, or at farthest when they arrive at the age of forty-five . . .

2. Every assistant shall keep a Journal, in which he shall regularly minute down the names and ages of all the slaves belonging to all the masters in his respective circuit, and also the date of every instrument executed and recorded for the manumission of the slaves, with the name of the court, Book and Folio, in which the said instruments respectively shall have been recorded: Which Journal shall be handed down in each circuit to the succeeding assistants.

3. In consideration that these rules form a new term of communion, every person concerned, who will not comply with them, shall have liberty quietly to withdraw himself from our Society within the twelve months succeeding the notice given as aforesaid: Otherwise the assistant shall exclude him in the Society.

4. No person so voluntarily withdrawn, or so excluded, shall ever partake of the Supper of the Lord with the Methodists, till he complies with the above requisitions.

5. No person holding slaves shall, in future, be admitted into Society or to the Lord's Supper, till he previously complies with these rules concerning Slavery . . .

Q. 43. What shall be done with those who buy or sell slaves, or give them away?

A.   They are immediately to be expelled: unless they buy them on purpose to free them . . .[7]

Q. 52. Why are not we more holy? Why do not we live in Eternity? Walk with God all the day long? Why are we not all devoted to God? Breathing the whole spirit of missionaries?

A.   Chiefly because we are enthusiasts; looking for the end without using the means. To touch only upon two or three instances: Who of you rises at four? Or even at five, when he does not preach? Do you recommend to all our societies the five o'clock hour for private prayer? Do you observe it? Or any other fix't time? Do not you find by experience that any time is no time? Do you know the obligation and benefit of fasting? How often do you practise it?

        The neglect of this alone is sufficient to account for our feebleness and faintness of Spirit. We are continually grieving the Holy Spirit of God by the habitual neglect of a plain duty. Let us amend from this hour! . . .

Q. 53. But how can I fast since it hurts my health?

A.   There are several degrees of fasting, which cannot hurt your health. We will instance in one. Let us every Friday (beginning on the next) avow this duty throughout the continent, by touching no tea, coffee or chocolate in the morning, but (if we want it) half a pint of milk or water-gruel. Let us dine on vegetables, and (if we need it) eat three or four ounces of flesh in the evening. At other times let us eat no flesh-suppers. These exceedingly tend to breed nervous disorders . . .

These *Minutes* gave birth to Episcopal Methodism in the United States.[8]

LESSON SIX

PUPILS' GUIDE

The Francis Asbury Memorial - "The Prophet of the Long Road"

I. Suggestions for Study

    a)   Read the lesson material carefully.

    b)   Look up Rehoboth, Delaware; Georgia; Pennsylvania; Maryland; New York; Charleston, South Carolina and England, United Kingdom on your map of the United States and the world at home.

II. Lesson material

    Text: Lesson 6 - The Francis Asbury Memorial

III. 1. The kind of man that Francis Asbury was:

    i)   What was Francis Asbury's mission in life, as described upon the rear of his famed statue? (Circle one)

        a)   Circuit Rider
        b)   Horseman
        c)   Preacher
        d)   The Prophet of the long Road

    ii)   How did our U.S. Congress eulogize Francis Asbury's life and work, as engraved upon the base of his statue? (Fill in the blanks)

        a)   His _____ journeying through _____, _____ and _____ from 1771 to 1816, greatly promoted _____, _____, _____, and _____ in the American _____.

    iii)   In Francis Asbury's May 21, 1792 Journal entry, he tells us that he felt a barrenness of soul because: (Circle one)

        a)   They prayed too much and talked too little
        b)   They rode 160 miles
        c)   They talked too much and prayed too little
        d)   He had a violent headache

iv) In Francis Asbury's June 1, 1792 Journal entry, he states that he "turned out the poor horses to pasture and rest, after riding them nearly–" (Circle one)

   a) 50 miles in 10 days
   b) 100 miles in 15 days
   c) 200 miles in 20 days
   d) 300 miles in 8 days

v) Asbury's Sunday, June 11, 1792 Journal entry states that he "felt the death of that district, and saw what was wanting there." The district was wanting: (Consult your text and fill in the blanks)

   a) _____, and the preaching a _____ and full _____ and the _____ of the doctrine of _____.

vi) In Asbury's Sunday, June 11, 1792 Journal entry, he writes that he also feels the want of time and places to pursue his practice of: (Circle one)

   a) Personal improvement
   b) Balanced meals
   c) Solitary prayer
   d) Horsemanship

vii) In Asbury's Sunday, July 16, 1792 Journal entry, he relates that he began to read and delight in the Bible between the ages of: (Circle one)

   a) 5 and 6
   b) 6 and 7
   c) 8 and 9
   d) 20 and 21

viii) In the same Journal entry, Asbury tells us about his school-master, who drove him to:

   a) Retaliate
   b) Fail his studies
   c) Pray
   d) Run away

ix) In Francis Asbury's July 16, 1792 Journal entry, he describes the Lord (Jesus Christ's) enemies as: (Circle all correct answers)

   a) Preachers of the Gospel
   b) The wicked

c) Clergymen
d) Carnal professors
e) Pastors
f) Carnal ministers
g) Apostates

x) In Francis Asbury's December 7 and 8, 1799 Journal entry, what does he state that the well-being of future generations depended upon? (Consult your text and fill in the blanks)

a) A decided tone to the _____, _____ and _____ opinions should be given by the _____ _____ of the country.

xi) What were the two divisions of this discourse, respectively? (Circle two)

a) What great things many Christians had done
b) What God had done for many Christians
c) Their faithfulness and good stewardship
d) Their unfaithfulness and complaints

xii) The heart-distressing information described in Asbury's January 1, 1800 Journal entry, was a result of:

a) The floods in South Carolina
b) The lack of funds
c) The death of George Washington
d) The death of King George III

xiii) In the same Journal entry, Francis Asbury portrays in detail the life and character of our first president, George Washington, as follows: (Consult your text and fill in the blanks)

a) Washington, the _____, _____ chief, the _____ friend, first _____ and temporal _____ of his country under _____ protection and _____. A universal _____ sat upon the faces of the _____ of Charleston; the _____ clothed in _____, the _____ muffled, the _____ _____, a public _____ decreed to be _____ on Friday, 14th of this _____, a marble _____ to be placed in some _____ situation. These were the _____ of sorrow, and _____ the marks of _____ _____ by his _____ fellow-citizens to the _____ of this great _____. I am disposed to lose _____ of all but _____:

matchless _____! At all times he _____ the
_____ of God, and never was he ashamed of his
_____ : we believe he _____, not fearing
_____ . In his _____ he ordered the
_____ of his _____, a true son of
_____ in all _____ .

xiv) In Asbury's above Journal entry, what are the character traits ascribed to George Washington? (Circle all correct answers)

a) Hot-tempered
b) Calm
c) Impulsive
d) Intrepid
e) Interested friend
f) Disinterested friend
g) Weak
h) Great
i) Insignificant
j) Matchless

xv) In the above Journal entry, of whom, states Asbury, was George Washington not ashamed during his life? (Circle one)

a) Congress
b) The Supreme Court
c) His Redeemer, Jesus Christ
d) The Executive Branch of the Government

xvi) The answer to Question 42 in the *Minutes of Several Conversations* between the Reverend Thomas Coke and the Reverend Francis Asbury, states that the practice of holding our fellow-creatures in slavery is contrary to: (Circle all correct answers)

a) The Buddhist religion
b) The Golden Law of God
c) Confucius' writings
d) All the Law and the Prophets (in the Bible)
e) The Koran
f) The unalienable rights of mankind
g) Every principle of the American Revolution
h) The principles of the French Revolution

xvii)   In the answer to Question 42 of the *Minutes of Several Conversations* between the Reverend Thomas Coke and the Reverend Francis Asbury, what was thought their most bounden duty? (Consult your text and fill in the blanks)

a)   We therefore think it our most bounden duty to _____ _____ some _____ _____ to extirpate this _____ from among us: And for that _____ we add the _____ to the _____ of our _____ . . .

xviii) Item 5 of the Answers to Question 42 of the *Minutes of Several Conversations* between the Reverend Thomas Coke and the Reverend Francis Asbury, states that no person holding slaves in future shall: (Circle two)

a)   Be rewarded
b)   Be praised
c)   Be admitted into Society
d)   Be decorated
e)   Be admitted to the Lord's Supper

xix)   What does the above tell us regarding the Methodist Episcopal Church in America's stance on the question of slavery? Slavery was: (Circle all correct answers)

a)   Accepted
b)   Abhorred
c)   Financially beneficial
d)   Denounced
e)   Tolerated
f)   Condemned
g)   Against God's Word, the Bible

xx)   The answer to Question 43 of the *Minutes of Several Conversations* between the Reverend Thomas Coke and the Reverend Francis Asbury, regarding those who buy or sell slaves or give them away, is: (Consult your text and fill in the blanks)

a)   They are _____ to be _____: unless they _____ them on _____ to _____ them . . .

xxi)   Question 52 of the *Minutes of Several Conversations* between the Reverend Thomas Coke and the Reverend Francis Asbury deals with 5 "why's" concerning true Christianity. What are they? (Consult your text and fill in the blanks)

a)   Why are not we _____ _____?
b)   Why do not we live in _____ ?
c)   Walk with _____ all the _____ _____?
d)   Why are we not all _____ to _____ ?
e)   Breathing the whole _____ of _____?

xxii)   The answer to Question 52 of the *Minutes of Several Conversations* between the Reverend Thomas Coke and the Reverend Francis Asbury, is as follows: Because we are: (Circle two)

a)   Too religious
b)   Too separate from the world mindset
c)   Enthusiasts
d)   We are looking for the end without using the means

xxiii) In the answer to Question 52 of the *Minutes of Several Conversations* between the Reverend Thomas Coke and the Reverend Francis Asbury; the neglect of what, alone, was sufficient to account for their feebleness and faintness of Spirit? (Circle one)

a)   Corporate prayer
b)   Worshipping God
c)   Bible Study
d)   Confession of sin
e)   Private prayer and fasting

xxiv)   The answer to Question 53 of the *Minutes* between the Reverend Thomas Coke and the Reverend Francis Asbury affirms that there are several degrees of a certain practise which cannot hurt one's health. This practice is: (Circle one)

a)   Sports
b)   Recreation
c)   Eating
d)   Running
e)   Fasting
f)   Studying

2. Christian Character Traits:

Select 10 Christian virtues, values and morals evidenced in the life and work of Francis Asbury: (List them below)

a. _____   f. _____

b. _____   g. _____

c. _____   h. _____

d. _____   i. _____

e. _____   j. _____

IV. Illustrate your work with pictures, outline map, models and drawings.

V. Memory quotation: (from Act of Congress)

His continuous journeying through cities, villages and settlements from 1771 to 1816 greatly promoted patriotism, education, morality and religion in the American Republic.

The Robert A. Taft Memorial on Capitol Hill

The Bronze Statue of Robert A. Taft

Tribute
to an
American

The Robert A. Taft Memorial

The first and largest of 27 bells to be installed on the Robert A. Taft Memorial on the Capitol grounds is hoisted into place.

LESSON 7

THE ROBERT A. TAFT MEMORIAL

An 11-foot bronze statue of Senator Robert A. Taft, son of past President and Supreme Court Chief Justice William Howard Taft, stands out in quiet strength and beauty on the slope leading up to the Capitol's predominance. The tall, matchbox-like carillon behind it towers 100 feet above the figure. Twenty-seven, beautifully-matched bells mark each hour and quarter hour as they pass by.

Hymns and Carols

On various occasions each Sunday and at noon each day of the week, hymns to the honor and glory of God are played, such as: *Nearer My God to Thee; O God Our Help in Ages Past; Take Time to Be Holy; Come, Thou Mighty King; Faith of Our Fathers; The Hymn of the Republic; God of Our Fathers; Awake my Soul; The Star-spangled Banner; America; Holy God we Praise Thy Name; God Bless America; America my Country*; and *America the Beautiful*. During the week celebrating Christmas each year, carols ring out their joyous praise for a Messiah. Included in this repertoire are old-fashioned favorites such as: *O Come Emmanuel; O Little Town of Bethlehem; O Worship the King, Silent Night; The First Noel, Adeste Fideles; I Heard the Bells on Christmas Day; Away in the Manger*; and *Hark the Herald Angels Sing*. This impressive memorial was presented by the people of the United States to Congress.[1]

The Largest Bell is Installed

At the installation of the largest of the 27 bells of the Taft Carillon, the following poem appeared in the August 13, 1956 issue of the Capitol Hill *Roll Call*:

The Test of the Bells
The bells ring
   Across the HILL . . .
Testing for the Taft Memorial
   Carillon . . .
For quality, fidelity of pitch,
   as the world of music measures such . . .

As also measured was he,
   Senator Taft of the Carillon . . .
A Senator's Senator . . .
   Stilled is his voice
But now the bells speak for him . . .

Bells calling the hour

As bells ring also along the corridors,
Senate and House,
Summons to duty,
Challenge to stand up and be counted . . .

The new, but eternal Independence bells . . .
Like the Carillon bells,
The call for a quorum of all patriots,
For the muster of all patriots,
Under God a new birth of Freedom.

Thomas Quinn Beesley

Inscriptions Upon the Memorial

The Robert A. Taft Memorial Carillon, dedicated on April 14, 1959, pays tribute to a great American. The handsome bronze statue of Senator Taft is the work of noted sculptor Wheeler Williams. Above it are inscribed these words:

This Memorial to Robert A. Taft, presented by the people to the Congress of the United States, stands as a tribute to the honesty, indomitable courage and high principles of free government symbolized by his life.

Inscribed upon the North Facade of the Carillon Tower, is Senator Taft's admonition on maintaining our great Republic:

If we wish to make democracy permanent in this country, let us abide by the fundamental principles laid down in the Constitution. Let us see that the State is the servant of its people and that the people are not the servants of the State.

Taft's views on Freedom are etched upon the South Facade of the Tower:

Liberty has been the key to our progress in the past, and is the key to our progress in the future. If we can preserve liberty in all its essentials, there is no limit to the future of the American people.

Taft's Famous Words

Among the writings and speeches of Robert A. Taft are to be found his views on *The Object of Government*, and *A Christian Code for Government*, respectively, excerpted below:

The Object of Government

The only object of government is to serve the people and help them to become a greater people in the best sense. We want a better people, people of strong character – God-fearing, industrious, self-reliant, honorable and intelligent. A reasonable standard of material welfare for all families is essential today as the basis for the development of both happiness and character.[2]

and

A Christian Code of Government

We need only a government inspired by the principles of the Pilgrim Fathers – a government which is honest to the core and furnishes a moral and religious leadership to the people, a government inspired by the dominating purpose that it will maintain at all costs the liberty of its people from foreign and domestic threat.[3]

Senator Taft penned these lines concerning *Fact*:

Fact

Fact has neither latitude, longitude nor expansion. You're right or you're wrong; you can't be nearly either.[4]

Dedication Speeches

At the Dedication Ceremonies, President Dwight D. Eisenhower presented the memorial to Congress, stating, "I would feel remiss if I failed to give some expression to the very great admiration and affection I formed for the Senator . . ."[5]

The Honorable Herbert Hoover expounded upon Senator Taft's integrity and courage, affirming that:

Robert A. Taft was an official with a social conscience. He not only would not desert his post; he never deserted his people.

Of course, he bore his cross. He was denounced as an isolationist, as a reactionary, as an enemy of the poor and a friend of the rich. These attacks never shook him, because of his philosophy and moral attitude toward life. His conscience was always clear. He was one who lost no sleep nights worrying that he would be found out. He lost much sleep over the fate of his country.

He knew to the end that his was a moral attitude toward life and men and that he had given to his country his last full measure of devotion.

And so upon this hill where long he served the American people stands this monument not to his greatness but to his virtue. Who is great and who is small in a Republic? It hardly matters. What does matter is that the essential virtues among men and women which made this country strong, which built great cities and verdant farms out of a wilderness, which stand for moral principles in public life, be preserved by reminders of such men as Robert A. Taft. Fortunately, in the belfry of this monument there is a magnificent carillon.

When these great bells ring out, it will be a summons to integrity and courage.[6]

LESSON SEVEN

PUPILS' GUIDE

The Robert A. Taft Memorial - "O God our Help in Ages Past"

I. Suggestions for Study

a) Read the lesson material carefully.
b) Look up the State of Ohio; and Capitol Hill, in Washington, D.C., on your map of the United States at home.

II. Lesson material

Text: Lesson 7 - The Robert A. Taft Memorial

III. 1. The kind of man that Robert A. Taft was:

i) Who was Robert A. Taft? Robert A. Taft was: (Circle all correct answers)

a) A foreigner
b) An American
c) A Congressman from California
d) A Senator from Ohio
e) The son of a past U.S. president
f) The son of a former U.N. Ambassador
g) The son of a past U.S. Supreme Court Chief Justice

ii) Robert A. Taft's bronze statue is how many feet tall, against a Carillon of how many feet? (Circle one)

a) 6 feet; 50 feet
b) 8 feet; 70 feet
c) 11 feet; 100 feet
d) 15 feet; 150 feet

iii) How many bells are housed in the Robert A. Taft Carillon? (Circle one)

a) 10
b) 27
c) 35
d) 50

iv)   What is played upon the Robert A. Taft Carillon bells on various occasions each Sunday and at noon each day? (Circle one)

a)   Rock 'n Roll
b)   Jazz
c)   Hymns to the glory of Almighty God
d)   Dixieland

v)   Name the titles of the music played upon the Robert A. Taft Memorial on Capitol Hill. (Fill in the blanks)

a)   Nearer my _____ to _____.
b)   O _____ our _____ in ages _____.
c)   Take _____ to be _____.
d)   The _____ of the _____.
e)   _____ of our _____.
f)   Awake _____ _____.
g)   The _____ Banner.
h)   _____.
i)   Holy _____ we _____ Thy _____.
j)   _____ bless _____.
k)   _____, my _____.
l)   _____, the _____.
m)   Come, Thou mighty _____.
n)   _____ of our _____.

vi)   How many times does Almighty God of the Bible appear in these titles of music? (Circle one)

a)   Once
b)   Three times
c)   Five times
d)   Seven times

vii)   How many times does "America" appear in these titles of music?

a)   Once
b)   Three times
c)   Four times
d)   Six times

viii) During the week celebrating Christmas each year, what songs are played on the Robert A. Taft Memorial Carillon on Capitol Hill? (Circle one)

    a) Country western
    b) Opera
    c) Waltzes
    d) Carols glorifying Jesus Christ, the Messiah

ix) Name the titles of the music played upon the Robert A. Taft Memorial during Christmas Week each year:

    a) O Come _____ .
    b) O Little _____ of _____ .
    c) O Worship the _____ .
    d) _____ Night.
    e) The First _____ .
    f) I Heard the _____ on _____ Day.
    g) _____ in the _____ .
    h) _____ Fideles.
    i) _____ the _____ _____ Sing.

x) What does the name "Emmanuel" mean? From what New Testament Scripture does it come? (Circle two)

    a) King of Kings   e) Galatians 2:20
    b) The Ruler of Israel   f) Colossians 1:17
    c) God with us   g) John 1:14
    d) The King of the Jews   h) Matthew 1:23

xi) When, by whom, to whom and for what purpose was the Robert A. Taft Memorial Carillon presented? (Fill in the blanks)

    a) April 14, _____ . This Memorial to _____ presented by the _____ to the _____ of the _____ _____ , stands as a _____ to the _____ , indomitable _____ and high _____ of _____ government _____ by his _____ .

xii) What are Robert A. Taft's admonitions on maintaining a great Republic, as inscribed upon the North Facade of the Carillon Tower? (Fill in the blanks)

    a) If we _____ to make _____ _____ in this country, let us _____ by the fundamental _____ laid down in the _____ . Let us see

that the _____ is the _____ of its _____ and
that the _____ are not the _____ of the
_____.

xiii)   Upon the South Facade of the Carillon Tower, Robert A. Taft's inscribed
        views on Freedom are as follows: (Fill in the blanks)

   a)   _____ has been the _____ to our _____
        in the _____, and is the _____ to our _____
        in the _____. If we can preserve _____ in all its
        _____, there is no _____ to the _____ of
        the _____ people.

xiv)   What is a Christian code of government according to Robert A. Taft's
        writings? (Fill in the blanks)

   a)   We need only a _____ inspired by the _____
        of the _____ Fathers. A _____ which is
        _____ to the core and furnishes a _____ and
        _____ leadership to the people, a _____
        inspired by the _____ purpose that it will
        _____ at all costs the _____ of its
        _____ from _____ and domestic threat.

2. Christian Character Traits:

Select 10 Christian virtues, values and morals evidenced in the life and deeds of
Robert A. Taft: (List them below)

a. _____   f. _____

b. _____   g. _____

c. _____   h. _____

d. _____   i. _____

e. _____   j. _____

IV. Illustrate your work with pictures, outline map, models and drawings.

V. Memory quotation: (From Robert A. Taft's writings)

We need only a government inspired by the principles of the Pilgrim Fathers. A
government which is honest to the core and furnishes a moral and religious
leadership to the people . . .

Arlington National Cemetery - Robert E. Lee's home on the hilltop

The Christian Heritage Of Our Nation - History Curriculum

Arlington National Cemetery

President John F. Kennedy's Tombsite - Arlington National Cemetery

The Christian Heritage Of Our Nation - History Curriculum

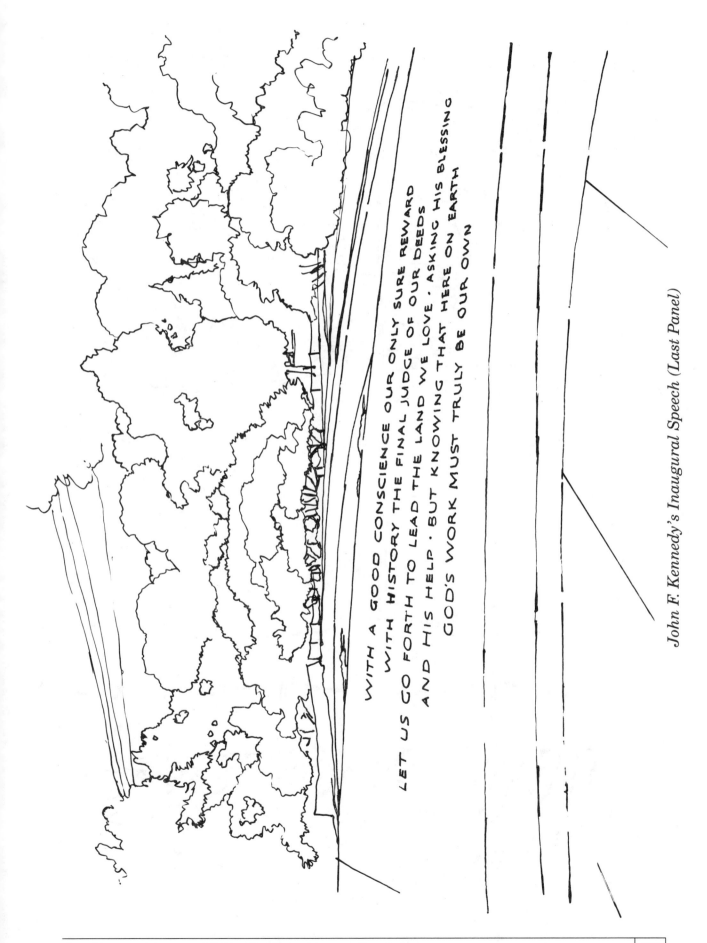

WITH A GOOD CONSCIENCE OUR ONLY SURE REWARD
WITH HISTORY THE FINAL JUDGE OF OUR DEEDS
LET US GO FORTH TO LEAD THE LAND WE LOVE · ASKING HIS BLESSING
AND HIS HELP · BUT KNOWING THAT HERE ON EARTH
GOD'S WORK MUST TRULY BE OUR OWN

John F. Kennedy's Inaugural Speech (Last Panel)

Robert Francis Kennedy's Tombsite

The Christian Heritage Of Our Nation - History Curriculum

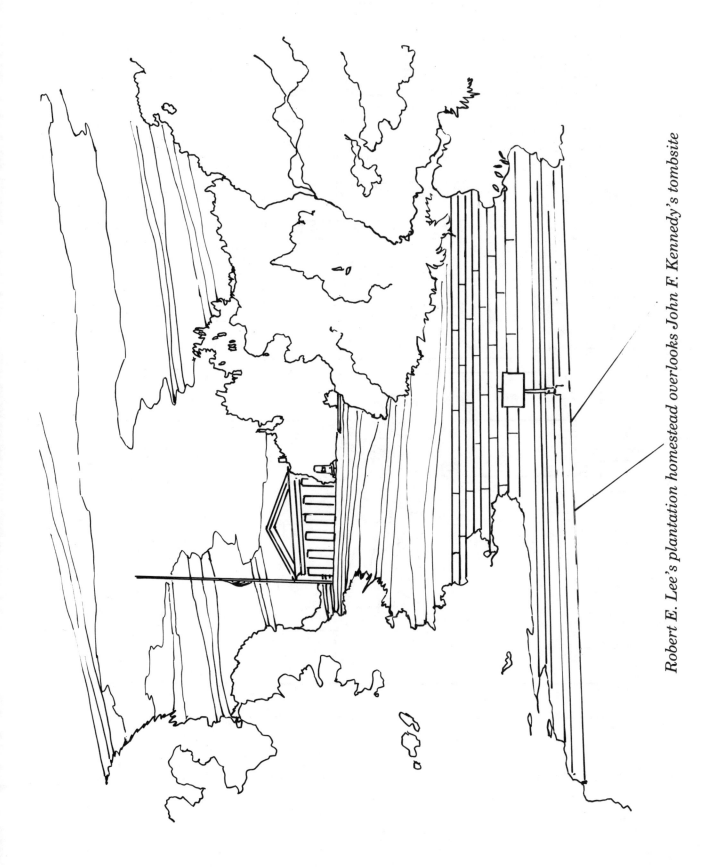

Robert E. Lee's plantation homestead overlooks John F. Kennedy's tombsite

The Tomb of the Unknown Soldier

The Christian Heritage Of Our Nation - History Curriculum

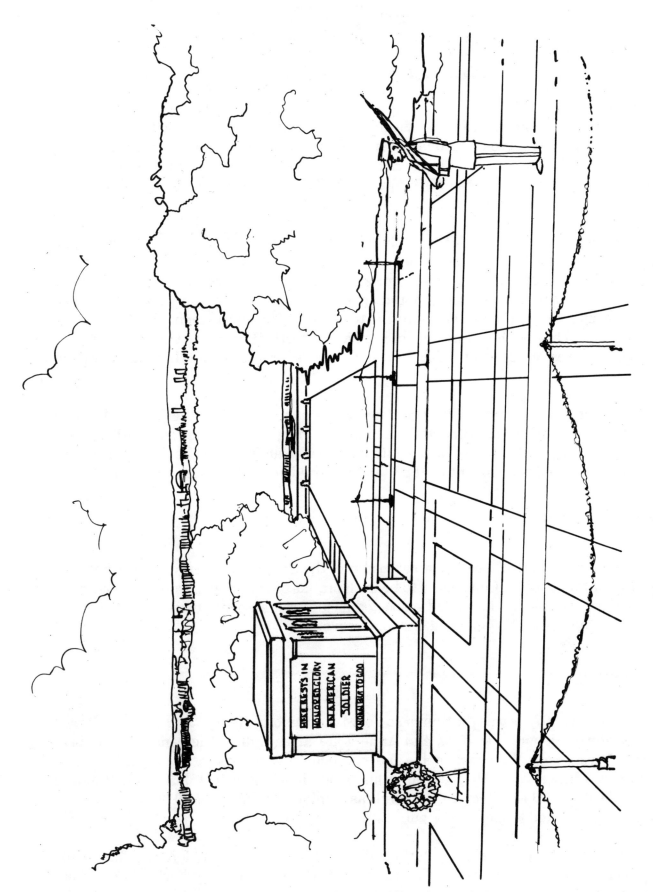

The Tomb of the Unknown Soldier - Arlington National Cemetery

LESSON 8

ARLINGTON NATIONAL CEMETERY

Across the Potomac River in Virginia, in a direct straight line with the Lincoln Memorial, lies Arlington National Cemetery. This site was the original 1,100 acre plantation belonging to Gen. Robert E. Lee, who married Mary Anne Randolph Custis, only surviving child of George Washington Park Custis, (George Washington's adopted grandson), and Mary Lee Fitzhugh.

At the break of the Civil War, Robert E. Lee resigned from the U.S. Army, stating that he could not lift his hand against family and friends of his native Virginia. His plantation home unoccupied, Union forces soon took over the premises. A law required that all private property owners should appear in person to pay their taxes. Mrs. Lee sent a cousin to pay the taxes amounting to $97.04. The government turned it down, however, purchasing the estate on public auction shortly thereafter. Union troops soon took over the estate. It was thus that Robert E. Lee's Arlington home became a national cemetery.

Twenty years later, Custis Lee, Gen. Lee's son, took his father's last Will and Testament to the Supreme Court. The court's ruling reinstated Lee as rightful owner of this estate. Unable to live on the site of a now-established cemetery, however, Lee sold it to the U.S. government in 1883 for a hundred and fifty thousand dollars.

Robert E. Lee's Genius

General Robert E. Lee, the great leader of the Confederate army in the Civil War, was a military genius. Considered to be in the ranks of the greatest military leaders in all history, he was also loved and respected as a Christian gentleman in the north, as well as in his native Virginia and the southern states.

Lee's Origins

Born in 1807, he was the fourth son of Major General Henry "Light Horse Harry" Lee, a Revolutionary War hero, and Anne Hill Carter, a direct descendant of Robert "King" Carter, one of the most noble and significant figures of Virginia's golden age in the early 18th century. He grew up in his family home built in 1795, an outstanding example of federal architecture. It stands as a unique landmark at 607 Oronoco Street in Alexandria, and is open to the public.

When Robert was six, his father, ill and broken in spirit, left the family for Barbados and never returned. The former hero died on his way back when Robert was 11, so that he was raised by his mother from age six. Anne Hill Carter, one of the little-celebrated heroines of America, brought up her five children almost single-handedly, giving them a magnificent example of Christian virtue, and molding their characters upon Scripture truth.

Lee's Formative Years

Fitzhugh Lee, a distinguished contemporary, wrote the following regarding Lee's early life:

> If he inherited much from a long and illustrious line of paternal ancestors, he no less fell heir to the strong characteristics of his mother's family, one of the oldest and best in Virginia. The unselfishness, generosity, purity, and faithfulness of the Virginia Carters are widely known, and they have always been "true to all occasions true." In his mother was personified all the gentle and sweet traits of a noble woman. Her whole life was admirable, and her love for her children beyond all other thoughts. To her watchful care they were early confided by the long absence and death of her distinguished husband.
>
> Robert was four years old when his father removed the family to Alexandria, six when he visited the West Indies for his health, and eleven when he died. If he was early trained in the way he should go, his mother trained him. If he was "always good," as his father wrote, she labored to keep him so. If his principles were sound and his life a success, to her, more than to any other, should the praise be given. . . As Robert grew in years he grew in grace; he was like the young tree whose roots, firmly imbedded in the earth, hold it straight from the hour it was first planted till it develops into majestic proportions. With the fostering care of such a mother the son must go straight, for she had planted him in the soil of truth, morality, and religion, so that his boyhood was marked by everything that produces nobility of character in manhood. The handsome boy was studious and sedate, was popular with other boys, stood high in the estimation of his teachers, and his early inspiration was good, for his first thoughts were directed upon subjects by an excellent mother.

At age 18, Lee entered the United States Military Academy, West Point, as a cadet to train for his distinguished career. In the 1830's he became a lieutenant. Lee married Mary Ann Randolph Custis, only surviving child of George Washington Parke Custis, who was George Washington's adopted grandson. They had seven children.

Though deeply devoted to his family, Lee's military career required long separations from his loved ones, taking him to many parts of the country. In 1846, when the United States declared war on Mexico, Lee was called into active duty, and his bravery and military skills won him recognition and promotion.

Lee greatly loved the Union, having devoted his adult life to its service as a soldier. He was opposed to secession. The following excerpt is from a letter he wrote from Texas where he was stationed, to his favorite cousin, Martha Custis Williams just months before the Civil War began:

January 22, 1861

God alone can save us from our folly, selfishness & shortsightedness. The last accounts seem to show that we have barely escaped anarchy to be plunged into civil war. What will be the result I cannot conjecture. I only see that a federal calamity is upon us, & fear that the country will have to pass through for its sins a fiery ordeal. I am unable to realize that our people will destroy a government inaugurated by the blood & wisdom of our patriot fathers, that has given us peace & prosperity at home, power & security aboard, & under which we have acquired a colossal strength unequalled in the history of mankind. I wish to live under no other government, & there is no sacrifice I am not ready to make for the preservation of the Union save that of honour. If a disruption takes place, I shall go back in sorrow to my people & share the misery of my native state, & save in her defence there will be one soldier less in the world than now. I wish for no other flag than the "Star–spangled Banner," and no other air than "Hail Columbia." I still hope the wisdom and patriotism of the nation will yet save it.[2]

On Christmas day, 1862, Lee wrote to his wife from Frederickburg:

Christmas Day, 1862

My heart is filled with gratitude to Almighty God for His unspeakable mercies with which He has blessed us in this day, for those He has granted us from the beginning of life, and particularly for those He has vouchsafed us during the past year. What should have become of us without his crowning help and protection? Oh, if our people would only recognize it and cease from self-boasting and adulation, how strong would be my belief in final success and happiness to our country! But what a cruel thing is war; to separate and destroy families and friends, and mar the purest joys and happiness God has granted us in this world; to fill our hearts with hatred instead of love for our neighbors, and to devastate the fair face of this beautiful world! I pray that, on this day when only peace and good-will are preached to mankind, better thoughts may fill the hearts of our enemies and turn them to peace. Our army was never in such good health and condition since I have been attached to it. I believe they share with me my disappointment that the enemy did not renew the combat on the 13th. I was holding back all day and husbanding our strength and ammunition for the great struggle, for which I thought I was preparing. Had I divined that was to have been his only effort, he would have had more of it. My heart bleeds at the death of every one of our gallant men.[3]

The Battle of Gettysburg

The Battle of Gettysburg in July of 1863 was the greatest battle of the Civil War. The Southern army of 75,000 men met the North's 90,000 in Union territory. Lasting three days, the Confederates had the advantage for the first two days, pushing the Union back, but on the third day the Union gained the victory, and the Confederate troops were left with no choice but to retreat back to Virginia in a dreary rainstorm, having lost over 20,000 men, dead or wounded. Lee accepted full responsibility for the defeat as shown in this letter to Jefferson Davis, written on July 31 from Camp Culpepper:

July 31, 1863

No blame can be attached to the army for its failure to accomplish what was projected by me, nor should it be censored for the unreasonable expectations of the public—I am alone to blame, in perhaps expecting too much of its prowess & valor. It however, in my opinion, achieved under the guidance of the Most High a general success, though it did not win a victory. I thought at the time that the latter was practicable. I still think if all things could have worked together it would have been accomplished. But with the knowledge I then had, & in the circumstances I was then placed, I do not know what better course I could have pursued. With my present knowledge, & could I have foreseen that the attack on the last day would have failed to drive the enemy from his position, I should certainly have tried some other course. What the ultimate result would have been is not so clear to me. Our loss has been very heavy, that of the enemy's is proportionately so. His crippled condition enabled us to retire from the country, comparatively unmolested . . . [4]

Robert E. Lee Proclaims
Day of Fasting, Humiliation and Prayer

Gettysburg marked a turning point in the war; the South no longer had the battle against the North. Though there would be another two years of fighting, the North began getting an upper hand with their superior resources and manpower. On August 21, Jefferson Davis called for a day of fasting and prayer. Lee issued the following order regarding it:

General Order No. 83

Headquarters Army Northern Virginia, August 13, 1863

The President of the Confederate States has, in the name of the people, appointed the 21st day of August as a day of fasting, humiliation, and prayer. A strict observance of the day is enjoined upon the officers and soldiers of this army. All military duties, except such as are absolutely necessary, will be suspended. The commanding officers of brigades and regiments are requested to cause divine services, suitable to the occasion, to be performed in their respective commands.

Soldiers! We have sinned against Almighty God. We have forgotten His signal mercies, and have cultivated a revengeful, haughty and boastful spirit. We have not remembered that the defenders of a just cause should be pure in His eyes; that "our times are in His hands;" and we have relied too much on our own arms for the achievement of our independence. God is our only refuge and our strength. Let us humble ourselves before Him. Let us confess our many sins, and beseech Him to give us a higher courage, a purer patriotism, and more determined will; that He will convert the hearts of our enemies; that He will hasten the time when war, with its sorrows and sufferings, shall cease, and that He will give us a name and place among the nations of the earth.[5]

Chaplain Jones of the Confederate Army reported the following regarding the spiritual revival which resulted from this day of fasting, humiliation and prayer:

We can never forget the effect produced by the reading of this order at the solemn services of that memorable fast day. A precious revival was already in progress in many of the commands. The day was almost universally observed; the attendance upon preaching and other services was very large; the solemn attention and starting tear attested the deep interest felt; and the work of grace among the troops widened and deepened, and went gloriously on until there had been at least fifteen thousand professions of faith in Christ as a personal Saviour. How far these grand results were due to this fast-day, or to the quiet influence and fervent prayers of the commanding general, eternity alone shall reveal.[6]

Lee's Christianity

Author Benjamin Howell Griswold, Jr. in his book, *The Spirit of Lee and Jackson*, wrote:

. . . Lee and Jackson were both professing Christians—most men of their day were that—but on the premise that these men not only professed Christianity, but actually practised it and endeavored in every way to live according to its much neglected tenets. They were great readers of the Bible, and nearly every act of their lives was directed by their interpretation of its maxims. This was true of their actions not only at home toward their family and neighbors, but even in the camp and on the battlefield toward their enemies . . . Humility, Purity, Peacemaking, Love of Righteousness—virtues neglected—if not a little despised today, seem to have exalted these men and lifted them from the depths of defeat to the pinnacle of fame . . .[7]

The Christian Heritage Of Our Nation - History Curriculum

Robert E. Lee's Death

Robert E. Lee's last days were written by Colonel William Preston Johnston for Reverend J.W. Jones in his *Personal Reminiscences of General Robert E. Lee, 1874.* Colonel Johnston was an intimate friend of the general and a distinguished member of the faculty of his college. He was one of those at the bedside of the dying general. It is being excerpted below in order to shed further light on Lee's true character and Christian comportment:

> The death of General Lee was not due to any sudden cause, but was the result of agencies dating as far back as 1863 . . . In October, 1869, he was again attacked by inflammation of the heart-sac, accompanied by muscular rheumatism of the back, right side, and arms. The action of the heart was weakened by this attack . . . His decline was rapid, yet gentle; and soon after nine o'clock on the morning of October 12th, he closed his eyes, and his soul passed peacefully from earth . . . General Lee's closing hours were consonant with his noble and disciplined life. Never was more beautifully displayed how a long and severe education of mind and character enables the soul to pass with equal step through this supreme ordeal; never did the habits and qualities of a lifetime, solemnly gathered into a few last sad hours, more grandly maintain themselves amid the gloom and shadow of approaching death. The reticence, the self-contained composure, the obedience to proper authority, the magnanimity and the Christian meekness, that marked all his actions, still preserved their sway, in spite of the inroads of disease and the creeping lethargy that weighed down his faculties . . . Leaning trustfully upon the all-sustaining Arm, the man whose stature, measured by mortal standards, seemed so great, passed from this world of shadows to the realities of the Hereafter.[8]

Historic Arlington National Cemetery

About 260,000 people are buried here. Only retired military or those on active duty, the wives and widows of military, children of military under 18 years of age, and the recipients of the Gold Medal of Honor, the Distinguished Service Cross, the Distinguished Service Medal, the Navy Cross, the Silver Star and the Purple Heart, have the right to be buried at Arlington.

Most of the tombstones, that is, those of regular dimensions, are provided by the government. A circle upon the face of each shows forth a cross in the vast majority of cases, designating the individual's faith at time of death.

John F. Kennedy's Tombsite

John F. Kennedy lies buried on a hillside just below General Lee's lovely plantation home, overlooking the capital city which he admired. The site of Kennedy's tomb, executed by architect John Warnecke, exemplifies simplicity and pureness of design. A central plaque designates Kennedy's date of birth and death. The eternal flame, unique to all our military cemeteries across the land, stands guard at his graveside. To the right and left of Kennedy's tomb are plaques for his still-born daughter, and his son, Patrick Bouvier Kennedy, respectively. The latter child lived only two days, dying but a few months before his father's assassination. Famous excerpts from Kennedy's Inaugural Address are engraved upon a semi-circular wall directly facing his tomb.

On the day he was inaugurated into office, the 35th President of the United States spoke these words:

> And so, my fellow Americans, ask not what your country can do for you. Ask what you can do for your country. My fellow citizens of the world, ask not what America will do for you, but what together we can do for the freedom of man. Finally, whether you are citizens of America or citizens of the world, ask of us the same high standard of strength and sacrifice which we ask of you. With a good conscience our only sure reward, with history the final judge of our deeds, let us go forth to lead the land we love, asking His blessing and His help, but knowing that here in earth God's work must truly be our own.
> **John F. Kennedy, President, United States of America**

Robert Francis Kennedy's Tombsite

Adjacent to John Kennedy's tomb is the simple grave of his brother Robert. A plain wooden cross is what he desired. It is painted white. A white marble plaque bears his name, date of birth and death. Opposite the tomb, inscriptions etched in stone represent famous human rights speeches made by Robert Kennedy. The first was delivered in South Africa, in 1966, and the second in Indianapolis, Indiana, in 1968.

The Tomb of the Unknown Soldier

A steep climb to the summit of *Arlington National Cemetery* takes us to the Tomb of the Unknown Soldier of the first and second World Wars; the Korean War and the Vietnam War. This seventy-two ton block of carved white marble bears the poignant inscription:

> Here lies in Honored Glory an American Soldier known but to God

An Honor Guard, the Third United States Infantry and official Presidential Unit resolutely guards this sacred tombsite, twenty-four hours a day. The inspection and changing of the guard is a memorable occasion for all who witness this moving ceremony.

The Christian Heritage Of Our Nation - History Curriculum

LESSON EIGHT

PUPILS' GUIDE

Arlington National Cemetery – Homesite of Robert E. Lee

I. Suggestions for Study

    a)   Read the lesson material carefully.

    b)   Look up Arlington, Virginia; Lexington, Fredericksburg, Culpeper, Virginia; Gettysburg, Pennsylvania; and West Point, New York.

II. Lesson material

    Text: Lesson 8 - Arlington National Cemetery

III. 1. The kind of man Robert E. Lee was:

    i)   Arlington National Cemetery is the site of: (Consult your text and fill in the blanks)

        a)   The original _____ _____ _____ belonging to _____ ___ _____, who married _____ _____ _____ _____, only surviving child of _____ _____ _____ _____, (George Washington's adopted _____), and _____ _____ _____.

    ii)   Why did Robert E. Lee resign from the U.S. army at the break of the Civil War? Because: (Consult your text and fill in the blanks)

        a)   He stated that he could not _____ _____ _____ against _____ and _____ of his _____ _____.

    iii)   What happened to Robert E. Lee's plantation home after the break of the Civil War? (Consult your text and fill in the blanks)

        a)   A _____ required that all _____ _____ _____ should appear in _____ to pay their _____. _____ sent a _____ to pay the _____ amounting to _____. _____ _____ turned it down, however, _____ _____ _____ on _____ _____ shortly _____. Union _____

soon took over the _____. It was thus that
_____ ____ _____ _____ home became a
national _____.

iv) What did Custis Lee, Robert E. Lee's son, do twenty years later? (Consult your text and fill in the blanks)

a) Custis Lee took his father's _____ _____ _____
_____ to the _____ _____. The court's
_____ _____ Lee as _____ owner of this
_____.

v) What did Custis Lee do with Arlington National Cemetery after the Supreme Court's ruling? (Consult your text and fill in the blanks)

a) Unable to _____ on the _____ of a now-established
_____, _____ sold it to the _____
_____ in _____ for a _____ and
_____ thousand _____.

vi) How many people are currently buried at Arlington National Cemetery? (Circle one)

a) 200,000
b) 220,000
c) 250,000
d) 260,000

vii) Who qualify to have their mortal remains buried at Arlington National Cemetery? (Circle all correct answers)

a) Active military
b) Retired military
c) U.S. Presidents
d) Foreign heroes
e) Wives and widows of military
f) Children of military under 18 years of age
g) Recipients of medals of honor
h) Heads of State

viii) What do the tombstones at Arlington National Cemetery show upon their faces in the vast majority of cases? (Circle one)

a) A triangle
b) A rectangle
c) The cross of Jesus Christ

d)   A half moon

ix)   Whom does the Tomb of the Unknown Soldier acknowledge as Omiscient (All-knowing)? (Circle one)

a)   A Greek deity
b)   A Roman god
c)   Almighty God of the Bible
d)   Hercules

x)   Who was Robert E. Lee? (Circle all correct answers)

a)   A Virginian
b)   Leader of the Confederate Army
c)   A naval hero
d)   A military genius
e)   A surveyor
f)   A Christian
g)   Leader of the Union Army
h)   A General

xi)   Robert E. Lee was the son of: (Consult your text and fill in the blanks)

a)   _____ _____ Henry "_____ _____
     _____" Lee, a _____ War _____, and
     _____ _____ _____, a direct descendant of
     _____ " _____ " _____, one of the most
     _____ and _____ figures of _____ _____
     age in the early _____ century.

xii)   In Lee's 1862, Christmas Day letter written to his wife from Fredericksburg, to whom, and for what, is he grateful? (Circle one)

a)   The army, for its strength
b)   The government, for its protection
c)   Almighty God, for His mercies and blessings
d)   West Point Military Academy, for its training

xiii)   In Lee's January 22, 1861 letter to his cousin, Martha Custis Williams, whom does he state can save us; and from what? (Circle one)

a)   The Federal Government; calamity
b)   The media; bad publicity
c)   The Union; anarchy
d)   God alone; folly, selfishness, short-sightedness and sin

xiv)   On August 21, 1863, Jefferson Davis called for a Day of Fasting, Humiliation and Prayer. What was Robert E. Lee's reaction to it? (Consult your text and fill in the blanks)

    a)   Lee issued a General Order _____.
Headquarters _____ _____ _____,
August 13, 1863. The President _____ _____ _____
_____ has, in the name of the _____,
_____ the _____ day of _____ as a day of
_____ _____ and _____ . . . Soldiers! We
have _____ against _____ _____. We have
_____ his _____ mercies, and have
_____ a _____, _____ and
_____ spirit . . .

xv)   In this General Order, whom does Lee state is our only refuge and strength? (Circle one)

    a)   The Confederate Army
    b)   The cavalry
    c)   Stonewall Jackson
    d)   Almighty God

xvi)   According to Chaplain Jones of the Confederate Army, the result of this Day of Fasting, Humiliation and Prayer was a work of grace among the troops, which widened and deepened, causing at least: (Consult your text and fill in the blanks)

    a)   500 professions of faith in Christ as a personal Saviour
    b)   1,000 professions of faith in Christ as a personal Saviour
    c)   5,000 professions of faith in Christ as a personal Saviour
    d)   15,000 professions of faith in Christ as a personal Saviour

xvii)   What results does Chaplain Jones state "eternity alone shall reveal" in terms of Robert E. Lee's actions during this Day of Fasting, Humiliation and Prayer? (Circle one)

    a)   Lack of interest and participation
    b)   Absence
    c)   Quiet influence and fervent prayer
    d)   Resignation and "moment of silence."

xviii) Author Benjamin Howell Griswold, Jr. states that Robert E. Lee and Stonewall Jackson were great readers of: (Circle one)

    a) Newspapers
    b) Mystery stories
    c) The Bible
    d) Westerns

xix) What Biblical qualities does this author affirm Robert E. Lee practised, not only at home, but also in the camp, and toward his enemies, which lifted him to the pinnacle of fame? (Circle all correct answers)

    a) Arrogance   e) Peacemaking
    b) Humility   g) Mercilessness
    c) Revenge   h) Love of righteousness
    d) Purity

xx) Colonel William Preston Johnston was an intimate friend of Lee, and a distinguished faculty member of his college. In his *Personal Reminiscences of General Robert E. Lee, 1874,* his eyewitness account of the General's dying moments reflect Lee's true character traits in action: They are: (Circle all correct answers)

    a) Impatience
    b) Anger
    c) Reticence
    d) Hatred
    e) Self-contained composure
    f) Obedience to proper authority
    g) Boastfulness
    h) Magnanimity
    i) Bitterness
    j) Christian meekness

xxi) How did Robert E. Lee die, according to those at his bedside? (Consult your text and fill in the blanks)

    a) Leaning _____ upon the _____ _____, the man whose _____, measured by _____ _____, seemed so _____, passed from this _____ of _____ to the _____ of the _____.

xxii) "Leaning trustfully" upon whose "arm" does the above eye-witness account of Lee's death refer to? (Circle one)

   a) Brahman
   b) Stonewall Jackson
   c) Almighty God of the Bible
   d) Chaplain Jones

2. Christian Character Traits:

Select 10 Christian virtues, values and morals exemplified by Robert E. Lee in his daily life. List them below:

a. _____   f. _____

b. _____   g. _____

c. _____   h. _____

d. _____   i. _____

e. _____   j. _____

IV. Illustrate your work with pictures, outline map, models and drawings.

V. Memory Scripture:

> O Lord, my heart is not proud, Nor my eyes haughty; Nor do I involve myself in great matters, or in things too difficult for me. Surely I have composed and quieted my soul; Like a weaned child rests against his mother; My soul is like a weaned child within me.   Psalm 131:1-2

The Iwo Jima Memorial

The Iwo Jima Memorial

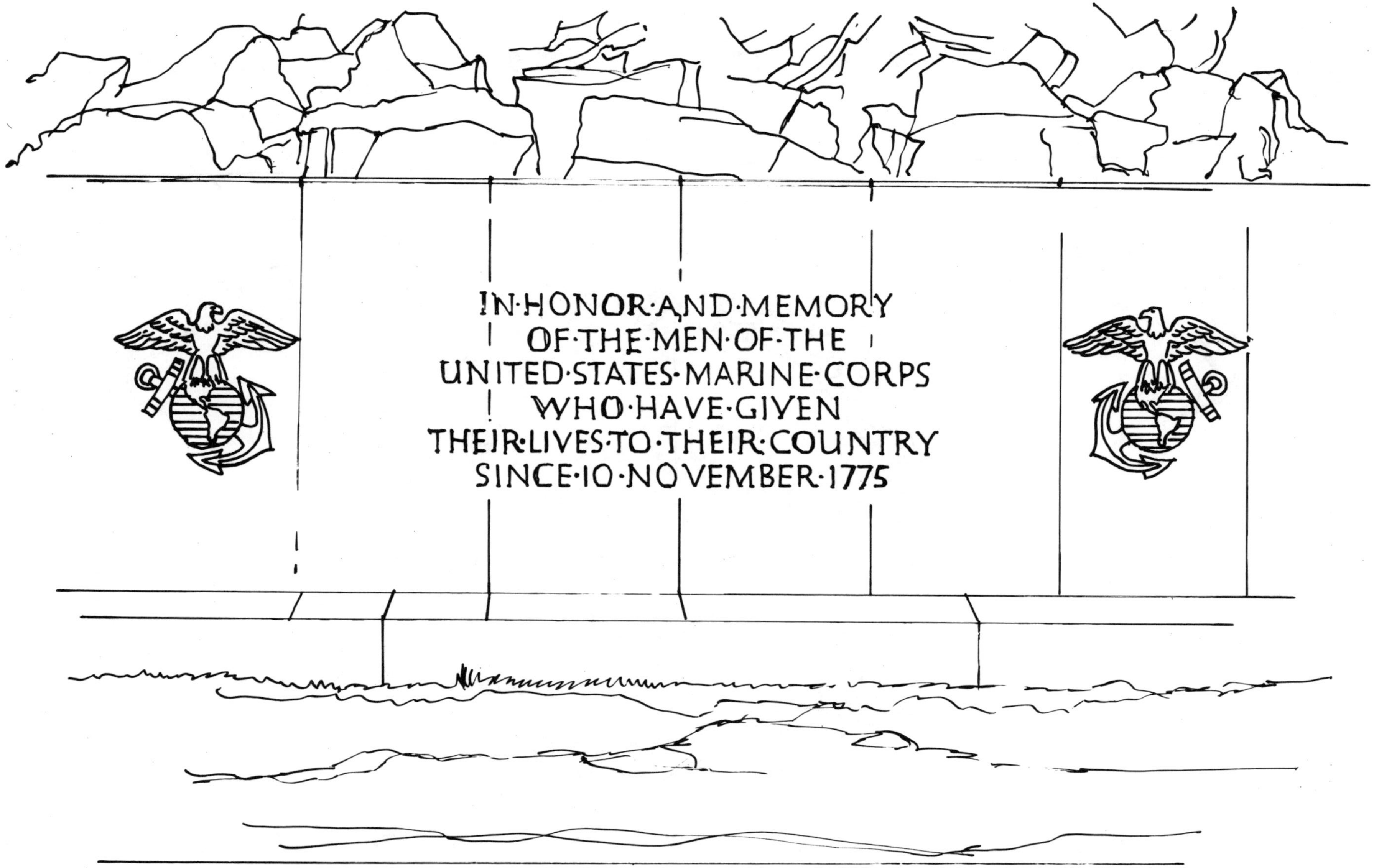

IN·HONOR·AND·MEMORY
OF·THE·MEN·OF·THE
UNITED·STATES·MARINE·CORPS
WHO·HAVE·GIVEN
THEIR·LIVES·TO·THEIR·COUNTRY
SINCE·10·NOVEMBER·1775

The Iwo Jima Memorial

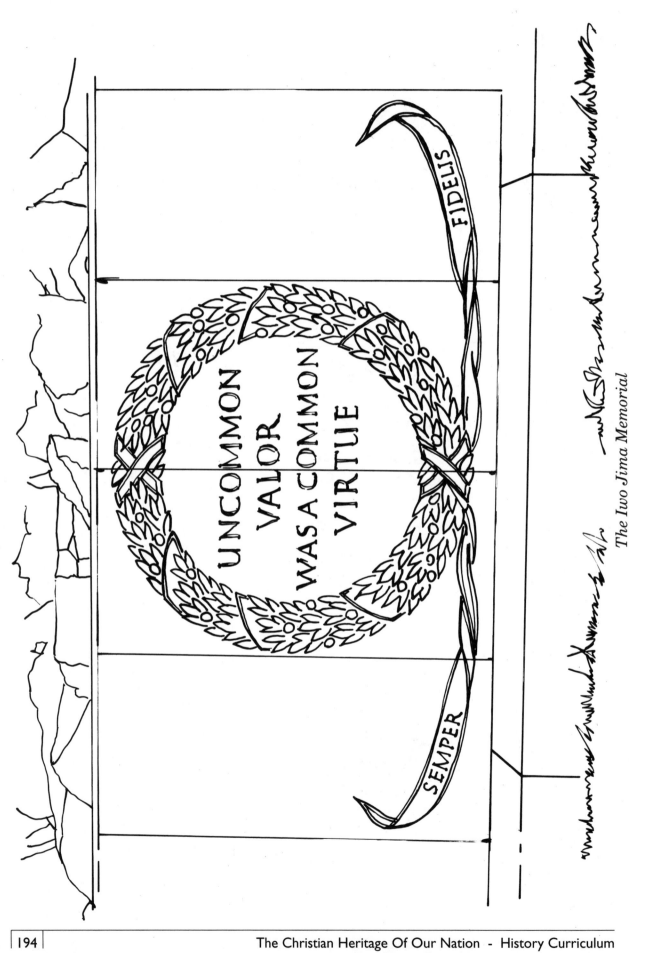

The Iwo Jima Memorial

LESSON 9

THE IWO JIMA MARINE CORPS MEMORIAL

"Uncommon Valor was a Common Virtue." Admiral Chester Nimitz

The above tribute was first expressed in a communique from Iwo Jima, applauding our servicemen as they battled ceaselessly to attain control of this strategic Japanese island. These noble attributes describing our valiant Marine Corps soldiers are prominently inscribed upon the base of the memorial, within a circular wreath.

Seven hundred and fifty miles south of Tokyo, Iwo Jima became the symbol of courage and sacrifice to the American people.

Undaunted American Courage and Sacrifice

On February 19, 1945, a force of approximately 71,245 men, 66,953 of them Marines, waited off the coast of this island which had been bombed and shelled 72 consecutive hours prior to their arrival.[1] For 25 days the battle raged. The final toll was a heavy one: 5,885 marines lost their lives, and a further 17,272 were injured, demonstrating the high price of liberty. A few days after the landing, five Marines, together with a Navy Corpsman, climbed laboriously to the top of Mount Suribachi with an iron pipe, to which had been attached the American flag. Their names are as follows: Private First Class Franklin Runyon Sousley; Corporal Ira Hamilton Hayes; Sergeant Michael Strank; Corporal Rene Arthur Gagnon, Corporal Harlon Henry Block and Pharmacist's Mate Second Class John Henry Bradley.[2] The Star-spangled Banner was firmly implanted into the grit and grime of Mount Suribachi's volcanic rock. Associated Press photographer, Joe Rosenthal, had followed this small band of men to the summit. His timely photograph became widely circulated and admired throughout the world. It symbolized undaunted American courage and sacrifice for the cause of freedom.[3]

Working from the original photograph, with the three surviving servicemen posing for him, sculptor Felix de Weldon molded an exact, life-like bronze image of this heroic epic. The entire work of art is upheld by a black granite pedestal, upon which these words are engraved in gold lettering:

> In Honor and Memory of the Men of the United States Marine Corps who have
> Given their Lives to their Country since 10 November, 1775.

Dedication ceremonies took place on November 10, 1954, commemorating the 179th anniversary of the Marine Corps. Each of the statues is 32 feet tall, the overall monument standing 78 feet in height. The M-1 rifle held by one of the figures is approximately 16 feet long, the carbines 12 feet long, and the canteens attached to their waists have a capacity to hold 32 quarts of water.[4]

On a hill overlooking the nation's capital, the Iwo Jima Memorial holds a timeless message for each American. It recalls in graphic detail, the high price of liberty, and the pride and courage with which our valiant soldiers have defended it for the past 200 years.

LESSON NINE

PUPILS' GUIDE

The Iwo Jima Memorial – "Uncommon Valor was a Common Virtue"

I. Suggestions for Study

    a)   Read the lesson material carefully.

    b)   Look up Hawaii; and Iwo Jima, Japan on your map of the United States and the world at home.

II. Lesson material

    Text: Lesson 9 - The Iwo Jima Memorial

III. 1. The kind of a nation that America is:

    i)   What does the word "valor" mean? (Circle all correct answers)

        a)   Cowardice
        b)   Deceit
        c)   Courage
        d)   Fear
        e)   Bravery

    ii)   What does the word "virtue" mean? (Circle all correct answers)

        a)   Qualities
        b)   Admirable character traits
        c)   Faults
        d)   Vice
        e)   Evil
        f)   Moral integrity

    iii)   Why did Admiral Chester Nimitz express the words "valor" and virtue" for our Marine Corps soldiers on Iwo Jima? (Fill in the blanks)

        a)   This _____ was first expressed in a _____ from Iwo Jima, _____ our _____ as they _____ ceaselessly to _____ _____ of this strategic _____ _____.

iv)   What does the epic on Iwo Jima symbolize to the world? (Consult your text and fill in the blanks)

  a)   Seven hundred and fifty miles _____ of _____, Iwo Jima became the _____ of _____ and _____ to the American _____ .

v)   When did this event occur: (Circle one)

  a)   January 20, 1943
  b)   July 15, 1944
  c)   December 12, 1944
  d)   February 19, 1945

vi)   For how long did this battle on Iwo Jima rage? (Circle one)

  a)   5 days
  b)   10 days
  c)   25 days
  d)   30 days

vii)   How many valiant United States soldiers lost their lives in defense of our freedoms, in the heroic battle of Iwo Jima? How many brave American soldiers were injured for this victory? (Circle one)

  a)   2,550; 14,330
  b)   10,255; 20,510
  c)   5,885; 17,272
  d)   7,925; 16,581

viii)   What event gained world recognition and renown after the victory on Iwo Jima? (Consult your text and fill in the blanks)

  a)   Five _____, together with a _____ _____, climbed _____ to the top of _____ _____ with an _____ _____, to which had been _____ the _____ _____ . . . The Star-spangled _____ was firmly _____ into the _____ and _____ of _____ _____ volcanic _____ .

ix)   What are the names of the six heroic soldiers who have become immortalized in the world-renowned photograph snapped on Iwo Jima: (Consult your text and fill in the blanks)

a)   Private _____ _____ _____ _____
     _____.

b)   Corporal _____ _____ _____.

c)   Sergeant _____ _____.

d)   Corporal _____ _____ _____.

e)   Corporal _____ _____ _____.

f)   Pharmacist's _____ _____ _____ _____
     _____ _____.

x)   Identify the famed Associated Press photographer who snapped this epic event on Iwo Jima: (Circle one)

a)   Guru Zen
b)   Abdul Ahlan
c)   Joe Rosenthal
d)   Kwang Chin

xi)   What became widely circulated and admired throughout the world? What did it symbolize? (Consult your text and fill in the blanks)

a)   _____ _____ timely _____ became
     widely _____ and admired _____ the
     _____. It symbolized _____ _____
     _____ and _____ for the cause of
     _____.

xii) What is the name of the great master sculptor of the Iwo Jima Memorial? (Circle one)

a)   Henri Matisse (French)
b)   Jose Luis Sanchez (Spanish)
c)   Aleijadinho (Brazilian)
d)   Felix de Weldon (American)

xiii) How did the great master sculptor execute his magnificent work of art? (Consult your text and fill in the blanks)

a)   _____ from the _____ _____, with
     the three _____ _____ _____ for
     him, sculptor _____ ___ _____ molded an
     _____, _____ bronze image of this _____
     _____.

xiv) What famous inscription appears in bold, gold lettering upon the Iwo Jima Memorial's pedestal? (Fill in the blanks)

a) In _____ and _____ of the _____ of the
    _____ _____ Marine _____ who have
    _____ _____ _____ to their _____
    since ____ November, _____ .

xv) When was the United States Marine Corps founded, and when did the dedication ceremonies of the Iwo Jima Memorial take place? (Circle one)

a) December 3, 1863;   December 3, 1963
b) August 10, 1812;   August 10, 1912
c) November 10, 1775;   November 10, 1954
d) January 20, 1787;   January 20, 1957

xvi) How tall is each one of the statues of the 6 heroic United States soldiers? How tall is the overall monument? (Circle one)

a) 48 feet;   85 feet
b) 32 feet;   78 feet
c) 25 feet;   60 feet
d) 10 feet;   30 feet

xvii) What did these six heroic United States soldiers use in lieu of a flagpost to hoist our Star-spangled Banner? (Circle one)

a) Driftwood
b) Coral cut from the reef
c) An iron pipe
d) The branch of a tree

xviii) Recall the timeless message which the Iwo Jima Memorial holds for each American as it proudly overlooks our nation's capital: (Consult your text and fill in the blanks).

a) The Iwo Jima Memorial recalls, in _____ _____ ,
    the high _____ of _____ , and the _____ and
    _____ with which our _____ _____
    have _____ it for the past _____ years.

2. Christian Character Traits

Select 10 Christian virtues, values and morals inherent in the heroic epic of Iwo Jima, February 19, 1945: (List them below)

a. _____   f. _____

b. _____   g. _____

c. _____   h. _____

d. _____   i. _____

e. _____   j. _____

IV. Illustrate your work with pictures, outline map, models and drawings.

V. Memory Inscription:

In honor and memory of the men of the United States Marine Corps who have given their lives to their country since 10 November, 1775.

The Netherlands Carillon - Gift of the people of Holland to the United States of America

The Netherlands Carillion - Forty-nine beautifully matched bells

LESSON 10

THE NETHERLANDS CARILLON

Overlooking our nation's capital, adjacent to the Marine Corps Memorial grounds, stands the Netherlands Carillon. In the Spring of 1952, Queen Juliana of the Netherlands presented a model of this Carillon to the people of the United States. At the time of its dedication, she expressed her gratitude to the United States for its timely help following the devastation of the Second World War:

> The Netherlands people from all strata have contributed to this gift, and the bells which are to follow come from various groups of the population: seamen, miners, farmers, flower-growers, fishermen, the armed services, teachers and scientists, financiers and shopkeepers, businessmen and drivers, pressmen, artists, women's organizations, sportsmen and civil servants, resistance people who cooperated with your troops, students, boys and girls, and little children. Each of the Dutch provinces wishes that one of the bells shall bear its name as well. The Antilles, the territories in the Caribbean, join in this present. And Surinam too wants to express its gratitude in its own way to the people of the United States.[1]

The world's greatest bell-founders, Pierre and Francois Hemony, lived in 17th century Holland. Each of the 49 bells in the carillon represents a province of Holland or a segment of Dutch society which donated it. Inscribed messages upon a number of these reflect their faith and trust in the Lord.

The Sixteenth Bell, extolling the Merchant Marine, has this to say:

> You who set your course between the stars and the waves pray the Lord for protection and a favorable wind.[2]

The Thirtieth Bell, dedicated to farmers, reads:

> They who resolutely sow new seed, will reap a rich harvest with the help of the Lord.[3]

The Thirty-second Bell is dedicated to the Arts. Its joyful statement is that—

> The breath of God is in their work and shows us, how they create for us out of nothing.[4]

LESSON TEN

PUPILS' GUIDE

The Netherlands Carillon – "God Created the Arts out of Nothing"

I. Suggestions for Study

    a)   Read the lesson material carefully.

    b)   Look up the Netherlands (Holland); Amsterdam, Rotterdam; and Washington, District of Columbia, on your map of the United States and the world at home.

II. Lesson material

    Text: Lesson 10 - The Netherlands Carillon

III. 1. The kind of a nation that America is:

    i)   The Netherlands Carillon overlooks: (Circle one)

        a)   Amsterdam
        b)   Rotterdam
        c)   Washington, D.C., our nation's capital
        d)   The great wall of China

    ii)   When, by whom, and to whom was this handsome Carillon presented? (Fill in the blanks)

        a)   In the _____ of _____, _____ _____ of the _____ presented a model of this Carillon to the _____ of the _____ _____.

    iii)   At the time of the dedication of the Netherlands Carillon, what feeling was expressed to the United States? (Circle two)

        a)   Hatred
        b)   Envy
        c)   Ridicule
        d)   Gratitude
        e)   Blame
        f)   Praise

iv)   At the dedication of the Netherlands Carillon, the sentiment expressed to the United States was due to her: (Circle one)

  a)   Warlike attitude
  b)   Interference in foreign policy
  c)   "Capitalistic" propaganda
  d)   Timely help following World War II

v)   According to the Dedication Speech, who contributed to this Carillon? (Consult your text and fill in the blanks)

  a)   The _____ _____ from all _____ have contributed to this _____, and the _____ which are to follow come from _____ _____ of the _____:

     _____, _____, _____, _____,

     _____, _____ _____ _____,

     _____ and _____, _____ and

     _____, _____ and _____,

     _____, _____, _____ organizations,

     _____ and _____ _____,

     _____ _____ who cooperated with your troops,

     _____, _____ and _____, and _____

     _____ ... The _____, the _____ in the

     _____, join in this _____. And _____ too

  wants to express its _____ in its own way to the

     _____ of the _____ _____.

vi)   How many groups contributed to the Netherlands Carillon? (Circle one)

  a)   5
  b)   12
  c)   24
  d)   10

vii)   What does this fact convey regarding the sentiments of the Netherlands people towards the United States? (Circle all correct answers)

  a)   Admiration
  b)   Reproach
  c)   Disinterest
  d)   Discredit
  e)   Praise
  f)   Thanks
  g)   Gratitude
  h)   Apathy
  i)   Dislike

j) Approval

k) Commendation

viii) Who wished their names to be inscribed upon the bells of the Netherlands Carillon? (Circle one)

    a) Environmentalists

    b) Marxist philosophers

    c) The Dutch Provinces

    d) Buddhist monks

ix) Name three bells of the Netherlands Carillon which bear inscriptions glorifying Almighty God of the Bible. (Circle three)

    a) 10th Bell

    b) 16th Bell

    c) 20th Bell

    d) 30th Bell

    e) 31th Bell

    f) 32nd Bell

x) Identify each of the three named Netherlands Carillon bells and their inscriptions glorifying God: (Consult your text and fill in the blanks)

    a) The _____ bell, extolling the _____ _____, has this to say: "You who _____ your course between the _____ and the _____, pray the _____ for protection and a _____ wind."

    b) The _____ bell, dedicated to _____, reads: "They who resolutely sow_____ _____, will reap a _____ _____ with the _____ of the _____."

    c) The _____ bell is dedicated to the _____. Its joyful _____ is that: "The _____ of _____ is in their _____ and _____ us, how they _____ for us out of _____."

2. Christian Character Traits

Select 10 Christian virtues, values and morals inherent in the gift of the Netherlands Carillon from the people of the Netherlands to the people of the United States: (List them below)

a. _____   f. _____

b. _____   g. _____

c. _____   h. _____

d. _____   i. _____

e. _____   j. _____

IV. *Illustrate your work with pictures, outline map, models and drawings.*

V. *Memory Inscription: The 32nd Bell is dedicated to the Arts:*

The breath of God is in their work, and shows us how they create for us out of nothing.

FOOTNOTES

Introduction

1 Hagner, Alexander B. *Street Nomenclature of Washington City.* Washington, 1897, p. 4.

2 Kite, Elizabeth Sarah. *L'Enfant and Washington (1791-1792).* Johns Hopkins Press, Baltimore, 1929.

3 Olszewski, George J. *The History of the Mall, Washington, D.C.* U.S. Department of Interior, National Park Service.

Lesson 1

1 Taft, William Howard. "Washington, its Beginning, its Growth and its Future." The National Geographic Magazine, March, 1915.

2 *Washington National Monument, Washington, D.C. Concise Description – Details in the Construction.* (Inscriptions on the four faces of the Aluminum point crowning apex of monument). From the Annual Reports of Colonel Lincoln Casey, Corps of Engineers, Engineer in Charge, February 21, 1885.

3 De Zapp, Rudolph. *The Washington Monument.* (Illustrated) An Authentic History of its origin and Construction, and a complete description of the Memorial Tablets. Washington, D.C.: The Caroline Publishing Company, 1900, p. 27.

4 Ibid.

5 Ibid.

6 Ibid. pp. 27, 28.

7 Ibid., p. 28

8 Ibid.

9 Ibid., p. 29

10 *Washington National Monument, Washington, D.C. Concise Description – Details in the Construction.* From the Annual Reports of Colonel Lincoln Casey, Corps of Engineers, Engineer in Charge, February 21, 1885. (Articles deposited in recess of the Cornerstone of Monument on July 4, 1848).

11 Ibid.

12 De Zapp, Rudolph. *The Washington Monument.* (Illustrated). An Authentic History of its origin and Construction, and a complete description of the Memorial Tablets. Washington, D.C.: The Caroline Publishing Company, 1900, pp. 7-26.

13 Moore, Charles (ed.) *George Washington's Rules of Civility and Decent Behaviour in Company and Conversation.* With Frontispiece and Facsimiles. Cambridge: The Riverside Press, 1926, pp. 3-21.

14 Millard, Catherine. *God's Signature over the Nation's Capital.* Officially Recorded Presidential Inaugural Scriptures compiled by Author. West Wilmington, PA: Sonrise Publications, 1988, p. 171.

15 Commager, Henry Steele. *Documents of American History.* F.S. Crofts and Company, 1934, pp. 151-152.

16 Ibid., p. 169.

17 Padover, Saul K. (ed.) *A Jefferson Profile.* New York: J. Day and Company, 1956, p. 227.

18 Documented from the published *General Orders of George Washington.* Mount Vernon Library, Mount Vernon, Virginia.

19 Adams, John. *Address to the United States Senate on the Death of Washington.* December 22, 1799 Newspaper Article.

20 A White House Release (Press Secretary).

21 Washington Memorial Chapel documentation, Valley Forge, Pennsylvania.

Lesson 2

1 October 3, 1863 Proclamation for Thanksgiving by the President of the United States of America, signed by the President, Abraham Lincoln. William A. Seward, Secretary of State. (Excerpted).

2 *In This Temple. A Guide Book to the Lincoln Memorial.* Museum Press, Inc., Washington, D.C. In cooperation with the Parks and History Association. n.d., pp. 32, 33.

3 Conklin, Edward F. U.S. Office of Public Buildings and Parks. Lincoln Memorial, Washington, D.C. U.S.G.P.O., 1927, p. 40.

4 Lincoln, Abraham. *Gettysburg Address.* Original Address, Rare Manuscript Division, Library of Congress, Washington, D.C.

5 Millard, Catherine. *The Rewriting of America's History.* Camp Hill: Horizon House Publishers, 1991, p. 167.

6 *First Baptist Church of Little Falls, New York, Handbook.* Sesquicentennial Services – 1879–1979. Rooted in the Past, Building in the Present, Reaching to the Future, p. 8.

7 Ibid.

8 Ibid.

9 Ibid.

[10] Matthew 7:1

[11] Matthew 18:7

[12] Revelation 16:7

[13] Lincoln, Abraham. *Second Inaugural Address.* Inscribed upon the inner North Wall, Lincoln Memorial, Washington, D.C.

[14] Conklin, Edward F. U.S. Office of Public Buildings and Parks. *Lincoln Memorial.* Washington, D.C. U.S.G.P.O., 1927, p. 45

[15] Ibid., p. 46

[16] Ibid.

[17] Ibid.

[18] Ibid.

[19] *The Encyclopedia Americana.* (Vol. 17) New York: Americana Corporation, 1940, p. 409.

[20] Millard, Catherine. *The Rewriting of America's History.* Camp Hill: Horizon House Publishers, 1991, p. 165.

[21] *The Encyclopedia Americana.* (Vol. 17) New York: Americana Corporation, 1940, p. 409.

[22] Ibid.

[23] Ibid.

[24] Wolf, William J. *The Religion of Abraham Lincoln.* New York: Seabury Press, 1963.

[25] Abraham Lincoln's 1847 Family Bible. Library of Congress Rare Book Collection, Washington, D.C.

[26] Ibid.

[27] Bernard, Kenneth A. *Lincoln and Music. The American Story Radio Program– Abraham Lincoln, 1809-1865*, pp.2-3; 5-6. Library of Congress Collection.

[28] *The Believer's Daily Treasure, or Texts of Scripture, arranged for every day in the year.* London: The Religious Tract Society, 1852, pp. 5-20

[29] Millard, Catherine. *The Rewriting of America's History.* Camp Hill: Horizon House, 1991, pp. 181-182.

Lesson 3

[1] Commager, Henry Steele. (ed.) *Documents of American History.* F.S. Crofts and Company, 1934, pp. 125-126.

² Longshore, Joseph, M.D. and Knowles, Benjamin. *The Centennial Liberty Bell, Independence Hall - Its Traditions and Associations.* Philadelphia: Claxton, Reuben and Haffelfinger, 1876, pp. 67-68.

³ Ibid.

⁴ Ibid.

⁵ Ibid.

⁶ Ibid.

⁷ Montague, Mary Louise. *John Witherspoon, Signer of the Declaration of Independence.* Washington, D.C.: H.L. and J.B. McQueen, Inc., 1932, p. 1.

⁸ Adams, John. *Speech delivered to Congress July 2, 1776.* Library of Congress Collection.

⁹ Wanamaker, John. *The Wanamaker Primer on Abraham Lincoln.* New York: John Wanamaker, 1909, pp. 98-100.

¹⁰ Lipscombe, Andrew A. (ed.) *The Writings of Thomas Jefferson.* (Vol. XVI). The Thomas Jefferson Memorial Association of the United States, Washington, D.C. 1904, pp. 281-282.

¹¹ Rayner, B.L. (ed.) *Sketches of the Life, Writings and Opinions of Thomas Jefferson* with selections of the most valuable portions of his voluminous and unrivalled correspondence. New York: A.W. Boardman, 1832, p. 518.

¹² Ibid., p. 516

¹³ Ibid., p. 398

¹⁴ Letters of Thomas Jefferson on Religion. (Compiled for Senator A. Willis Robertson, April 27, 1960.) The Williamsburg Foundation, Williamsburg, Virginia.

¹⁵ Jefferson, Thomas. *Catalogue of Paintings, etc. at Monticello.* Library of Congress Rare Book Collection, Washington, D.C.

¹⁶ Jefferson, Thomas. *A Summary View of the Rights of British America,* set forth in some Resolutions intended for the inspection of the present Delegates of the people of Virginia, now in Convention. By a native, and member of the House of Burgesses. Williamsburg. Printed by Clementinarind, 1774, pp. 15-16.

¹⁷ Jefferson, Thomas. *Autobiography.* Original in the Library of Congress Rare Manuscript Division, Washington, D.C.

¹⁸ Ibid.

¹⁹ Rayner, B.L. (ed.) *Sketches of the Life, Writings and Opinions of Thomas Jefferson,* p. 556.

Lesson 4

[1] Einstein, Albert, PhD. *Relativity - The Special and General Theory.* Translated by Robert W. Lawson, D.Sc., F. Inst. P., University of Sheffield, N.J.: Quinn and Boden Company, Inc., 1920. Introduction, p. vii.

[2] Ibid.

[3] Ibid.

[4] Ibid.

[5] Ibid.

[6] Einstein, Albert, PhD. *A Test Case for Humanity.* The Information Department, The Jewish Agency for Palestine, London: United Kingdom, 1939.

Lesson 5

[1] *Washington Evening Star.* "The Great Reformer" - The 400th Anniversary of Martin Luther's Birthday in Washington, D.C., November 10, 1883, p. 8.

[2] Ibid., pp. 9-10

[3] Ibid., p. 10

[4] Foxe, John. *Foxe's Book of Martyrs, or The Acts and Monuments of The Christian Church;* being a complete History of the Lives, Sufferings and Deaths of the Christian Martyrs; from the Commencement of Christianity to the present period. To which is added an account of the Inquisition, the Bartholomew Massacre in France, The General Persecution under Louis XIV, the massacres in the Irish Rebellions in the years 1641, and 1798. Rise, Progress and Persecutions of the people commonly called Quakers, together with an account of the Western Martyrology, or Bloody Assizes; with The Lives of some of the Early Eminent Reformers. In Two Volumes. (Vol. I) New York: Published by William Borradaile, 1829, pp. 642-645.

Lesson 6

[1] Asbury, Francis. *The Journal of the Reverend Francis Asbury,* Bishop of the Methodist Episcopal Church, from August 7, 1771 to December 7, 1815. In Three Volumes. (Volume II.) From July 15, 1786 to November 6, 1800. New York: Published by N. Banks and T. Mason for the Methodist Episcopal Church, 1821, p. 129.

[2] Ibid., pp. 130-131

[3] Ibid., p. 133

[4] Ibid., pp. 133-136

[5] Asbury, Francis. *The Journal and Letters of the Reverend Francis Asbury.* In Three Volumes (Volume II). The Journal, 1794-1816. Elmer T. Clark (ed.), Nashville: Abingdon Press, 1958, pp. 213-216.

[6] Ibid., p. 216.

[7] *Minutes of Several Conversations between the Reverend Thomas Coke, L.L.D., The Reverend Francis Asbury and others,* at a Conference begun in Baltimore, in the State of Maryland, on Monday the 27th of December, in the year 1784. Philadelphia: Printed by Charles Cist, in Arch Street, the Corner of Fourth Street, MDCCLXXXV, pp. 15; 17.

[8] Ibid., pp. 19-20.

Lesson 7

[1] Song Records for Automatic Player. Memorandum dated July 1, 1964, to Mr. Stewart, Architect of the Capitol, from Mr. White, Memorial Bell Tower. Office of the Architect of the Capitol, Washington, D.C.

[2] *A Tribute to an American.* Dedication Ceremonies and Speeches at the Inauguration of the Robert A. Taft Memorial. Office of the Architect of the Capitol, Washington, D.C.

[3] Ibid.

[4] Ibid.

[5] Ibid.

[6] Ibid.

Lesson 8

[1] Lee, Fitzhugh. *General Lee.* New York: D. Appleton and Company, 1894, pp. 20-22.

[2] Lattimore, Ralston B. (ed.) *The Story of Robert E. Lee,* as told in his own words and those of his contemporaries. Washington, D.C.: Colortone Press, 1964, p. 24.

[3] Ibid., p. 47.

[4] Ibid., p. 60.

[5] Ibid., p. 12.

[6] Ibid., p. 13.

[7] Griswold, Jr., Benjamin Howell. *The Spirit of Lee and Jackson.* Baltimore: The Norman Remington Company, 1927, pp. 12-13; 18.

[8] Lee, Robert E., Captain. *Recollections and Letters of General Robert E. Lee, by his Son.* New York: Doubleday, Page and Company, 1924, pp. 88, 89.

Lesson 9

[1] These Facts and Statistics have been verified with Ben Frank, Senior Historian, Marine Corps Oral History Program. May 17, 1984.

[2] Ibid.

[3] Ibid.

[4] Ibid.

Lesson 10

[1] Queen Juliana of the Netherlands' Dedication Speech (on record with the Department of the Interior, National Park Service, Washington, D.C.).

[2] *Inscriptions on the Bells of the Netherlands Carillon.* The Dutch verses by Ben van Eysselsteyn. (Courtesy of Paul Goeldner, Associate Regional Director, U.S. Department of Interior, National Park Service).

[3] Ibid.

[4] Ibid.

Addendum

[1] Suter, Henderson, Rev., Rector of Christ Church, Alexandria, Virginia. February 21, 1885. *Prayer at the Dedication of the Washington Monument.* Library of Congress Collection.

ANSWERS TO QUESTIONS

LESSON ONE

III.

1.   i)   b

     ii)   b

     iii) a   6. Sleep not when others speak, sit not when others stand, speak not when you should hold your peace, walk not on when others stop.

             b   22. Shew not yourself glad at the misfortune of another though he were your enemy.

             c   108. When you speak of God or His attributes, let it be seriously and with reverence. Honour and obey your natural parents altho they be poor.

             d   109. Let your recreations be manfull, not sinfull.

     iv) c; d; f; g

     v)   a   Fifty United States flags, proudly encircling the base, each one representing one of the fifty states in the Union.

     vi) c

     vii) c

     viii) a   26. "God and our Native Land."
United Sons of America. Instituted, 1845. Pennsylvania.

             b   27. Grand Division, Sons of Temperance, North Carolina. "Love, Purity, Fidelity."

             c   95. "Liberty, Independence, Virtue." Pennsylvania. (Founded 1681). By Deeds of Peace.

             d   98. The Surest Safeguard of the Liberty of our Country - Total Abstinence from all that Intoxicates. Sons of Temperance of Pennsylvania.

             e   104. "To Washington, the Great, Good and Just, by friendly BREMEN." (Germany)

             f   107. From the Templars of Honor and Temperance. Organized Dec. 5th 1845. "Truth, Love, Purity and Fidelity." Our Pledge: "We will not make, buy, sell or use as a beverage, any spiritous or malt liquors, wine, cider, or any other alcoholic liquor, and we will discountenance their manufacture, traffic and use, and this pledge we will maintain unto the end of life." Supreme Council of the Templars of Honor and Temperance. 1846.

g   124. China . . . It is evident that Washington was a remarkable man . . . Ah, who would not call him a hero? The United States of America regard it promotive of national virtue generally and extensively neither to establish titles of nobility and royalty nor to conform to the age . . . but instead deliver over their own public deliberations and inventions so that the like of such a nation one so remarkable does not exist in ancient or modern times. Among the people of the Great West can any man, in ancient or modern times, fail to pronounce WASHINGTON peerless?

This Stone is Presented by a Company of Christians and engraved at Ningpu . . . China . . . the Reign of the Emperor Heen Fung (July 12th, 1853.)

h   127. Holiness to the Lord.

i   133. Under the Auspices of Heaven and the Precepts of Washington, Kentucky will be the last to give up the Union. "United we stand, divided we fall."

j   156. The Memory of the Just is Blessed. Prov. 10:7. Presented by the children of the Sunday Schools of the Methodist Episcopal Church, in the City of New York, Feb. 22, '55.

k   158. From the Sabbath School Children of the Methodist E. Church in the City and Districts of Philadelphia, 4th July, 1853. A Preached Gospel. A Free Press. Washington. We revere his Memory. "Search the Scriptures." Suffer little children to come unto Me and forbid them not, for of such is the Kingdom of God. Luke XVIII:16. Train up a child in the way he should go, and when he is old, he will not depart from it. Prov. XXII:6.

ix)   a   5. Delaware. First to adopt, will be the last to desert the Constitution.

b   10. Alabama. A Union of Equality as adjusted by the Constitution.

c   11. The State of Louisiana. Ever faithful to the Constitution and the Union.

d   17.   State of Georgia. The Union as it was. The Constitution as it is.

e   47.   North Carolina.   Declaration of Independence. Mecklenburg, May, 1775. "Constitution."

f   80.   Anno 1850. By the City of Baltimore. May Heaven to this Union continue its Beneficence; May Brotherly Affection with Union be Perpetual; May the Free Constitution which is the work of our Ancestors be sacredly maintained and its Administration be stamped with Wisdom and Virtue.

g   96.   Declaration of Independence, Philadelphia, July 4th, 1776. Corporation of the City of Philadelphia.

x)   b; e; g; h; i; k

xi)   a; d; f; h

xii)   a; c; e; h

xiii)   Almighty God, we make our earnest prayer that Thou wilt keep the United States in Thy holy protection; that Thou wilt incline the hearts of the citizens to cultivate a spirit of subordination and obedience to government; and entertain a brotherly affection and love for one another and for their fellow citizens of the United States at large. And finally that Thou wilt most graciously be pleased to dispose us all to do justice, to love mercy, and to demean ourselves with that charity, humility and pacific temper of mind which were the characteristics of the Divine Author of our blessed religion, and without a humble imitation of whose example in these things we can never hope to be a happy nation. Grant our supplication, we beseech Thee, through Jesus Christ our Lord. Amen.

xiv)   He was incapable of fear, meeting personal dangers with the calmest unconcern. Perhaps the strongest feature in his character was prudence, never acting until every circumstance, every consideration, was maturely weighed; refraining if he saw a doubt, but, when once decided, going through with his purpose, whatever obstacles opposed. His integrity was most pure, his justice the most flexible I have ever known, no motive of interest or consanguinity, or friendship or hatred, being able to bias his decision. He was, in every sense of the words, a wise, a good and a great man.

xv)   d

xvi)   . . . May Heaven continue to you the choicest tokens of its beneficence: that your union and brotherly affection may be perpetual; . . . that the free Constitution, which is the work of your hands, may be sacredly maintained; that its administration in every department may be stamped with wisdom and virtue; that in fine, the happiness of the people of these states, under the auspices of liberty may be made complete by so careful a preservation and so prudent a use of this blessing as will acquire to them the glory of recommending it to the applause, the affection and adoption of every nation which is yet a stranger to it . . .

xvii)   c

xviii)   a; d; f; h; i; k; l

xix)   c

xx)   a Wisdom;
         b Virtue

2. *Christian Character Traits*

a.	Courage	f.	Prayerfulness
b.	Honesty	g.	Reverence of God
c.	Integrity	h.	Zeal
d.	Morality	i.	Patriotism
e.	Wisdom	j.	Objectivity

LESSON TWO

III.

1.   i)   c

      ii)   d

      iii)   In this Temple as in the hearts of the people for whom he saved the Union the memory of Abraham Lincoln is enshrined forever.

      iv)   b; d

      v)   a   I do, therefore, invite my fellow-citizens in every part of the United States, and also those who are sojourning in foreign lands, to set apart and observe the last Thursday in November next as a day of thanksgiving and praise to our beneficent Father who dwelleth in the heavens.

      vi)   b; c

      vii)   b; d; f

      viii) a   Let us judge not that we be not judged.

             b   Woe unto the world because of offenses; for it must needs be that offenses come, but woe to that man by whom the offense cometh.

            c   The judgments of the Lord are true and righteous altogether.

ix)   d

x)   a; c; e

xi)   c

xii)   a

xiii)   Fourscore and seven years ago, our fathers brought forth on this continent a new nation, conceived in liberty, and dedicated to the proposition that all men are created equal.

xiv)   c

xv)   c

xvi)   c

xvii)   b

xviii)   c

xix)   a   The Emancipation of a Race

            b   Reunion of North and South

xx)   c

xxi)   a   "Immortality."

                    "Faith," "Hope" and "Charity" stand by as a seated damsel receives the imperishable crown of immortality. The meaning here is that Eternal Life is acquired through faith in Christ, hope in Christ, and Christ's love that is shed abroad in our hearts to others after the Holy Spirit indwells the believer at salvation.

xxii)   c

xxiii)   a   There is a Fountain Filled with Blood

            b   When Shall I See Jesus and Reign with Him Above

            c   Father, What E'er of Earthly Bliss Thy Sovereign Will Denies

            d   Rock of Ages

xxiv)   a   He saw his duty as the Chief Magistrate of a great and imperilled people, and he determined to do his duty, and his whole duty, seeking the guidance and leaning upon the arm of Him of whom it is written, "He giveth power to the faint, and to them that have no might He increaseth strength." Yes, he leaned upon His arm, he recognized and received the truth that the "kingdom is the Lord's, and He is the governor among the nations." He remembered that "God is in history," and felt that nowhere had His hand and His mercy been so marvelously conspicuous as in the history of this nation . . .

xxv) c

2. *Christian Character Traits*

a.	Dependence upon God	f.	Humility
b.	Trust in God	g.	Glorification of God
c.	Fear of God	h.	Justice
d.	Love of Scripture	i.	Fairness
e.	Prayerfulness	j.	Self-sacrifice

LESSON THREE

III.

1. i) a   In 1943, the two-hundredth anniversary of Jefferson's birth was celebrated with the inauguration and grand opening of this building to the public.

ii) a   Jefferson reading his draft of the Declaration of Independence to the Committee appointed by the Continental Congress to evaluate the document: Benjamin Franklin, John Adams, Roger Sherman and Robert R. Livingston.

iii) c

iv) d

v) a   I have sworn upon the altar of God eternal hostility against every form of tyranny over the mind of man.

vi) c

vii) a   The Declaration of Independence; The Statutes for Religious Freedom; Jefferson's anti-slavery views; and his belief that institutions and organizations should advance with the progress of a civilization.

viii) d

ix) c

x) d

xi)   c; f; h

xii)   c

xiii)   d

xiv)   b;d

xv)   a   Contributions of money for the propagation of opinions which he disbelieves.

xvi)   a   Giving his contributions to the particular pastor whose morals he would like to pattern, and whose powers he feels most persuasive to righteousness.

xvii)   c

xviii) a

xix)   a   The event would be celebrated by succeeding generations as the great anniversary festival, commemorated as the day of deliverance by solemn acts of devotion to God Almighty from one end of the continent to the other, from this time forward forevermore.

xx)   a   It was that which gave promise that in due time the weights would be lifted from the shoulders of all men, and that all should have an equal chance. This is the sentiment embodied in the Declaration of Independence.

xxi)   a   Congress shall make no law respecting an establishment of religion or prohibiting the free exercise thereof.

xxii)   c

xxiii) c

xxiv)   a   In an off-the-record, non-political letter, written by Thomas Jefferson to the Danbury Baptist Association.

xxv)   a   Thomas Jefferson wrote this letter on January 1,1802, replying to their public address which applauded his stance for establishing religious freedom.

xxvi)   a   An assurance to the Danbury Baptists that he concurs with their belief of man being accountable to God alone for his mode of worship, without the government's coercion or interference.

xxvii) b; e; f;
        h; j; k;
        m; n; o

xxviii) c; f; h

xxix)   a   God who gave us life gave us liberty. Can the liberties of a nation be secure when we have removed a conviction that these liberties are the gift of God? Indeed I tremble for my country when I reflect that God is just. That His justice cannot sleep forever. Commerce between master and slave is despotism.

xxx)   c

xxxi)   a; c; e;
         f; g; h;
         i; j; k

xxxii)   a   . . . The abolition of domestic slavery is the great object of desire in those colonies where it was unhappily introduced in their infant state. But previous to the enfranchisement of the slaves we have, it is necessary to exclude all further importations from Africa; yet our repeated attempts to affect this by prohibitions, and by imposing duties which might amount to a prohibition, have been hitherto defeated by his majesty's negative: Thus preferring the immediate advantages of a few African corfairs (slaves), to the lasting interests of the American states, and to the rights of human nature deeply wounded by this infamous practise . . .

xxxiii) a   It is still in our power to direct the process of emancipation and deportation peaceably and in such slow degree as that the evil will wear off insensibly and their place be pari passu (slowly) filled with free white laborers. If, on the contrary, it is left to force itself on, human nature must shudder at the prospect held up . . . Commerce between master and slave is despotism.

xxxiv)   b; d; e;
         g; h; i

xxxv)   a   Lord, now lettest Thou Thy servant depart in peace.

xxxvi)   d

2.   Christian Character Traits

a.	Honor of God	f.	Respect of others
b.	Justice	g.	Defense of the tyrannized
c.	Love of others	h.	Fairness
d.	Self-sacrifice	i.	Denunciation of greed
e.	Reverence for God	j.	Denunciation of slavery

LESSON FOUR

III.

1. i)   c

    ii)   a   The more complex and intricate his calculations of the
                    universe became, the more assured he was of the reality of a
                    Supreme Creator.

    iii)   b

    iv)   b; d

    v)   c

    vi)   c

    vii)   d

    viii)   c

    ix)   a   A hot body weighs more than the same body when cool,
                    because when hot the atoms are moving at faster speeds, or
                    higher energy levels . . .

    x)   a   In addition to the mass, 99 percent of the energy of all
                    substances is locked in the nuclei, such as the power by which
                    a single lump of coal could run a liner across the Atlantic.

    xi)   c

    xii)   c

    xiii)   d

    xiv)   a   The first and only holy city, and Palestine is the place where
                    their original history, their sacred history, took place.

    xv)   a   Jerusalem is only the third holy city.

    xvi)   a   They trace their tradition back to Jewish origins, insofar as
                    after the Arab conquest of Jerusalem in 637, the "Omar
                    Mosque" the "Dome of the Rock" was erected by the Omayyad
                    Caliph Abd el Malek on the very place where the Jewish Ark
                    of the Covenant and the Temple of Solomon had stood . . .

    xvii)   a   A qiblah, a direction of prayer, only as long as he counted on
                    the Jews as the main supporters of his new creed; . . .

    xviii) d

    xix)   a   This tiny Palestinian country is the only place in the world
                    legitimately and most deeply connected with the Jewish

people, its religious foundation and its historic tradition as an independent people.

xx) a   In speaking up for a Jewish Palestine we want to promote the establishment of a place of refuge where persecuted human beings may find security and peace and the undisputed right to live under a law and order of their making. The experience of many centuries has taught us that this can be provided only by home rule and not by a foreign administration . . .

xxi) d

xxii) b

LESSON FIVE

III.

1.   i)   c

     ii)   c

    iii)   b

     iv)   d

      v)   a   The Protestant Reformation dates from the 31st October, 1517, the day on which Martin Luther nailed to the door of the church at Wittemberg his famous ninety-five theses.

     vi)   a   Pope Leo X in 1510 resorted to the plan of selling indulgences as a means of filling the empty treasury at Rome.

    vii)   d

   viii)   c

     ix)   a   Tetzel threatened to excommunicate and bring the most dreadful maledictions to bear against Luther and any others who dared question the efficacy of his indulgences.

      x)   d

     xi)   a   Martin Luther wrote out the ninety-five theses as subjects for discussion, at the coming holyday of All Saints and nailed them to the door of the church.

    xii)   1   Our Lord and Master, Jesus Christ, when He commands us to repent, intends that our whole lives shall be one of repentance.

2	This word cannot be understood of the sacrament of penance (i.e. confession and satisfaction) as administered by the priest.
4	Repentance and sorrow that is true penitence lasts as long as a man is displeased with himself; that is, while he passes from this to eternal life.
6	The pope can forgive no debt but can only declare and confirm the forgiveness which God Himself has given, except in cases that refer to himself. If he does otherwise, the debts remain unremoved and unforgiven.
8	The laws of ecclesiastical penance ought to be imposed solely on the living, and have no regard for the dead.
21	Therefore, the preachers of indulgences are in error when they say that in consequence of the pope's indulgences, men are liberated from all sin and saved.
27	They preach mere human folly who maintain that as soon as the money tinkles, avarice and love of gain arrive, increase and multiply. But the support and prayers of the church depend on God's will and good pleasure.
32	Those who fancy themselves sure of salvation by indulgences will go to perdition along with those who teach them so.
36	Every Christian who truly repents of his sins enjoys an entire remission both of the penalty and of the guilt, without any need of indulgences.
37	Every true Christian, whether dead or alive, participates in all the blessings of Christ, or of the church, by God's gift, and without a letter of indulgence.
45	We should teach Christians that whoever sees his neighbor in want and yet buys an indulgence, does not buy the pope's indulgence, but incurs God's anger.
51	We should teach Christians that the pope (as it is his duty) should distribute his own money to the poor whom the indulgence sellers are now stripping of their last farthing, even were he compelled to sell the mother church of St. Peter.
54	Injustice is done to the Word of God when as much or even more time is taken up in church in preaching indulgences than the Word of God.
56	The treasures of the church, out of which the pope distributes indulgences, are neither recognized nor pronounced satisfactory by the church of Christ.

xiii)	c	
xiv)	d	
xv)	c	
xvi)	d	
xvii)	c	
xviii)	c	
xix)	79	It is blasphemy to say that the cross adorned with the arms of the pope is as effectual as the cross of Christ.
xx)	c	
xxi)	d	
xxii)	c	
xxiii)	b	
xxiv)	a	Luther was a man of prodigious sagacity and acuteness, very warm, and formed for great undertakings; being a man, if ever there was one, whom nothing could daunt or intimidate. When the cause of religion was concerned, he never regarded whose love he was likely to gain, or whose displeasure to incur . . .

2. *Christian Character Traits*

a.	Prayerfulness	f.	Truthfulness
b.	Dependence upon God	g.	Zeal
c.	Devotion to Jesus Christ	h.	Holy boldness
d.	Sincerity	i.	Steadfastness
e.	Honesty	j.	Humility

LESSON SIX

III.

1.	i)	d	
	ii)	a	His continuous journeying through cities, villages and settlements from 1771 to 1816, greatly promoted patriotism, education, morality and religion in the American Republic.
	iii)	c	
	iv)	d	
	v)	a	Discipline, and the preaching a present and full salvation and

the enforcement of the doctrine of sanctification.

vi)   c

vii)   b

viii)   c

ix)   b; d; f; g

x)   a   A decided tone to the morals, manners and religious opinions should be given by the first settlers of the country.

xi)   b; d

xii)   c

xiii)   a   Washington, the calm, intrepid chief, the disinterested friend, first father and temporal saviour of his country under Divine protection and direction. A universal cloud sat upon the faces of the citizens of Charleston; the pulpits clothed in black, the bells muffled, the paraded soldiery, a public oration decreed to be delivered on Friday, 14th of this month, a marble statue to be placed in some proper situation. These were the expressions of sorrow, and these the marks of respect paid by his feeling fellow-citizens to the memory of this great man. I am disposed to lose sight of all but Washington: matchless man! At all times he acknowledged the providence of God, and never was he ashamed of his Redeemer: we believe he died, not fearing death. In his will he ordered the manumission of his slaves – a true son of liberty in all points.

xiv)   b; d; f;
        h; j

xv)   c

xvi)   b; d; f; g

xvii)   a   We therefore think it our most bounden duty to take immediately some effectual method to extirpate this abomination from among us: And for that purpose we add the following to the rules of our Society. . .

xviii) c; e

xix)   b; d; f; g

xx)   a   They are immediately to be expelled: unless they buy them on purpose to free them . . .

xxi)	a	Why are not we more holy?
	b	Why do not we live in Eternity?
	c	Walk with God all the day long?
	d	Why are we not all devoted to God?
	e	Breathing the whole spirit of missionaries?

xxii)   c; d

xxiii)   e

xxiv)   e

2.   *Christian Character Traits:*

a.	Deprivation	f.	Contentment
b.	Self-sacrifice	g.	Prayerfulness
c.	Mortification	h.	Zealousness
d.	Humility	i.	Perseverance
e.	Long-suffering	j.	Love of God

LESSON SEVEN

III.

1.   i)   b; d; e; g

ii)   c

iii)   b

iv)   c

v)   a   Nearer my God to Thee

b   O God our Help in ages Past

c   Take time to be Holy

d   The Hymn of the Republic

e   Faith of our Fathers

f   Awake my Soul

g   The Star-spangled Banner

h   America

i   Holy God we Praise Thy Name

	j	God bless America
	k	America, my Country
	l	America, the Beautiful
	m	Come, Thou Mighty King
	n	God of our Fathers
vi)	c	
vii)	b	
viii)	d	
ix)	a	O Come Emmanuel
	b	O Little Town of Bethlehem
	c	O Worship the King
	d	Silent Night
	e	The First Noel
	f	I Heard the Bells on Christmas Day
	g	Away in the Manger
	h	Adeste Fideles
	i	Hark the Herald Angels Sing

x)　　　　c; h

xi)　a　April 14, 1959. This Memorial to Robert A. Taft, presented by the people to the Congress of the United States, stands as a tribute to the honesty, indomitable courage and high principles of free government symbolized by his life.

xii)　a　If we wish to make democracy permanent in this country, let us abide by the fundamental principles laid down in the Constitution. Let us see that the State is the servant of its people and that the people are not the servants of the State.

xiii)　a　Liberty has been the key to our progress in the past, and is the key to our progress in the future. If we can preserve liberty in all its essentials, there is no limit to the future of the American people.

xiv)   a   We need only a government inspired by the principles of the Pilgrim Fathers – a government which is honest to the core and furnishes a moral and religious leadership to the people, a government inspired by the dominating purpose that it will maintain at all costs the liberty of its people from foreign and domestic threat.

2.   *Christian Character Traits*

a.	Honest	f.	Honorable
b.	Courageous	g.	Intelligent
c.	High-principled	h.	Moral
d.	God-fearing	i.	Long-suffering
e.	Responsible	j.	Loyal

LESSON EIGHT

III.

1.   i)   a   The original 1,100 acre plantation belonging to Robert E. Lee, who married Mary Ann Randolph Custis, only surviving child of George Washington Park Custis, (George Washington's adopted grandson), and Mary Lee Fitzhugh.

     ii)   a   He stated that he could not lift his hand against family and friends of his native Virginia.

     iii)   a   A law required that all private property owners should appear in person to pay their taxes. Mrs. Lee sent a cousin to pay the taxes amounting to $97.04. The government turned it down, however, purchasing the estate on public auction shortly thereafter. Union troops soon took over the estate. It was thus that Robert E. Lee's Arlington home became a national cemetery.

     iv)   a   Custis Lee took his father's last Will and Testament to the Supreme Court. The court's ruling reinstated Lee as rightful owner of this estate.

     v)   a   Unable to live on the site of a now-established cemetery, Lee sold it to the U.S. government in 1883 for a hundred and fifty thousand dollars.

     vi)   d

     vii)   a; b; e; f; g

viii)	c	
ix)	c	
x)	a; b; d; f; h	
xi)	a	Major General Henry "Light Horse Harry" Lee, a Revolutionary War hero, and Anne Hill Carter, a direct descendant of Robert "King" Carter, one of the most noble and significant figures of Virginia's Golden age in the early 18th century.
xii)	c	
xiii)	d	
xiv)	a	Lee issued a General Order No. 83. Headquarters Army Northern Virginia, August 13, 1863. The President of the Confederate States has, in the name of the people, appointed the 21st day of August as a day of fasting, humiliation and prayer . . . Soldiers! We have sinned against Almighty God. We have forgotten his signal mercies, and have cultivated a revengeful, haughty and boastful spirit . . .
xv)	d	
xvi)	d	
xvii)	c	
xviii)	c	
xix)	b; d; e; h	
xx)	c; e; f; h; j	
xxi)	a	Leaning trustfully upon the all-sustaining Arm, the man whose stature, measured by mortal standards seemed so great, passed from this world of shadows to the realities of the Hereafter.
xxii)	c	

2. ***Christian Character Traits***

a.	Meekness	f.	Trust in God
b.	Purity	g.	Love of Righteousness
c.	Self Control	h.	Prayerfulness
d.	Peacemaking	i.	Love of his Redeemer, Jesus Christ
e.	Obedience	j.	Love of the Bible

LESSON NINE

III.

1. i)   c; e

    ii)   a; b; f

    iii)   a   This tribute was first expressed in a communique from Iwo Jima, applauding our servicemen as they battled ceaselessly to attain control of this strategic Japanese island.

    iv)   a   Seven hundred and fifty miles south of Tokyo, Iwo Jima became the symbol of courage and sacrifice to the American people.

    v)   d

    vi)   c

    vii)   c

    viii) a   Five marines, together with a Navy Corpsman, climbed laboriously to the top of Mount Suribachi with an iron pipe, to which had been attached the American flag . . . The Star-spangled Banner was firmly implanted into the grit and grime of Mount Suribachi's volcanic rock.

    ix)   a   Private First Class Franklin Runyon Sousley.

           b   Corporal Ira Hamilton Hayes.

           c   Sergeant Michael Strank.

           d   Corporal Rene Arthur Gagnon.

           e   Corporal Harlan Henry Block

           f   Pharmacist's Mate Second Class John Henry Bradley.

    x)   c

    xi)   a   Joe Rosenthal's timely photograph became widely circulated and admired throughout the world. It symbolized undaunted American courage and sacrifice for the cause of freedom.

    xii)   d

    xiii) a   Working from the original photograph, with the three surviving servicemen posing for him, sculptor Felix de Weldon molded an exact, life-like bronze image of this heroic epic.

    xiv)   a   In Honor and Memory of the Men of the United States Marine Corps who have given their lives to their country since

10 November, 1775.

xv)	c	
xvi)	b	
xvii)	c	
xviii)	a	The Iwo Jima Memorial recalls, in graphic detail, the high price of liberty, and the pride and courage with which our valiant soldiers have defended it for the past 200 years.

2. *Christian Character Traits*

a.	Honor		f.	Self-sacrifice
b.	Faithfulness		g.	Courage
c.	Imagination		h.	Perseverance
d.	Patriotism		i.	Pluck
e.	Virtue		j.	Ingenuity

LESSON TEN

III.

1.	i)	c	
	ii)	a	In the Spring of 1952, Queen Juliana of the Netherlands presented a model of this Carillon to the people of the United States.
	iii)	d; f	
	iv)	d	
	v)	a	The Netherlands people from all strata have contributed to this gift, and the bells which are to follow come from various groups of the population: seamen, miners, farmers, flower-growers, fishermen, the armed services, teachers and scientists, financiers and shopkeepers, businessmen and drivers, pressmen, artists, women's organizations, sportsmen and civil servants, resistance people who cooperated with your troops, students, boys and girls, and little children . . . The Antilles, the territories in the Caribbean, join in this present. And Surinam too wants to express its gratitude in its own way to the people of the United States.
	vi)	c	
	vii)	a; e; f; g; j; k	

viii) c

ix) b; d; f

x) a The 16th bell, extolling the Merchant Marine, has this to say:
"You who set your course between the stars and the waves,
pray the Lord for protection and a favorable wind."

   b The 30th bell, dedicated to farmers, reads: "They who
resolutely sow new seed, will reap a rich harvest with the help
of the Lord."

   c The 32nd bell is dedicated to the Arts. Its joyful statement is
that: "The breath of God is in their Work and Shows us, how
they create for us out of Nothing."

2. *Christian Character Traits*

a.	Gratitude	f.	Self-sacrifice
b.	Benevolence	g.	Kindness
c.	Prayerfulness	h.	Respect
d.	Honor of God	i.	Joy
e.	Reciprocity	j.	Dedication

LESSON ONE

TEACHERS' GUIDE

5 CLASS SESSIONS

The Washington Monument – "Praise be to God!"

What you will need:

1. Text: Lesson 1 - The Christian Heritage of our Nation History Curriculum - Memorials.
2. Illustrations (attached).
3. "The Christian Heritage of our Nation" - Ten National Memorials #2 video.
4. A VCR player.
5. Thumb tacks or scotch tape.

I. Opening activities:

Affix the following enlarged illustrations to the walls of your classroom: (Permission is granted per teacher of *The Christian Heritage of our Nation History Curriculum – Memorials* course of study, to enlarge the attached illustrations for display upon the walls of the classroom.)

a) Our Nation's Capital from the Tidal Basin
b) The Washington Monument – with fifty U.S. flags around its base
c) The Twenty-fourth Landing Memorial Stone
d) "Train up a Child in the Way he should go . . . " (Prov. 22:6)
e) "The Memory of the Blessed will last . . . " (Prov. 10:7)
f) "Suffer the Little Children to Come unto Me . . ." (Luke 18:16)
g) The Washington Monument from the Reflecting Pool

Write out upon a chalk board Proverbs 22:6:

Train up a child in the way he should go, and when he is old he will not depart from it.

The above illustrations are to be displayed prior to your students' arrival. Attention should be focused upon the Christian meaning and significance of these major landmarks of America's history, prominently displayed in the sculpture and architecture of the Washington Monument.

Allow your students the liberty to ascertain what these visual reenactments of our nation's history and heritage depict.

II. *Textual Reenactment: (30 minutes allotted)*

Select passages from the text on the original writings, addresses and proclamations of George Washington. The aim of this lesson is to portray the father of our nation in his true light, leading your students to come to their own conclusion regarding the authentic Christian identity of George Washington; that is, to prove for themselves that George Washington's life was governed by Scripture and prayer.

III. *Visual Reenactment: (15 minutes allotted)*

a)   Alert your students to the fact they will now be seeing the visual reenactments of a number of these Christian themes in the architecture, inscriptions and sculpture of the Washington Monument, together with the narrated text, memorialized for all Americans at a national historic site of foremost significance.

b)   Play, at the first Class Session, "The Christian Heritage of our Nation" - Ten National Memorials #2 video. (First Memorial).

IV. *Forum Discussion, Questions, Clarifications and Answers: (15 minutes allotted)*

a)   Allow your students free rein in discussing their prior concepts, ideas and views on the history and heritage of America, from current textbooks, articles and television productions comparing them to the above Lesson One - Plan (I). Select passages from the original writings, addresses and proclamations of George Washington, together with the visual reenactments of the Christian themes depicted in the architecture and sculpture of this foremost national memorial.

b)   Answer all questions pertaining to the above lesson clearly, concisely and accurately, based upon your thorough study, knowledge and understanding of George Washington's true Christian identity and commitment to Jesus Christ, from the original texts provided.

c)   Assign Lesson 1 text, together with PUPILS' GUIDES (attached), to your students for critical analysis and reflective study. These should be completed and returned prior to Lesson 2.

d)   Before closing the lesson, ask your students to reflect upon the question: "From the original texts presented, and the visual reenactments of the authentic history and heritage inherent in the sculpture, inscriptions and architecture of the Washington Monument, was George Washington's first allegiance to God, Christ and the Bible, or to politics?"

LESSON TWO

5 CLASS SESSIONS

The Lincoln Memorial – Abraham Lincoln, Emancipator of The Slaves

What you will need:

1. Text: Lesson 2 - The Christian Heritage of our Nation History Curriculum - Memorials.
2. Illustrations (attached).
3. "The Christian Heritage of our Nation" - Ten National Memorials #2 video.
4. A VCR player.
5. Thumb tacks or scotch tape.

I. Opening Activities:

Affix the following enlarged illustrations and photographs to the walls of your classroom:

a) The Lincoln Memorial
b) The Statue of Abraham Lincoln by Daniel Chester French
c) Abraham Lincoln's Church - The New York Avenue Presbyterian Church
d) Lincoln's hand-autographed Devotional – "The Believer's Daily Treasure"
e) Lincoln's Gettysburg Address (Inner, South Wall)
f) "Emancipation of a Race" painting
g) "Immortality" painting
h) "Justice and the Law" painting
i) Lincoln's Second Inaugural Address (Third panel)
j) "Reunion" painting
k) "Reunion of the North and the South" painting
l) "Charity" painting
m) "Fraternity" painting
n) The "One Nation Under God" stained-glass window
o) The Reflecting Pool - Lincoln Memorial
p) The Pledge of Allegiance to Our Flag
q) Reverend Francis Bellamy's Original Pledge of Allegiance
r) Reverend Francis Bellamy's Church - First Baptist Church of Little Falls, New York.

Write upon a chalk board: Matthew 18:7, Abraham Lincoln's theme Scripture in his Second Inaugural Address:

Woe unto the world because of offenses; for it must needs be that offenses come, but woe to that man by whom the offense cometh.

These are to be displayed prior to your students' arrival. Attention should be focused upon the Christian themes inherent in the architecture, sculpture and paintings of this major national landmark memorializing Lincoln's famous writings, addresses and Christian way of life. Allow your students the liberty to ascertain what these visual reenactments of America's history and heritage depict.

II. Textual Reenactment: (30 minutes allotted)

Select passages from the text on the original writings, addresses and proclamations of Abraham Lincoln, reenacting these events through his own words. The aim of this lesson is to portray the Emancipator of the Slaves in his true light, leading your students to come to their own conclusion regarding the authentic Christian identity of Abraham Lincoln; that is, to prove for themselves that Abraham Lincoln's life was governed by Scripture and prayer.

III. Visual Reenactment: (15 minutes allotted)

a)   Alert your students to the fact they will now be seeing the visual reenactment of the Christian themes in the architecture, sculpture and paintings of this major national memorial, together with the narrated text, affirming Abraham Lincoln's identity as the Emancipator of the Slaves.

b)   Play, at the first class session, "The Christian Heritage of our Nation" - Ten National Memorials #2 video. (Second Memorial)

IV. Forum Discussion, Questions, Clarifications and Answers: (15 minutes allotted)

a)   Allow your students free rein in discussing their prior concepts, ideas and views on Abraham Lincoln, Emancipator of the Slaves, from current textbooks, articles and television productions; comparing them to the above Lesson Two - Plan (II). Select Passages from the original writings of Abraham Lincoln, together with the visual reenactments of the Christian themes depicted in the architecture, sculpture and paintings of this foremost national memorial.

b)   Answer all questions pertaining to the above lesson clearly, concisely and accurately, based upon your thorough study, knowledge and understanding of Abraham Lincoln's true Christian identity and commitment to Jesus Christ, from the original texts provided.

c)   Assign Lesson 2 text, together with PUPILS' GUIDES (attached) to your students for critical analysis and reflective study. These should be completed and returned prior to Lesson 3.

d)   Before closing the lesson, ask your students to reflect upon the question:

"From the original historical writings, addresses and proclamations of Lincoln presented, and the visual reenactments of the Christian themes depicted in the architecture, sculpture and paintings of this foremost national memorial, was his first allegiance to God, Christ and the Bible, or to politics?"

LESSON THREE

TEACHERS' GUIDE

5 CLASS SESSIONS

The Thomas Jefferson Memorial —
Author of the Declaration of Independence

What you will need:

1. Text: Lesson 3 - The Christian Heritage of our Nation History Curriculum - Memorials.
2. Illustrations (attached).
3. "The Christian Heritage of our Nation" - Ten National Memorials #2 video.
4. A VCR player.
5. Thumb tacks or scotch tape.

I. Opening activities:

Affix the following illustrations to the walls of your classroom:

a) The Jefferson Memorial from the Tidal Basin
b) The Jefferson Memorial - his favorite style of architecture
c) The Jefferson Memorial - Adolph Weinman's sculpture
d) The Bronze Statue of Jefferson - "The Declaration of Independence"
e) The Jefferson Memorial - "Statutes for Religious Freedom"
f) The Jefferson Memorial - Words from his "Notes on Virginia" and "Autobiography"
g) The Jefferson Memorial overlooking our Nation's Capital

Write upon a chalk board: Jefferson's words from his *Notes on Virginia*:

> God who gave us life gave us liberty. Can the liberties of a nation be secure when we have removed a conviction that these liberties are the gift of God? Indeed I tremble for my country when I reflect that God is just. That His justice cannot sleep forever . . .

The above illustrations are to be displayed prior to your students' arrival. Attention should be focused upon the Christian meaning and significance of these predominant sculptural inscriptions and masterpieces within and without the Jefferson Memorial. Allow your students the liberty to ascertain what these visual reenactments of America's history and heritage depict.

II. Textual Reenactment: *(30 minutes allotted)*

Select passages from the text on the original writings, addresses and proclamations of Thomas Jefferson, reenacting these events through his own words. The aim of this lesson is to portray the author of the Declaration of Independence in his true light, leading your students to come to their own conclusions regarding the authentic identity of Thomas Jefferson; that is, to prove for themselves that Thomas Jefferson's words were governed by Scripture.

III. Visual Reenactment: *(15 minutes allotted)*

a)   Alert your students to the fact they will now be seeing the visual reenactments of a number of these inscriptions and masterpieces, together with the narrated text, memorialized for all Americans at a national historic site of foremost significance.

b)   Play, at the first Class Session "The Christian Heritage of our Nation" - Ten National Memorials #2 video. (Third Memorial)

IV. Forum Discussion, Questions, Clarifications and Answers: *(15 minutes allotted)*

a)   Allow your students free rein in discussing their prior concepts, ideas and views on Thomas Jefferson, author of the Declaration of Independence, from current textbooks, articles and television productions; comparing them to the above Lesson Three - Plan (III). Select passages from the original writings of Thomas Jefferson, together with the visual reenactments of the Christian themes depicted in the inscriptions and masterpieces of this foremost national memorial.

b)   Answer all questions pertaining to the above lesson clearly, concisely and accurately, based upon your thorough study, knowledge and understanding of Thomas Jefferson's true identity, from the original texts provided.

c)   Assign Lesson 3 text, together with PUPILS' GUIDES (attached), to your students for critical analysis and reflective study. These should be completed and returned prior to Lesson 4.

d)   Before closing the lesson, ask your students to reflect upon the question: "From the original historical writings, addresses and proclamations of Jefferson presented, as depicted in the inscriptions and masterpieces of this foremost national memorial, was his first allegiance to God, or to politics?"

LESSON FOUR

2 CLASS SESSIONS

The Albert Einstein Memorial – Einstein's Energy Formula

What you will need:

1. Text: Lesson 4 – The Christian Heritage of our Nation History Curriculum - Memorials.
2. Illustrations (attached).
3. "The Christian Heritage of our Nation" - Ten National Memorials #2 video.
4. A VCR player.
5. Thumb tacks or scotch tape.

I. Opening activities:

Affix the following illustrations to the walls of your classroom:

a) The Bronze Statue of Albert Einstein by Robert Berks.

Write out upon a chalk board:

> The more complex and intricate his calculations of the universe became, the more assured he was of the reality of a Supreme Creator.

These are to be displayed prior to your students' arrival. Attention should be focused upon the meaning and significance of this important landmark of America's scientific history, prominently displayed in front of the National Academy of Sciences, on Constitution Avenue in our nation's capital. Allow your students the liberty to ascertain what this visual reenactment of our nation's scientific history depicts.

II. Textual Reenactment: (30 minutes allotted)

Select passages from the text on the biographical material, news article and original writings of Albert Einstein. The aim of this lesson is to portray the historical events depicted in this work of art in their true light, leading your students to come to their own conclusions regarding the authentic identity and life of Albert Einstein.

III. Visual Reenactment: *(15 minutes allotted)*

a) Alert your students to the fact they will now be seeing the visual reenactment of this historic landmark, together with the narrated text, memorialized for all Americans at a national historic site of significance.

b) Play, at the first class session "The Christian Heritage of our Nation" - Ten National Memorials #2 video. (Fourth Landmark.)

IV. Forum Discussion, Questions, Clarifications and Answers: *(15 minutes allotted).*

a) Allow your students free rein in discussing their prior concepts, ideas and views on the authentic biography and scientific history of Albert Einstein, from current textbooks, articles and television productions, comparing them to the above Lesson Four - Plan (IV). Select passages from the text on the biographical material, news article and original writings of Albert Einstein, together with the visual reenactment of the brilliant scientist, at this National Memorial.

b) Answer all questions pertaining to the above lesson clearly, concisely and accurately, based upon your thorough study, knowledge and understanding of the texts provided.

c) Assign Lesson 4 text, together with PUPILS' GUIDES (attached), to your students for critical analysis and reflective study. These should be completed and returned prior to Lesson 5.

d) Before closing the lesson, ask your students to reflect upon the question: "From the original texts presented and the visual reenactment of the life and work of Albert Einstein, to whom does this brilliant master-mind attribute the creation of the universe, and sovereignty over it – God, or evolution?"

LESSON FIVE

3 CLASS SESSIONS

The Martin Luther Memorial - "A Mighty Fortress is our God"

What you will need:

1. Text: Lesson 5 - The Christian Heritage of our Nation History Curriculum - Memorials.
2. Illustrations (attached).
3. "The Christian Heritage of our Nation" - Ten National Memorials #2 video.
4. A VCR player.
5. Thumb tacks or scotch tape.

I. *Opening activities:*

Affix the following illustrations to the walls of your classroom:

a) The Martin Luther Statue in our Nation's Capital.
b) The Martin Luther Statue - his right hand upon a Bible.

Write out upon a chalk board:

> A mighty fortress is our God
> A bulwark never failing
> A helper He amid the flood
> Of mortal ills prevailing -

These are to be displayed prior to your students' arrival. Attention should be focused upon the Christian meaning and significance of this major landmark of our history, prominently portrayed in the handsome bronze statue of Martin Luther in our nation's capital. Allow your students the liberty to ascertain what this visual reenactment of our history and heritage depict.

II. *Textual Reenactment: (30 minutes allotted)*

Select passages from the text on the original historical documentation pertaining to Martin Luther. The aim of this lesson is to portray the historical events reflected in the life and work of Martin Luther, leading your students to come to their own conclusions regarding the authentic Christian identity of this great leader of the Protestant Reformation.

III. Visual Reenactment: (15 minutes allotted)

a) Alert your students to the fact they will now be seeing the visual reenactment of this Christian Memorial, together with the narrated text, memorialized for all Americans at a national historic site of foremost importance.

b) Play, at the first Class Session. "The Christian Heritage of our Nation" - Ten National Memorials #2 video. (Fifth Memorial.)

IV. Forum Discussion, Questions, Clarifications and Answers: (15 minutes allotted)

a) Allow your students free rein in discussing their prior concepts, ideas and views on Martin Luther, from current textbooks, articles and television productions; comparing them to the above Lesson Five - Plan (V). Select passages from the text on original documentation pertaining to Martin Luther and from the great master sculptor's own interpretation, in this sculptural masterpiece depicting the Reformer's true identity.

b) Answer all questions pertaining to the above lesson clearly, concisely and accurately, based upon your thorough study, knowledge and understanding of the life and deeds of Martin Luther.

c) Assign Lesson 5 text, together with PUPILS' GUIDES (attached), to your students for critical analysis and reflective study. These should be completed and returned prior to Lesson 6.

d) Before closing the lesson, ask your students to reflect upon the question: "From the original texts presented and the visual reenactment of the authentic identity of Martin Luther, was his first allegiance to God, Christ and the Bible, or to mammon?"

LESSON SIX

TEACHERS' GUIDE

3 CLASS SESSIONS

The Francis Asbury Memorial - "The Prophet of the Long Road."

What you will need:

1. Text: Lesson 6 - The Christian Heritage of our Nation History Curriculum - Memorials.
2. Illustrations (attached).
3. "The Christian Heritage of our Nation" – Ten National Memorials #2 video.
4. A VCR player.
5. Thumb tacks or scotch tape.

I. Opening activities:

Affix the following illustrations to the walls of your classroom:

a) The Francis Asbury Memorial Statue in our Nation's Capital
b) The Equestrian Statue of Francis Asbury - his right hand holding a Bible
c) The portrait of Francis Asbury

Write out upon a chalk board:

> His continuous journeying through cities, villages and settlements from 1771 to 1816 greatly promoted patriotism, education, morality, and religion in the American Republic. Act of Congress.

These are to be displayed prior to your students' arrival. Attention should be focused upon the Christian meaning and significance of this major landmark of America's history. Allow your students the liberty to ascertain what this memorial in our nation's history and heritage depicts.

II. Textual Reenactment: (30 minutes allotted)

Select passages from the text on the original Journal entries and Minutes expounding upon the Christian life and deeds of Francis Asbury, reenacting these events through his own words. The aim of this lesson is to portray "The Prophet of the Long Road" in his true light, leading your students to their own conclusion regarding the authentic Christian identity of Francis Asbury; that is, to prove for themselves that Asbury's life was governed by Scripture and prayer.

III. Visual Reenactment: *(15 minutes allotted)*

a)   Alert your students to the fact they will now be seeing the visual reenactment of this national historic memorial of foremost significance.

b)   Play "The Christian Heritage of our Nation" - Ten National Memorials #2 video. (Sixth Memorial).

IV. Forum Discussion, Questions, Clarifications and Answers: *(15 minutes allotted)*

a)   Allow your students free rein in discussing their prior concepts, ideas and views on Francis Asbury, "The Prophet of the Long Road," from current textbooks, articles and television productions; comparing them to the above Lesson Six - Plan (VI) text on the original Christian history and heritage of Francis Asbury - "The Prophet of the Long Road."

b)   Answer all questions pertaining to the above lesson clearly, concisely and accurately, based upon your thorough study, knowledge and understanding of Francis Asbury's true Christian identity, his commitment to Jesus Christ and the Great Commission.

c)   Assign Lesson 6 text, together with PUPILS' GUIDES (attached), to your students for critical analysis and reflective study. These should be completed and returned prior to Lesson 7.

d)   Before closing the lesson, ask your students to reflect upon the question: "From the original texts presented, and the visual reenactment of the authentic history and heritage of the life and deeds of Francis Asbury, was his first allegiance to God, Christ and the Bible, or to mammon?"

LESSON SEVEN

TEACHERS' GUIDE

2 CLASS SESSIONS

The Robert A. Taft Memorial - "O God our Help in Ages Past"

What you will need:

1. Text: Lesson 7 - The Christian Heritage of our Nation History Curriculum - Memorials.
2. Illustrations (attached).
3. "The Christian Heritage of our Nation" - Ten National Memorials #2 video.
4. A VCR player.
5. Thumb tacks or scotch tape.

I. Opening activities:

Affix the following illustrations to the walls of your classroom:

a) The Robert A. Taft Memorial on Capitol Hill
b) The Bronze Statue of Robert A. Taft
c) The Robert A. Taft Memorial - "A Tribute to an American"
d) The Hoisting of the First Bell - Robert A. Taft Memorial.

Write out upon a chalk board Robert A. Taft's words:

> We need only a government inspired by the principles of the Pilgrim Fathers – a government which is honest to the core and furnishes a moral and religious leadership to the people . . .

These are to be displayed prior to your students' arrival. Attention should be focused upon the Christian meaning and significance of this major landmark and symbol of America's history, prominently memorialized in the life and deeds of Robert A. Taft.

Allow your students the liberty to ascertain what these visual reenactments of our nation's history and heritage depict.

II. Textual Reenactment: (30 minutes allotted)

Select passages from the text on the original writings of Robert A. Taft, and those who knew him, reenacting these events through his own words. The aim of this lesson is to portray this famous American son in his true light, leading your students to come to their own conclusions regarding the authentic identity of Robert A. Taft.

III. Visual Reenactment: (15 minutes allotted)

a) Alert your students to the fact they will now be seeing a visual reenactment of the architecture and sculpture of the national memorial, together with the narrated text, memorialized for all Americans at this national historic site.

b) Play, at the first Class Session, "The Christian Heritage of our Nation" - Ten National Memorials #2 video. (Seventh Memorial).

IV. Forum Discussion, Questions, Clarifications and Answers: (15 minutes allotted)

a) Allow your students free rein in discussing their prior concepts, ideas and views on Robert A. Taft, from current textbooks, articles and/or television productions; comparing them to the above Lesson Seven - Plan (VII). Select passages from the original writings of Robert A. Taft, and those who knew him, and from the great master sculptors' and artists' renditions at this national historic memorial.

b) Answer all questions pertaining to the above lesson clearly, concisely and accurately, based upon your thorough study, knowledge and understanding of the texts provided.

c) Assign Lesson 7 text, together with PUPILS' GUIDES (attached) to your students for critical analysis and reflective study. These should be completed and returned prior to Lesson 8.

d) Before closing the lesson, ask your students to reflect upon the question: "From the original texts presented and the visual reenactment of the life and deeds of Robert A. Taft, mirrored in the sculptural, artistic and musical themes of the only memorial on Capitol Hill, is America's first allegiance to God, or to politics?

LESSON EIGHT

TEACHERS' GUIDE

4 CLASS SESSIONS

Arlington National Cemetery - Robert E. Lee's Plantation Homesite

What you will need:

1. Text: Lesson 8 - The Christian Heritage of our Nation History Curriculum-Memorials.
2. Illustrations (attached).
3. "The Christian Heritage of our Nation" - Ten National Memorials #2 video.
4. A VCR player.
5. Thumb tacks or scotch tape.

I. Opening activities:

Affix the following illustrations to the walls of your classroom:

a) Arlington National Cemetery - Robert E. Lee's home on hilltop
b) Arlington National Cemetery
c) President John F. Kennedy's tombsite
d) John F. Kennedy's Inaugural Speech - (Last panel)
e) Robert Francis Kennedy's tombsite
f) Robert E. Lee's plantation homestead
g) The Tomb of the Unknown Soldier
h) The Changing of the Guard

Write upon a chalk board:

> O Lord, my heart is not proud, nor my eyes haughty; nor do I involve myself in great matters, or in things too difficult for me. Surely I have composed and quieted my soul; Like a weaned child rests against his mother, my soul is like a weaned child within me.   Psalm 131:1-2

These are to be displayed prior to your students' arrival. Attention should be focused upon the Christian meaning and significance of these historic events and landmarks, memorialized at Arlington National Cemetery, Robert E. Lee's plantation homesite.

Allow your students the liberty to ascertain what these visual reenactments of our nation's history and heritage depict.

II. Textual Reenactment: (30 minutes allotted)

Select passages from the text memorializing and commemorating personages and events of foremost historic significance to our nation. The aim of this lesson is to study the historical events of America's past in their true light, leading your students to come to their own conclusions regarding the authentic Christian emphasis and identity woven into the warp and woof of Arlington National Cemetery.

III. Visual Reenactment: (15 minutes allotted)

a) Alert your students to the fact they will now be seeing the visual reenactments of the historic legacy of Arlington National Cemetery, together with the narrated text, in order to better understand the meaning and import of this national historic site.

b) Play, at the first Class Session, "The Christian Heritage of Our Nation" - Ten National Memorials #2 video. (Eighth Memorial).

IV. Forum Discussion, Questions, Clarifications and Answers: (15 minutes allotted)

a) Allow your students free rein in discussing their prior concepts, ideas and views on the history and heritage of Arlington National Cemetery (Robert E. Lee's homesite), from current textbooks, articles and television productions, comparing them to the above Lesson Eight - Plan (VIII). Select passages from the original writings of Robert E. Lee, and those who knew him, together with the visual reenactments depicted in the sculptural, artistic and patriotic themes of this foremost national memorial.

b) Answer all questions pertaining to the above lesson clearly, concisely and accurately, based upon your thorough study, knowledge and understanding of the texts provided.

c) Assign Lesson 8 text, together with PUPILS' GUIDES (attached) to your students for critical analysis and reflective study. These should be completed and returned prior to Lesson 9.

d) Before closing the lesson, ask your students to reflect upon the question: "From the original texts presented and the visual reenactments of the authentic American heritage and history of Arlington National Cemetery, is America's *first* allegiance to Almighty God and Jesus Christ, or to the military?"

LESSON NINE

TEACHERS' GUIDE

2 CLASS SESSIONS

The Iwo Jima Memorial - "Uncommon Valor was a Common Virtue"

What you will need:

1. Text: Lesson 9 - The Christian Heritage of our Nation History Curriculum- Memorials.
2. Illustrations (attached).
3. "The Christian Heritage of our Nation" - Ten National Memorials #2 video.
4. A VCR player.
5. Thumb tacks or scotch tape.

I. Opening Activities:

Affix the following illustrations to the walls of your classroom:

a) The Iwo Jima Memorial
b) The Iwo Jima Memorial - Raising of the U.S. Flag
c) The Iwo Jima Memorial - Inscription upon the Base
d) The Iwo Jima Memorial - "Uncommon Valor was a Common Virtue."

Write out upon a chalk board:

> In Honor and Memory of the Men of the United States Marine Corps who have Given their Lives to their Country since 10 November, 1775.

These are to be displayed prior to your students' arrival. Attention should be focused upon the authentic meaning and significance of this major landmark of America's history, memorializing the valiant men of our United States Marine Corps.

Allow your students the liberty to ascertain what this visual reenactment of our nation's history and heritage depicts.

II. Textual Reenactment: (30 minutes allotted)

Select passages from the text on the authentic meaning of this historic event, and the visual reenactment, from the sculptor's own life-like interpretation. The aim of this lesson is to portray the historical events memorialized in this famous sculpture in their true light, leading your students to come to their own conclusions regarding the true identity of America.

III. Visual Reenactment: (15 minutes allotted)

a) Alert your students to the fact they will now be seeing a visual reenactment of the sculptural and artistic themes of this national landmark, together with the narrated text, memorialized for all Americans at a national historic site of significance.

b) Play, at the first Class Session, "The Christian Heritage of our Nation" - Ten National Memorials #2 video. (Ninth Memorial).

IV. Forum Discussion, Questions, Clarifications and Answers: (15 minutes allotted)

a) Allow your students free rein in discussing their prior concepts, ideas and views on this epic of America's history, from current textbooks, articles and television productions, comparing them to the above Lesson Nine - Plan (IX). Select passages from the text on the original meaning of the great master artists' own interpretation of the victory on Iwo Jima, as depicted at this national historic site.

b) Answer all questions pertaining to the above lesson clearly, concisely and accurately, based upon your thorough study, knowledge and understanding of the text provided.

c) Assign Lesson 9 text, together with PUPILS' GUIDES (attached) to your students for critical analysis and reflective study. These should be completed and returned prior to Lesson 10.

d) Before closing the lesson, ask your students to reflect upon the question: "From the original texts presented and the visual reenactment of the authentic historic event on Iwo Jima, as seen in this scuptural masterpiece; is America's first allegiance to God and virtue, or to tyranny and cowardice?"

LESSON TEN

TEACHERS' GUIDE

I CLASS SESSION
The Netherlands Carillon

What you will need:

1. Text: Lesson 10 - The Christian Heritage of our Nation History Curriculum-Memorials.
2. Illustrations (attached).
3. "The Christian Heritage of our Nation" - Ten National Memorials #2 video.
4. A VCR player.
5. Thumb tacks or scotch tape.

I. *Opening Activities:*

Affix the following enlarged illustrations to the walls of your classroom:

a) The Netherlands Carillon
b) The Netherlands Carillon - Forty-nine beautifully-matched bells.

Write upon a chalk board:

> The Breath of God is in their Work and Shows us, how they Create for us out of Nothing. (Inscription upon the 32nd Bell).

II. *Textual Reenactment: (30 minutes allotted)*

Select passages from the text on the historic meaning behind Holland's valuable gift of the Netherlands Carillon to the United States. The aim of this lesson is to portray the United States in her true light, leading your students to come to their own conclusion regarding the authentic identity of their own country; that is, to prove for themselves that America is a Republic under God.

These are to be displayed prior to your students' arrival. Attention should be focused upon the Christian themes inherent in the sculptural and artistic themes of the Netherlands Carillon, memorializing America's timely help to Holland after World War II. Allow your students the liberty to ascertain what these visual reminders of America's history depict.

III. Visual Reenactment: (15 minutes allotted)

Alert your students to the fact they will now be seeing the visual reenactments of these sculptural and artistic themes, together with the narrated text, in a national historic landmark of significance.

Play "The Christian Heritage of our Nation" – Ten National Memorials #2 video (Tenth Memorial).

IV. Forum Discussion, Questions, Clarifications and Answers: (15 minutes allotted)

a)   Allow your students free rein in discussing their prior concepts, ideas and views on the United States of America, their country; in public, and non-public school textbooks, articles and television productions, comparing them to the above Lesson Ten - Plan (X). Select passages from the text, together with the visual reenactments of the Christian themes portrayed in the art and sculpture of this national memorial.

b)   Answer all questions pertaining to the above lesson clearly, concisely and accurately, based upon your thorough study, knowledge and understanding of the text provided.

c)   Assign Lesson 10 text, together with PUPILS' GUIDES (attached), to your students for critical analysis and reflective study. These should be completed and returned prior to the end of this course of study.

d)   Before closing the lesson, ask your students to reflect upon the question: "From the original dedication speech at the Netherlands Carillon delivered by Queen Juliana of the Netherlands, and the sculptural and artistic themes inherent in this national memorial, is America's *first* Allegiance to God, and to helping others, or to self?"

ADDENDUM

P R A Y E R

AT THE DEDICATION OF THE

WASHINGTON MONUMENT

—BY—

Rev. Henderson Suter, Rector of Christ Church[*]

ALEXANDRIA, VA., FEB. 21, 1885.

Almighty God, Ruler of nations and of men, by whose providence our fathers were led to this goodly land–and by whom they were guided and sustained in their efforts to secure their liberties, accept, this day, the grateful homage of us, the inheritors of their well-earned rights.

Them and their leaders Thou didst choose. With courage and patriotism Thou didst inspire all ; but, we to-day, while unmindful of none, are specially called to acknowledge as Thy gift, George Washington.

In honor of him, Thy servant, the nation of Thy planting and of his thought and prayers, has built this monument, and we, to-day, in that nation's behalf, speak to his God and ours, in prayer and thanks.

As we stand beneath the lofty height of this memorial work, and mark the symmetry of its form, we would remember Washington's high character, and all the virtues which, in him, builded-up the man.

A leader fearing God ; a patriot unstained by self ; a statesman wishing only the right, he has left us an example for whose following, we supplicate thy help, for ourselves and for all who are now, and shall hereafter be, the instruments of Thy providence to this land and nation.

In so far as he followed the inspirations of wisdom and of virtue, may we follow him and may his character be to the latest generation, a model for the soldier, for the civilian and for the man,–that, in our armies may be trust in God, in our civilians integrity and among our people, that home life which exhorteth praise ; and so, all those blessings which he coveted for his people and his kind, be the heritage of us and of our children, forever.

O God the high and mighty Ruler of the Universe, bless to-day, and henceforth, Thy servant the President of the United States and all others in authority.

To our Congress ever give wisdom. Direct and prosper all their consultations.

May our judges be able men, such as fear God, men of truth–governed in judgment only by the laws.

May our juries be incorruptible, ever mindful of the solemnity of the oath, and of the great interests depending on its keeping.

May no magistrate, or officer, having rights to maintain or order to secure, ever "wrest the judgement of the poor," or favor the rich man in his cause.

O God, throughout our land, let amity continually reign. Bind ever the one part, to the other part. Heal every wound, opened by human frailty, or by human wrong. Let the feeling of brotherhood have the mastery over all selfish ends, that with one mind and one heart, the North and the South and the East and the West, may seek the good of the common country, and work out that destiny, which has been allotted us among the nations of the earth.

[*] George and Martha Washington's church.

Merciful Father, from whom "all good thoughts and good desires come," let the principles of religion and virtue, find firm root, and grow among our people. May they heed the words of their own Washington, and never "indulge the supposition, that morality can be maintained without religion," or forget that "to political prosperity, religion and morality are indispensable supports." Deepen in them reverence for Thy character. Impress a sense of Thy power. Create a desire for Thy favor, and let it be realized that man's highest honor, is to be a servant of God, and that to fear Him and keep his commandments, is our whole duty.

O God, in all our relations with the nations of the earth, let honor and justice rule us. May their wisdom be our guide and our good their choice. Emulative only in the high purpose of bettering the condition of man, may they and we dwell together in unity and concord.

Bless all efforts to widen the sphere of knowledge, that true wisdom may be garnered by our people and nature yield her secrets for man's good and Thy glory.

In all our seminaries of learning–our schools and colleges–may men arise, who shall be able to hand down to the generations following all that time has given.

And look upon our land. Give us the rain and the fruitful season. Let no blight fall upon the tree–no disease upon the cattle–no pestilence upon man.

To honor Thee O God, we this day yield our homage and offer our praise.

Our Fathers, "cried unto Thee and were delivered."

"They trusted in Thee and were not confounded."–and we, their children, gathered by this monument, to-day, the silent reminder of Thy gifts, ask Thy blessing, O Ruler of nations and men, in the name of Him through whom Thou hast taught us to pray, and, may no private or public sins cause Thee to hide thy face from us ; but from them, turn Thou us, and in our repentance, forgive.

To our prayers, we add our thanks, our thanks for mercies many and manifold.

Thou didst not set Thy love upon us, and choose us because we were more in number than any people, but because Thou wouldst raise us up to be an asylum for the oppressed, and for a light to those in darkness living.

For this great honor, O God, we thank Thee.

Not for our righteousness hast Thou upheld us hitherto, and saved from those evils which wreck the nations; but, because Thou hadst a favor unto us.

For this great mercy, O God, we thank Thee.

Not solely through man's wisdom have the great principles of human liberty been embodied for our government, and every man become the peer of his fellow man before the law; but, because Thou hast ordered it.

For this great mercy, O God, we thank Thee.

And now our Father, let this assembly, the representatives of the thousands whom thou hast blessed, go hence, to-day, their duty done, joyful and glad of heart, for all the goodness that the Lord hath done for this great nation.

And for the generations to come–yet unborn–may this monument which we dedicate, to-day, to the memory of George Washington, stand as a witness for those virtues and that patriotism, which lived, shall secure for them Liberty and Union forever.

Amen[1]

HISTORY OF THE UNITED STATES OF AMERICA - MOUNT RUSHMORE HISTORIC PLAQUE

Almighty God, from this pulpit of stone the American people render thanksgiving and praise for the new era of civilization brought forth upon this continent. Centuries of tyrannical oppression sent to these shores God-fearing men to seek in freedom the guidance of the benevolent hand in the progress toward wisdom, goodness toward men, and piety toward God.

1776 - Consequently, on July 4, 1776, our forefathers promulgated a principle never before successfully asserted, that life, liberty, equality and pursuit of happiness were the birthrights of all mankind. In this Declaration of Independence, formulated by Jefferson, beat a heart for all humanity. It declared this country free from British rule and announced the inalienable sovereignty of the people. Freedom's soldiers victoriously consecrated this land with their life's blood to be free forevermore.

1787 - Then, in 1787, for the first time a government was formed that derived its just powers from the consent of the governed. General Washington and representatives from the thirteen states formed this sacred constitution, which embodies our faith in God and in mankind by giving equal participation in government to all citizens, distributing the powers of governing threefold, securing freedom of speech and of the press, establishing the right to worship the Infinite according to conscience, and assuring this nation's general welfare against an embattled world. This chart of national guidance has for 145 years weathered the ravages of time. Its supreme trial came under pressure of Civil War, 1861-65. The deadly doctrines of secession and slavery were then purged away in blood. The seal of the union's finality set by President Lincoln, was accomplished like all our triumphs of law and humanity, through the wisdom and the power of an honest, Christian heart.

Farsighted American statesmanship acquired by treaties, vast wilderness territories where progressive, adventurous Americans spread civilization and Christianity.

1850 - Texas willingly ceded the disputed Rio Grande region, thus ending the dramatic acquisition of the west.

1867 - Alaska was purchased from Russia.

1904 - The Panama Canal Zone was purchased as authorized by President Theodore Roosevelt, whereupon our people built a navigable highway to conveniently enable the world's people to share the fruits of the earth and of human industry. Now, these areas are welded into a nation possessing unity, liberty, power, integrity and faith in God with responsible development of character and the steady performance of humanitarian duty.

Holding no fear of the economic and political, chaotic clouds hovering over the earth, the consecrated Americans dedicate this nation before God, to exalt righteousness and to maintain mankind's constituted liberties so long as the earth shall endure.

– William Andrew Burkett
Author

This 560-word "History of the United States of America, 1776-1904," was chosen in 1935 by a nationwide competition conducted by the Mount Rushmore National Memorial Inscription Committee, the President of the United States, Chairman. This plaque was presented by the National Historical Foundation, July 4, 1971.

The Christian Heritage Of Our Nation - History Curriculum

About the Author

Dr. Catherine Millard is the founder and president of Christian Heritage Tours, Inc., and Christian Heritage Ministries. She has spent fifteen years as a scholar at the Library of Congress, researching the authentic Christian history and heritage of the United States. In 1995, she was elected to "Who's Who among students in American Universities and Colleges" for outstanding academic achievement in the realm of Christian education. Dr. Millard is also the recipient of the 1990 George Washington Honor Medal and the 1992 Faith and Freedom Religious Heritage of America Award, for significant contributions in affirming and strengthening the biblical principles in American life.

She is the author of books on America's original history, to include *The Rewriting of America's History, A Children's Companion Guide to America's History, Great American Statesmen and Heroes,* and *The Christian Heritage of Our Nation History Curriculum - Landmarks;* as well as six video documentaries on the subject. Dr. Millard has lectured and taught the original Christian heritage and history of America extensively in colleges, universities and schools throughout the nation.

If you or your group is going to be in the Washington, D.C. area; Philadelphia, Valley Forge or Gettyburg, PA; or Jamestown, Williamsburg, Yorktown, Virginia and would like to take part in an exciting tour that points out the true history of our country, complete with all references to the Biblical foundations of our land, contact Christian Heritage Tours, Inc., 6597 Forest Dew Court, Springfield, Virginia 22152, or call (703) 455-0333.

Catherine Millard is also available to provide teaching seminars, lectures, and multimedia presentations to your school or organization, on the subject of America's Christian heritage and history. You may contact her through the above address:

FOR ADDITIONAL COPIES OF
The Christian Heritage of Our Nation History Curriculum - Memorials
call or write Christian Heritage Ministries or go to your local Christian bookstore.
(703) 455-0333